Play the Game Right

The Biography of "Butch" van Breda Kolff

Paul A. Luscombe

P.A.L. Publishing Co.   ISBN: 0-9704372-0-X

Table of Contents

Acknowledgments	v
Foreword Dean Smith	ix
Introduction	xi
Chapter 1: The Formative Years 1922–1951	1
Chapter 2: The Early Lafayette Years 1951–1955	35
Chapter 3: The Early Hofstra College Years 1955–1962	67
Chapter 4: The Princeton Years 1962–1967	83
Chapter 5: The NBA Years: The Lakers 1967–1969	115
Chapter 6: The NBA Years: The Pistons 1969–1974	139
Chapter 7: The NBA Years: The Jazz 1974–1982	153
Chapter 8: The Later Lafayette Years 1984–1988	179
Chapter 9: The Later Hofstra Years 1988–1994	207
Chapter 10: Retirement? 1994–present	225
Resources	253
Sources of Material	257

Acknowledgments

In constructing the Biography of Willem van Breda Kolff, many of Butch's friends have expressed what an important influence he has made on their lives, particularly as younger men seeking to find their respective identities. From Lafayette College, conversations on the phone and personal letters from his coaching pupils were extremely supportive of Butch's coaching style. All-American Jim Radcliff mentioned that Butch taught him never to second-guess his life's decisions. At Princeton, Chris Thomforde praised the coach for combining a disciplined intensity for the game while at the same time instilling an element of fun. Hofstra's captain of its 23-1 team from 40 years ago—Steve Balber—echoed similar sentiments. Others interviewed or supplying letters include Cary Ahl, George Young, Stu Murray, Dave Jones, Corky Galtere, Eddie Knapp, Ernie Peters, Tony Duckett, Matt Roberts, and Andy Wescoe (Lafayette); Steve Dunn, Bill Thieben, and John Uustol (Hofstra); and Art Hyland and Gary Walters (Princeton). Kurt Kehl of the Princeton University Athletic Communication staff was very helpful as a "fact finder."

Butch van Breda Kolff was likewise admired and respected by his peers. Dean Smith says he is one of the best collegiate coaches in history. Bobby Knight regards him as the "best college coach I ever saw." Pete Carril dedicated his autobiography to Butch. Joe Lapchick recognized his talents and directed him toward coaching.

Making friends was a natural process for VBK. Generally speaking, he sustained these friendships throughout his life, while continuing to add new ones along the way. Ted Winpenny, his childhood friend from the Montclair Athletic Club, still stays in touch with Butch. From the early Lafayette years, he continues to gather with Cary Ahl and Pete Carril, among others. From Hofstra, he visits with Bill Thieben and Steve Balber. From the later Lafayette years, he sees John Leone and Judy Campbell. He still plays golf with "Crash Helmet" Bill Claren, a teammate of his from the Verona Inn days. During retirement, he continues to make new friends on a regular daily basis, as evidenced by his friendship with Tom Bertrand. Tom was instrumental in filling in some information about Butch's NBA experiences with the Pistons, The Jazz, and the Memphis Tams.

Many successful figures of the business and sports world have achieved their status through capitulation and compromise, stepping aside in certain times, and being aggressive at others. Butch always stated what he believed and took action accordingly. As such, he experienced many confrontational situations, particularly in the arena of professional basketball. Above all, he was a purist who "played the game right." As Steve Balber said, "He didn't play the best players. He played the players who played best together."

He was a genius at coaching. The phrase "organized confusion" captured Butch's self-analysis of his coaching style. He coached over 1300 games, college and professional, over a 44 year span. He coached Princeton to the Final Four and the #5 slot in the nation. He was the first and only coach to jump from the Ivy League to be the Head Coach of an NBA franchise. He coached the Lakers to two NBA championship finals. He has the best percentage won-lost seasons on record at both Lafayette (23-3) and Hofstra (23-1). His achievements of turning around the Pistons and the Jazz are a credit to his record.

His critics cite his courtside manner, his animated antics, and his constant battle with the referees. For sure, his passion for the sport led to this behavior rather than any deliberate attempt at showmanship. His passion led to impatience in dealing with the likes of Alan Mendelson of the Jazz. In the same vein, he was intolerant of the per-

Acknowledgments **vii**

functory details of the Athletic Director's job at the University of New Orleans. Oddly enough, he rarely if ever countered criticism and frequently took the blame of the team upon himself.

Above all, he played the game of basketball and the game of life right.

Lafayette Hall-of-Fame Member Marty Zippel was one of the first "test readers" to review my manuscript, and his encouragement to complete the project was certainly motivationall. My fellow-Lafayette sports writer Doug Hobby was extremely vital in helping me proofread the text and thus meet our production deadline. And last but by no means least, my wife Cinnie's endless search for a prime-time publisher, her persistent phone calls in tracking down stories relating to Butch, and her positive spirit kept the project moving along to completion.

Foreword

Dean Smith leads the list of all-time NCAA coaches with 879 total victories. He led the University of North Carolina to 25 NCAA Tournaments in 34 years, reaching the Final Four 10 times and winning the championship twice (1982, 1993). He coached the U.S. Olympic team to the gold medal in 1976.

Butch van Breda Kolff is one of the best basketball coaches in history! He certainly "did it his way" (as the song goes) and did do it with a love for the game. A truly special, unique coach!

Dean Smith

P.S. The University of North Carolina played his great Princeton teams, so we know!

(During the 1967 season, the Smith-led Tar Heals played VBK's Princeton Tigers two times, and the teams split the "series" 1-1. UNC finished #3 in the country and Princeton wound up #5.)

About the Author

After 36 years on Wall Street, Paul Luscombe retired in 1999 from Morgan Stanley Dean Witter. Throughout those 36 years, Paul had been a consistent writer for the *Lafayette Alumni News*. An active Lafayette alumnus, Paul currently is the chairman of the Lafayette College Maroon Club Athletic Hall of Fame. The position involves extensive research of biographical information about the various athletes and coaches who are candidates for the Hall.

As an undergraduate at Lafayette, Paul was Sports Editor and Managing Editor for *The Lafayette,* the student semi-weekly newspaper. After receiving his bachelor's degree in philosophy, Paul went on to the Wharton School (University of Pennsylvania) where he obtained his MBA in finance. While at Wharton, Paul was editor in chief of the student newspaper (*The Wharton Advocate*) supported by the MBA Club.

The van Breda Kolff biography (*Play the Game Right*) is the second writing project for Paul. He also wrote a short humor book entitled *Give Dad a Mulligan*.

Introduction

The classic sports David and Goliath story is truly exemplified by little Lafayette College's upset of NCAA basketball power Notre Dame on January 4, 1988. Defeating 15-point favorite Notre Dame was an amazing achievement for Lafayette, a college of 1000 male students (approximately 2000 overall), none of whom were on athletic scholarship. If ever there were a ranking of great "underdog" wins in college basketball history, Lafayette's conquest of the Irish would have to be near the top of the list.

Butch van Breda Kolff was the coach for Lafayette, Digger Phelps was the coach for Notre Dame.

Following the victory, the Lafayette College bookstore reprinted the tape of the entire game, which actually was a televised broadcast on Chicago's WGN9. Although I witnessed the game in person, I purchased the tape and now, almost anytime I have guests with any affiliation with Lafayette, and to a lesser extent Notre Dame, I bring out the tape to provide the evening's entertainment. Furthermore, in mid-1999, upon retirement from 36 years on Wall Street, I found myself again watching the game on rainy days or simply to pass the time. Soon, I began to feel as if I knew Coach Butch van Breda Kolff. Indeed, I had an inkling of how he coached a basketball team.

At first, I decided to write up the Lafayette-Notre Dame game, intending to submit it to the Lafayette Maroon Club for publication in its newly anticipated Sports Journal. But as I delved into the background of Butch van Breda Kolff, I began to realize what an interesting personality he was and is. In no time, I was in the embryonic stages of a biography, a biography of a man I had never really known.

After securing his home phone number from John Leone, Butch's assistant at Lafayette and subsequent head coach for 4 years, on or about March 15, 2000, I telephoned Butch van Breda Kolff (VBK) on the premise that I had interest in writing his biography. By way of background, I had written Butch and sent him a rough draft manuscript outlining my approach to his biography. Upon hearing my story, Butch was quite receptive and he said, "Let's get moving on this!"

Within a month, I met VBK at his home in Florida and I immediately learned how easy it was for Butch to make friends. In just a few hours, VBK laid his entire life story in front of me, not so much by bragging but rather by showing me an endless array of scrapbooks depicting his many stops along the college and professional basketball circuit. Also included were positions with a small high school team in Mississippi and a women's professional team in New Orleans.

What follows is the result of my investigating the details of those many scrapbooks as well as developing other sources of background information on Butch. Chronicling the accomplishments of Coach van Breda Kolff, writing of his volatile career, and being a part of his life-style were experiences that will stay with me forever.

Chapter 1

The Formative Years Circa 1922–1951

"I've never been one to live in the past. I don't even live in the future. What happens now is the main thing. If we have a good year, great!"

Butch van Breda Kolff[1]

A little more than five minutes remained in the fourth quarter of the seventh and deciding game of the 1969 NBA championship series between the Los Angeles Lakers and the Boston Celtics. In their previous six meetings, the two teams had captured three wins apiece. After a season of over 100 games, the championship aspirations of the players, the coaches, and all the fans were to be determined by the outcome of this one encounter.

As the clock ran down, the Celtics appeared in control of the contest and led the lethargic Lakers by seven points. At this point, the virtually indestructible Wilt "The Stilt" Chamberlain informed Laker Coach Butch van Breda Kolff that he had an injured knee and essentially pulled himself from the game. Butch replaced Wilt with another 7-footer—Mel Counts—and soon the energized Lakers had reduced the deficit to 103-102 with 3:07 left in the contest. The Lakers had recaptured the momentum. Suddenly stalled, the Celtics called a "time-out."

---

[1] As quoted in van Breda Kolff article by George Gurtner in the *New Orleans Magazine*, Oct. 1982

BUTCH VAN BREDA KOLFF
WHAT A
SWEET OLD BUTCH
OF A CAREER!

1951-1955	1955-1962	1062-1967	1967-1969	1969-1972	1972-1973	1973-1974
LAFAYETTE COLLEGE	HOFSTRA UNIVERSITY	PRINCETON UNIVERSITY	LOS ANGELES LAKERS	DETROIT PISTONS	PHOENIX SUNS	MEMPHIS TAMS

1974-1977	1977-1979	1979-1982	1983-1984	1984-1988	1988-1994
NEW ORLEANS JAZZ	UNIVERSITY OF NEW ORLEANS	NEW ORLEANS PRIDE	PICAYUNE HIGH SCHOOL	LAFAYETTE COLLEGE	HOFSTRA UNIVERSITY

OVERALL COACHING RECORD
WINS	LOSSES
773	585

"Sweet Old Butch" Basketball Record. Compiled by John Leonne

At that point, clearly visible to the 17,368 hometown fans and a national TV audience, Wilt informed Butch that he wanted to reenter the game. His leg suddenly felt fine. Without hesitation, Butch glared at the legendary Wilt and said, "No. We're playing better without you. Sit down." Wilt reluctantly took his place on the bench and the game continued.

The game remained tight for the next few minutes. As time was about to expire, the Lakers trapped Celtic star John Havlicek and deflected the ball from his hands, but directly into those of substitute forward Don Nelson positioned at the foul line. Almost in one continuous motion, Nelson caught the ball and quickly fired a shovel shot which hit the back of the rim, bounced high in the air, and dropped straight through the net effectively giving the Celts the deciding basket. The seventh game victory and the NBA championship belonged to the Celtics by a score of 108-106.

The hometown Laker crowd was stunned into silence. The Lakers' owner went ballistic! *Sports Illustrated* branded Butch's keeping Wilt on the bench as "probably the single most controversial courtside decision ever made by a professional basketball coach." Butch never backed down from his course of action. He liked the team he had on the floor, he had the momentum, he took a gamble and lost. He could live with his convictions.

On March 19, 1969, just a few weeks after the decisive game, Butch van Breda Kolff resigned his position as Coach of the Los Angeles Lakers. As the apparent scapegoat for the Laker defeat, he undoubtedly felt the heat emanating from the Laker front office.

Twelve years after coaching the NBA championship game, Butch van Breda Kolff (pronounced von bread a cough) was teaching history and coaching basketball at Picayune Memorial High School in Mississippi. It was Butch's first job after a two-year period of unemployment, the longest and most depressing years of his life. From the heights of the hoop world, Butch's career had spiraled downward to an inconspicuous dot on the basketball map.

Nonetheless, Butch loved his job in Picayune. Though far from the national spotlight, Butch took great satisfaction in teaching the fundamentals of basketball to his youthful players. The discipline, the teachings and his authoritative booming voice engulfed the fatherless void which shackled their young Mississippi lives. Although this was his first coaching job at the high school level, his style and focus remained the same. Above all, he relished teaching the boys how to *play the game right*. Butch thrived on his new coaching assignment and was by no means demeaned by his latest twist of fate. Perhaps best of all, was the satisfaction of being addressed as "Coach". It was music to his ears.

On the sidelines, Butch continued to proactively coach his team, praising them for crisp passing on offense and frantically encouraging them to get back on defense. Slam-dunking was not included in the "art form" known as basketball, and he shuddered at any incidents of "show boating".

In one of Picayune's mid-season games, Butch's center—6'4" Pat Collins—attempting to slam dunk the ball at the end of a breakaway, jammed the ball against the back of the rim and watched it carom back to the foul line. During the ensuing "time out," Collins—anticipating the wrath of VBK—immediately apologized to the coach. "I'm sorry coach." The coach had no tolerance for "hot-dogging." Withholding any open comments, Butch sarcastically laughed at his repentant player. The team eventually went on to post a 14-8 record. More importantly, they learned how to *play the game right.*

☆ ☆ ☆

Late in the evening, in October of 1944, as marine corps buddies Lafayette King and Butch van Breda Kolff raced back to the military airport in Pensacola Florida, they were well aware of the consequences of being "absent without leave" while the nation was at war. They were desperate to make the flight assigned to bringing the Cherry Point football team back to its home base in North Carolina. Lafayette had starred in the game while Butch acted as "equipment manager," but they had become separated from the nucleus of the team while checking out the social scene of downtown Pensacola. The young marines enjoyed themselves tremendously, but now rued having stayed so long at the pubs in the seaside town. They had simply lost track of time.

When the two marines arrived on the runway, they discovered that their team plane had taken off without them. For sure, they would be classified as "AWOL"—facing possible court-martial and a dishonorable discharge—if they were not at reveille the next morning. Using all the resources at their disposal, they approached the pilot of a nearby Navy cargo plane and pleaded their case. The two were willing to stow away anywhere on board just to get back on time.

But the pilot played the game by the book. He revealed that the cargo on board his plane was already at the limit, and he just couldn't tolerate an extra 400 pounds. He also mentioned that he only had one seat available, and that preference would be made for Navy over Marine personnel. Unfortunately for Butch and

Lafayette, two sailors appeared and outlined essentially the same predicament about the need for a ride to their home base in Virginia. Lafayette and Butch were "shut out" as far as the cargo plane was concerned. When the two sailors begged the pilot for a ride, he reiterated that only one of them could make the trip. There was room for a combined total of 23 passengers and crew on board, and that was all he would take.

The sailors agreed to settle the matter with a coin flip. As Butch and his friend Lafayette watched, Sailor #1 flipped a coin into the air and shouted, "Call it!" Sailor #2 yelled out, "Tails." And "tails" it was! With his right two fingers elevated to form the "V" sign, the ecstatic Sailor #2 raced up the loading stairway to snare the last available seat.

Sailor #1 simply extended his middle finger in the air in protest.

Lafayette King, Butch, and the ill-fated Sailor #1 watched enviously as the cargo plane rolled down the runway and ascended into the darkened late evening sky. Suddenly, within seconds of takeoff, a fighter-bomber appeared immediately overhead and the bloated cargo plane was unable to veer from its course. A huge explosion ensued as the two planes collided and burst into flames, crashing quickly into Pensacola Bay. Butch and his pals shook with horror as the planes sank quickly out of view. A lone stream of gray smoke, silhouetted against the moonlight, was all they could see. No survivors of the crash were found following an extensive search. All 23 on board the cargo plane, which might have carried Butch and Lafayette had they been more persuasive, were dead.

Having suddenly lost interest in the flying option, Lafayette and Butch decided that hitchhiking was their only means of possibly making North Carolina by morning, and so they set out to pound the highways. As they thought of the personnel on the cargo plane, they trembled at the possibility of being a stowaway on the vessel. They inwardly thanked the now deceased cargo pilot for denying them passage.

The two marines—exhausted, sleepless, but alive—miraculously made roll call the next morning.

Undoubtedly, the tragedy left a lasting impression on the psyche of Butch van Breda Kolff. That life or death could be decided by a "coin flip"—a simple 50-50 probability—left him with a more or less fatalistic outlook on life.

Some twenty-five years after the cargo plane crash, Butch flipped a mental coin and benched the immortal Wilt "The Stilt" Chamberlain. He could survive the consequences of his decision. In the course of his life, he frequently said, "Oh, what the hell!" Likewise, he emerged from the low point in his career in Picayune. Winning the game at hand, playing with the cards that are dealt, reacting to situations—those became just some of the trademarks of Butch van Breda Kolff.

The soccer team representing the Kingdom of the Netherlands was not listed among the pre-tournament favorites at the 1912 Olympics held in Stockholm, Sweden. But spearheaded by the outstanding efforts of Jan Gualtherius van Breda Kolff, the Dutch athletes won enough of their games to finish third in the standings. In recognition of their achievement, the Netherlands players were awarded bronze medals. At the time, when baseball held the undisputed claim as America's "national pastime," soccer held a similar position in Holland as that country's most important sport. At the age of 17, Jan van Breda Kolff was equivalent to a national hero.

Jan also excelled at tennis, and was a junior tennis champion in Holland prior to his Olympic success in soccer. While en route to a tennis tournament, a fluke incident on a Dutch train resulted in a large piece of luggage falling on his right shoulder. Thereafter, the velocity of his once powerful serve was greatly diminished. However, he continued to rely on his extremely effective ground stroke to garner several Dutch tennis titles.

The individual star of the 1912 Olympics was Jim Thorpe, the legendary multisport athlete from Carlisle, Pennsylvania. Thorpe accumulated more than twice as many points as his nearest competitors in the decathlon and pentathlon events. Although his gold medals were later rescinded on the basis of his accepting a $25 paycheck while playing semi-professional baseball, Thorpe's achievements were forever etched on the hearts of all Americans and sports fans around the globe.

Normally held every four years, the Olympics did not take place in 1916 because of World War I. The next round of Olympic games occurred in 1920 at Antwerp, Belgium. By this point, some eight years later, Jan van Breda Kolff and his wife Catherine had migrated to the United States and settled in Montclair, New Jersey, where they lived at 186 Christopher Street. In their living room, prominently displayed over the mantel, was Jan's bronze medal from the 1912 Olympics.

When the van Breda Kolffs arrived from Holland in 1920, Warren G. Harding had just been elected President of the United States. Harding's victorious campaign slogan was "Return to Normalcy," which captured the national sentiment following the idealistic policies and foreign involvement of President Woodrow Wilson. In August 1923, Harding died of complications from food poisoning and pneumonia. He was succeeded by Vice President Calvin Coolidge, who was later elected President in 1924, capturing fifty-four percent of the popular vote.

The Eighteenth Amendment to the Constitution prohibited alcoholic beverages in the United States. The amendment essentially spawned an underworld of illegal imports and bars (known as "speakeasies") and soon the period became known as "The Roaring Twenties." The Roaring Twenties were renowned for contraband liquor, knee-length skirts, and hedonistic behavioral standards. Al Jolson appeared in the first important sound motion picture, *The Jazz Singer*. His versions of "Swanee" and "Toot Toot Tootsie!" symbolized the era. "The Charleston" was a dance that helped many Americans forget the ravages of World War I.

After a brief recession in 1921, the nation experienced rising business profits as a result of labor-saving devices in the manufacturing and farm sectors of the economy. The automobile industry soared from its infancy during this time. Radios were soon in every household. From 1925 to 1929, stock market prices soared three-fold. A "national prosperity" had taken the country by storm, and Coolidge's phrase "The business of the United States is business" succinctly captured the mood of the country.

☆ ☆ ☆

Mountainside Hospital was a prominent medical facility servicing the Montclair area. All of its various medical departments were located within the municipal boundaries of Montclair—except the pediatrics ward, which was located in Glen Ridge. And so, on October 28, 1922, Willem Heindrik van Breda Kolff was officially born in Glen Ridge, New Jersey, an early product of the Roaring Twenties.

Throughout his youth, Willem (hereafter referred to as "Butch" or "VBK") was consciously aware and proud of his father's Olympic achievement. The symbolism inherent in the bronze medal acted like a catalyst, motivating Butch to athletic excellence and perfection.

The van Breda Kolffs were attracted to the Dutch colonial architecture on Christopher Street as well as the proximity of the Walnut Street train station, which provided Butch's father with a convenient commute to Wall Street. Every Monday through Friday, Mr. van Breda Kolff donned his Hamburg hat and his velvet collared topcoat and within about an hour he was at his desk at Goldman Sachs & Co. He had plenty of time to organize his day before the market opened. Butch, however, exhibited little interest in pursuing a career on Wall Street, where his father was a successful stockbroker with Goldman and later on with Orvis Brothers. As his life and his career unfolded, Butch found money matters and formal attire to be of secondary importance. He seemed more interested in making $5 in a basketball shoot-out than in building a retirement nest egg or playing the role of a businessman.

When Butch's father finished his dinner, he almost always lit up a cigarette and poured through stacks of financial reports relating to the stock market. Before the night was over, he had smoked several cigarettes and consumed a vast amount of data. Butch, on the other hand, was addicted to the sports pages of the *Herald Tribune* and he virtually memorized baseball box scores and any other statistics that the newspaper provided. He constantly sought to stay ahead of his Montclair buddies, with whom he had a continuous battle of "twenty questions" concerning the latest sports trivia. Often, he would arise early in the morning to see if any new baseball players were being brought up from the minors. If so, he would quickly call one of his friends and stump him with the name of the relatively unknown player. In the rare case where he overslept, sometimes his pals would stump him. Butch said of his collection of friends, "We didn't excel at school, but we knew every player in the baseball world!"

Throughout Butch's well-traveled career, he was always hesitant to talk about his own personal finances. He disliked discussing the details of any contracts he had negotiated when taking on a new coaching slot. Moreover, he refrained from publicly criticizing employers who probably underpaid him for his services. During Butch's youth, Wall Street was considerably more secretive than currently. Wall Street consisted almost entirely of partnership-owned companies, large and small, which weren't required to report their earnings to the public. Goldman Sachs retained this right to privacy until they finally went public in 1999. Perhaps this syndrome of financial confidentiality was subtly transmitted from the elder VBK to his son. Butch's father frequently spoke of the 1912 Olympics and Jim Thorpe, but rarely mentioned any details of his position on Wall Street. Butch credited his father's strictness as the source of his own competitive zeal, most of which was expressed through the sports medium.

During Butch's youth, the van Breda Kolffs took at least eight trips to the Netherlands via the Holland America Lines. The prize ship of the line was the *Neiw Amsterdam,* and others included the *Ryandam, Volendam, Veendam,* and *Rotterdam*. Depending on the ship, the voyage usually took eight to nine days each way. Butch greatly enjoyed the trips, particularly the sporting activities such as deck tennis, ping-pong, swimming, and the like. Butch attended school overseas on some of the excursions. The trips seemed to strengthen his ties to his Dutch heritage, but conceivably could have disrupted the discipline of a more structured educational program.

Butch's father frequently boasted about his family's ties to the United States diplomatic corps in the Netherlands, often citing the latter's heroism in the wake of the Nazi invasion in 1939. Butch's older sister, "Miesje," was officially named Maria Helena Joannna van Breda Kolff. She is approximately two years older than Butch (about eighty years old) and lives in Chatham, Massachusetts, on Cape Cod. His younger sister Marjorie, is eight years younger (about seventy years old) and lives in Madison, Wisconsin.

Montclair New Jersey

During Butch's early youth, Montclair was a prominent suburb on the New Jersey landscape. Two country clubs, The Montclair Golf Club (Verona) and the Upper Montclair Golf Club (Clifton), both adopted the Montclair name even though they were located outside the town's borders. Just the name *Montclair* implied an element of prestige. Beautiful mansions and estates punctuated Upper Mountain Avenue on the bluff overlooking the town. Many of the wealthier residents sent their offspring to privately endowed Montclair Academy. The town's downtown shopping area was renowned for its exclusivity, particularly the elegant branch of Hahne's department store. The Montclair National Bank & Trust managed the financial matters for many local residents.

Including Butch's father, many executives were attracted by the Delaware Lackawanna & Western rail link connecting Montclair with New York City. Without doubt,

The Formative Years: Circa 1922–1951

the railroad provided Montclair with a cosmopolitan atmosphere, although some critics implied the railroad's initials (DLW) stood for "Delay Linger & Wait"! Montclair's proximity to the Garden State Parkway, which was completed in the mid-1950s, added to the town's allure.

The 1930 census listed Montclair Township's population at 42,017, and generally speaking, most demographers expected the community's population base to hit 50,000 by 1950. In the early 1950s, the community's high school became a perennial sports power as coaching legends Clary Anderson (football) and Butch Fortunato (basketball) produced consistent state champions. For the record, Anderson coached ten undefeated football teams and compiled a 197-22-5 record during his twenty-five-year tenure at Montclair. All the high schools in the area— Nutley, Bloomfield, Clifton, East Orange and Orange— felt that Montclair was the team to beat.

Montclair also had its own YMCA on Park Avenue near the center of town. The "Y" added to the regional sports presence of the town as many basketball leagues prospered while using the facility as their home site.

Young Butch van Breda Kolff was indeed wrapped up in the athletic emphasis of Montclair, New Jersey. Early on, thanks to a tip from one of his pals, he secured a junior membership at the Upper Montclair Golf Club, and he was able to play all summer long for a mere pittance.

In addition to his other athletic skills, Butch always maintained a fundamentally sound golf game, generally scoring in the low to mid 80s. Once he shot an 84 at the Pine Valley Golf Club near Clementon, New Jersey. *Golf Digest* and many other golf publications have consistently rated Pine Valley as the most difficult course in the United States, possibly in the world.

More importantly, he thoroughly utilized the extensive facilities of the Montclair Athletic Club (or MAC) at 201 Valley Road. The site was virtually a microcosm of an Olympic campus. Here Butch played basketball, tennis, soccer, baseball, football, and any sport you can name, even bowling and squash. The presence of two dedicated doubles squash courts illustrated the extent of the club's participation in a multitude of sports. In essence, Butch could create his own version of the decathlon. Prominent tennis tournaments such as the Eastern Junior Clay Tennis Championships, which included several Davis Cup stars, were held at the club. One year, Butch was defeated in the Interscholastic State Finals by Eddie Moylan, who later achieved tennis stardom with the Davis Cup. Additionally, Moylan went on to secure a Wimbleton Doubles Title (with Tom Faulkenberg) in the summer of 1945. In his late seventies, Moyer still competes in local senior tennis events.

At a young age, Butch dedicated his life to sports. Every free moment he spent at the Athletic Club. When the game was basketball, some events entailed organized teams, uniforms, refs, and all. At other times, Butch was involved with a game of "two on two" or "three on three." Sometimes, the group would just play "stoop ball" in the rain, fantasizing that a major league game was at stake.

Among the regulars at the Club, Ted Winpenny was one of Butch's closest friends. Like Butch, Ted was a sports fanatic who embraced all the facilities of the MAC. Frequently, Butch and Ted were the only two on the basketball court, and so the two buddies engaged in the game of "Ghost." The game consists of each player taking a shot at the basket, and—if made—the other player must make the same shot from the identical distance while using the same shooting hand. For example, if Butch sank his jump shot from 15 feet, then Ted would also have to make a fifteen-footer using his less-than-familiar left hand. If Ted missed, he would be saddled with the letter "G." The first player to miss five shots—thus spelling out the word "G-H-O-S-T"—lost the game. Since Butch was lefty and Ted was right-handed, the game was like a drill in ambidexterity, forcing each player to shoot from his opposite side.

Winpenny recalls one of the basketball games in the winter of 1937 when along with Butch he represented the MAC in a junior sports exhibition. The MAC team edged the Montclair Vikings by 32-28. "I particularly recall this game because it was one of the few times I ever outscored Butch." He

The Formative Years: Circa 1922–1951   **13**

At the age of 15, Butch (left) played tennis for the Montclair Athletic Club team in 1937 along with his friends Bruce Doe and Ted Winpenny (right). Credit: Montclair AC photographer

Sixty-three years later, Butch and Winpenny are shown in front of Butch's Sun City FLA house during the 2000 Thanksgiving Weekend. Credit: Anonymous friend of Butch

further added, "Butch was a big-tall guard who relished feeding his teammates, and I was known as a 'basket hanger.'" Winpenny regarded Butch as the "World's Second Greatest Athlete," ranking Kyle Rote as the world's number one.

Blue jeans, gym shorts, t-shirts, and any other form of playground attire dominated the young VBK's wardrobe.

MONTCLAIR ATHLETIC CLUB JUNIORS VS MONTCLAIR VIKINGS BOX SCORE FROM MARCH 1937

Montclair Athletic Club Juniors				Montclair Vikings			
Player	FG	FT	PTS	Player	FG	FT	PTS
Winpenny, F	3	3	9	Cousins, F	4	1	9
D. Daly, F	3	2	8	Bachman, F	1	0	2
Connell, C	1	0	2	Hemleh, C	4	4	12
Van Breda Kolff, G	3	1	7	Longton, G	2	1	5
Crane, G	1	4	6	McIntosh, G	0	0	0
Totals	11	10	32	Totals	11	6	28

His hair was never combed. He was a constant bead of perspiration. Frequently, he used the "Y" for a shower just to clean up. Above all, he loved sports, he loved games, and Montclair provided him with the outlet.

Additionally, young VBK constantly played "catch" with his neighborhood buddies on Christopher Street outside his home. When his father called him to come in for dinner, he would yell, "Broer, come in now!" *Broer* is a generic Dutch nickname and Bill's friends interpreted *Broer* to be "Butch." As Butch's life moved on, he tried to shed the nickname, preferring to be called "Van." But Butch was the name that stuck. He would be forever known as Butch.

Once in his teens, given his focus on athletics and his physical stature—6'2" and 175 pounds—Butch became a star of several athletic teams at Montclair High School. Basketball and soccer were his strongest suits, with tennis ranking about third. Being left-handed helped him with his jump shot, but also gave him an excuse to forgo taking notes in class. Since he predated the invention of the ballpoint pen, he dreaded smearing the ink as he curled his left hand in order to write. Regardless, Butch much preferred the playing fields at the Montclair Athletic Club to the library. He *hated* to study!

KEY DATES IN THE LIFE OF WILLEM (BUTCH) VAN BREDA KOLFF (UP TO APRIL 1951)

Birthday	October 28, 1922
High school graduation	June, 1940
Hill school graduation	June, 1941
Enter Princeton University	September, 1941
Enlist U.S. Marine Corps	July, 1943
Reenter Princeton Univ.	September, 1946
Signs with NY Knicks	February, 1947
Marries Florence Smith	April 17, 1945
Twins are born	August 27, 1949
Accepts coaching job at Lafayette College	April, 1951

Nonetheless, as college time approached, Butch's father—a source of constant motivation—encouraged him to apply to Princeton University. Since Butch's grades were average at best, it was decided that he should take a post-graduate year at the Hill School in Pottstown, Pennsylvania, to better prepare for the rigors of an educational institution such as Princeton. A year later, Butch's friend Ted Winpenny also took the prep school route in hopes of gaining admission to Princeton. Ted opted for the Lawrenceville School, located just a few miles from the Princeton campus in Lawrenceville, New Jersey.

At the Hill School, Butch studied harder than any time in his life. "The Hill School was like a prison," he remarked. However, he played sports as well, and he credits the soccer coach at Hill with the development of his soon-to-be recognized soccer skills. "Coach Robert Cowperthwaite really taught me everything about the game of soccer," Butch reminisced later in life.

Frank Montgomery, a vice president with the National Biscuit Company, lived directly across the street from the van Breda Kolff family. Mr. Montgomery mentioned to Butch's dad that the company was looking for a summer sales assistant in its Jersey City operation. In the late 1930s, the concept of the "supermarket" was just evolving. Butch's new job entailed traveling with a full time salesman and "shelf stocking" per the requests of the supermarket managers. For his efforts, he was paid $22 a week. At the end of the workday, Butch would join his salesman at a local pub. While the salesman had beers, the underage Butch drank a "million" Cokes! It was Butch's first exposure to the outside business world.

In the spring of 1941, Butch was still "on the bubble" as far as his acceptance at Princeton was concerned. During the summer, he took additional exams to test his qualification level. He considered Dartmouth, which was then the powerhouse basketball team among the Ivies. Coached by Ozzie Cowles, the Big Green made it all the way to the finals of the 1944 NCAA only to lose to Utah 42-40 in the championship. But a hassle over a phantom summer job caused Butch to lose interest in Dartmouth. Finally, two days before fall classes were about to begin, Butch's application to Princeton was accepted. He was literally the last one in the door. While Butch completed his duties at the Nabisco Company, his dad had to rush home from Goldman Sachs, secure some clothing for his son, rush back to Jersey City, and whisk him off to Princeton for registration. Nonetheless, his father, the consummate Tiger fan, was euphoric!

Princeton University: Phase I

In his early years at Princeton, Butch could hardly resist trying out for any given athletic team or simply finding a "pick-up game." He became a pitcher on the baseball team. He was an outstanding soccer player. Ultimately, his coaching lessons at the Hill School paid off when he was named to the All-American soccer team in 1946 and was chosen as the Player of the Year of the Eastern Intercollegiate League (the official name of the "Ivy League" prior to 1954).

Soccer was a good sport for the van Breda Kolffs. Butch was an All-American collegiate player and his father Jan was an Olympic champion. Later in life, Butch extolled the virtues of the game of soccer for the youth of America. He believed that soccer caused fewer injuries for young players. He felt that soccer could be played effectively by big men and small men alike. Unlike football, a game of "specialists," soccer allowed everyone to get into the full swing of the contest. "Everyone touches the ball."

As his career evolved, while coaching basketball at the collegiate level, Butch often performed double duty by acting as coach of the soccer team. Likewise, as a conditioning vehicle, he had his collegiate basketball teams work out with the soccer team. Cal Ripken Jr., the iron man of major league baseball, is the son-in-law of one of his college soccer coaching products at Lafayette College.

Basketball was fast becoming his favorite sport, however, as he relished playing for veteran Coach Cappy Cappon. Cappy had learned the game during the time when a center jump followed every basket scored. Throughout his coaching history, Cappy relied on an "Iron Man Five," rarely substituted, and used players who were "tough, gritty, aggressive, and smart." Sports writers joked about Cappon's reliance on five players. They often noted that, if Princeton were to have an annual award for the best "Sixth Man" on the team, they would have a six-way tie among all the bench warmers. He stressed defense as the major aspect of winning basketball, and the balding coach's principles left a lasting impression on VBK.

Before long, Butch was elected Captain of the Princeton basketball team. The Tiger offensive star of the team was John S. "Bud" Palmer, a "tall, dark, and handsome" pivot man who possessed many "spin moves" from within the key. The name "Palmer" was built into the Princeton infrastructure, with Bud's family line tracking back to the original name on the recently rebuilt Tiger football stadium. Palmer carried over his skills to the original New York Knickerbockers, and later on was instrumental in bringing Butch to the Knicks. Palmer also possessed a marvelous speaking voice. Upon retirement as an active player, he assumed the TV broadcast responsibilities for both the Knicks and the New York Rangers. His silver-toned broadcasts of the games were probably the finest in the league.

Tragedy struck the van Breda Kolff household during the spring semester of Butch's freshman year. For years, his mother Catherine had been suffering from coughing spasms and was frequently bed-ridden. The symptoms of tuberculosis and the appropriate medication were discovered too late to help Mrs. van Breda Kolff. She died at the very young age of forty-six.

Coupled with his unlimited appetite for athletics, his mother's death impaired Butch's academic pursuits. Before long he became overextended at Princeton. His grades suffered dramatically from all the sporting activity, and eventually he was forced to withdraw from Princeton for scholastic reasons. He tried to improve his grade point average by attending summer school, but later on discovered that Princeton didn't accept summer grades when determining athletic eligibility. Discouraged, Butch let his studies slip even further. In a rare display of modesty, Butch later confessed, "I had a little difficulty with academics. I *hated* to study. All I cared about was sports!" Butch was never one to make excuses for his shortcomings in life.

Compared to many of his coaching peers, Butch van Breda Kolff grew up in a relatively comfortable environment. His father had a prominent position on Wall Street. The van Breda Kolffs lived in a beautiful home in suburban Montclair. A college education at one of the nation's most prestigious schools awaited him. Others in the coaching ranks came from much humbler beginnings. Press Maravich, father of Pistol Pete, and a successful college coach at North Carolina State and LSU, was born into a sweatshop environment of Aliquippa, PA, and the liquid heat of the Jones & Laughlin Steel Company. Pete Carril, for thirty years the coach at Princeton University, was brought up in South Bethlehem, PA, near the furnaces of the Bethlehem Steel Company. The next phase of Butch's life, a 2 1/2 year tour of duty in the US Marine Corps, soon imparted a heavy dose of humility and mental toughness to his resumé.

The United States Marine Corps

In mid-1943, Butch van Breda Kolff enlisted in the United States Marine Corps. Upon completion of boot camp at Parris Island, Butch was a combat-ready soldier. Indeed, he was "gung ho" and prepared to take on the U.S. enemies of World War II. During basic training, the polite lexicon of Montclair society was relegated to his subconscious while his vocabulary expanded to include every profanity known to man. Overnight, Butch's speaking mannerisms became quite guttural.

Initially, however, Butch was assigned away from direct combat, and he received his orders to report to the Military Police division (i.e., MPs) of the Marines. He soon attained the rank of drill sergeant. For sure, the position helped him cultivate his now famous booming vocal chords. As a basketball coach, Butch's players could always hear his voice over the din of the crowd.

A large portion of Butch's "tough guy" reputation and appearance stems from his Marine Corps background. As a drill sergeant, he directly confronted life's problems without ever giving thought to a compromising solution. Life required quick and authoritative reactions. Unfortunately for Butch, many of these confrontational occurrences took place when he was an NBA coach. He refused to bow to the power structure of corporate basketball. Owners and general managers of NBA teams loved his win-loss records, but they cringed whenever Butch criticized a trade or a waiver of a specific player. "You're fired!" was an expedient way of dealing with Butch's stubborn nature. After all, he was Dutch.

Behind this rough façade lived a very gregarious Butch van Breda Kolff. He always greatly enjoyed making and keeping friends. He yearned to reach out to people. His outgoing nature was a strong asset in the recruitment process. He enjoyed the American pub scene, preferring an earthy workingman's bar to an elitist lounge with tablecloths. He regarded having a few beers with his team as part of the solidarity of the unit.

Following his initial training at Parris Island, Butch suddenly received notice that he was to be transferred to Cherry Point, North Carolina. At first, he tried to negate the transfer, but discovered through inquiry that Cherry Point was the Marine aviation center and housed all the athletic activities for the Marines in that region. He was off to Cherry Point in a heart-beat. Soon, athletics overrode the ostensible military purpose of his existence. He immediately made the post tennis team. Then, he became integral to the basketball team of the Cherry Point Marine Base. In 1944, the Cherry Point Flying Leathernecks were Butch's "MOS" (i.e., *military occupational specialty*) as he traveled extensively while representing the team. Because of the extent of the war, many college and professional basketball players participated in the games. Butch particularly recalls roughing it up with Bones McKinney. A rebounding phenom, Bones later led the University of North Carolina to the finals of the NCAA only to lose to Oklahoma A&M. He subsequently starred for Red Auerbach's Washington Capitals.

Butch saw no combat while in the Marines. His final assignment was with the United States occupational force in Japan. Sports became an active part of Butch's life in Japan as well.

"Princeton University: Phase II

Once he completed his military obligation, Butch returned to Princeton for a second try. Unfortunately, he signed up for a course in geology not realizing that his professor was the new head of the department. He was tough! Butch figured the study of rocks just couldn't be that difficult. Butch had no problem conceptualizing the game of basketball, but he just couldn't handle the theories associated with the study of the earth's surface. Soon he flunked out of Princeton for the second time. Although he had a broad vocabulary, undoubtedly fortified by doing so many crossword puzzles, Princeton required more of a studying effort than Butch was willing to give.

He ultimately completed his undergraduate degree at New York University where he majored in physical education. "That was a major I could handle," he commented. Actually, Butch took some biology courses at NYU and fared considerably better than he did with geology at Princeton. He recalls slicing up a dead cat and studying its parts. Butch received his NYU degree at night when not playing for the Knicks. At the time, NYU was a basketball power in its own right. The Violets were led by All-American Adolph Shayes, who went on to star for the Syracuse Nats. After Shayes retired as an active player, he became the "Supervisor of Referees" in the NBA. In the decade from 1967–77, Dolf became very familiar with the name Butch van Breda Kolff.

The Original New York Knickerbockers:

In early 1946, the New York Knickerbocker franchise was being organized, and ultimately was up and running for the 1946–47 season. The Knicks were originally part of the Basketball Association of America (BAA), which merged with the National Basketball League after the 1948–49 season. The Knicks' first year coach was Neil Cohalen, who was replaced by the immortal Joe Lapchick for the 1947-48 season. Among the outstanding players on the team were Princeton's Bud Palmer along with Carl Braun and Ernie "Doc" Vanderweghe (Colgate) and Harry "The Horse" Galatin (NE Missouri State).

Many of the franchises in the league had financial difficulties, and the inflation adjusted salaries of the players fell well short of the those experienced by today's stars.

Many players held down second jobs, or pursued second careers. Ernie Vanderweghe, for example, played in the league while studying for his medical degree. The Pittsburgh Ironers and the Providence Steamrollers were among the franchises that failed for financial reasons. Thanks to Bud Palmer's recommendation, the original Knick franchise signed Butch van Breda Kolff following his dismissal from Princeton. Young VBK was soon wearing number 17 for the Knicks. Butch liked the number 17 because that was his father's age when he won the Olympic bronze metal. He played sixteen games for the Knicks after signing in February 1947. He helped the team achieve a 33-27 record and a second place finish in the Eastern Division of the league.

Butch immediately made his mark on the Knicks. He was listed in their initial media guide as the first Knick player to have a technical foul called against him. Some twenty-five years later he was tagged with forty technical fouls to set the NBA record. Butch argues that Kevin Laughery holds the record. Apparently, Kevin holds the record for most technicals in one game (six) whereas VBK's single game mark was four. (Two technicals are cause for ejection from a game. In both Kevin and Butch's situations, the technicals continued on as they were leaving the arena!)

Until 1950, Butch played against the likes of the Minneapolis Lakers, the Ft. Wayne Zollner Pistons, and the Rochester Royals. The Lakers were led by bespectacled George Mikan and a cast of stars including Slater Martin, Jim Pollard, and "Whitey" Skoog. No teams existed west of the St. Louis Hawks. Long bus trips to anywhere in the Eastern Hemisphere were a way of life for the players. Many star players from the college ranks opted to play in the AAU (Amateur Athletic Union) while representing such companies as the Phillips Oil Corp. Oklahoma A&M's George Kurland, one of the games's initial 7-footers, elected to play for the Phillips 66ers in lieu of accepting a professional offer.

Louis Effrat of the *New York Times* aptly wrote of Butch's early role as a Knickerbocker. "He definitely belonged and from the outset won respect as a 'smart player,' a fellow whose quest for knowledge never lagged." Knick's Coach Joe Lapchick, a man of few words, repeatedly said of Butch, "He's a pro."

The respect for Butch's abilities was probably best exhibited in intrasquad scrimmages or pick-up games. When choosing up teams, Butch invariable was the first player selected.

Butch's official program stats listed him as 6'3" and weighing 185 pounds. Butch claimed that both numbers were exaggerated, probably by one inch and ten pounds respectively. Over the course of Butch's NBA playing career, he averaged a mere 4.7 points per game. As a scorer, the 1948–49 season was his best as he averaged 7.3 points per game during the regular season and 8.2 during the

Butch as Knick. Photo from Dec. 12, 1948 *Herald Tribune*—Frank

Butch as Knick. Photo from Dec. 12, 1948 *Herald Tribune*—Frank

playoffs. For the record, his shooting percentage was .305 from the field and .669 from the foul line.

But Butch claimed he provided "value added" to the team through his non-scoring skills. In fact, he disparaged most of the familiar basketball statistics since they only acknowledge when a player "touches the ball." He was more an advocate of what he referred to as the "slob" skills. "Slob skills" were described as getting back on de-

PROGRAM STATISTICS

Willem Van Breda Kolff   "Butch"   (Princeton and NYU)
Birthplace: Glen Ridge,   Height: 6 ft. 3 in.   Born: Oct. 28, 1922
New Jersey

	G	FGA	FGM	Pct.	FTA	FTM	Pct.	A	Pts	Avg.
1946–47	16	34	7	.206	17	11	.647	6	25	1.6
1947–48	44	192	53	.276	120	74	.617	29	180	4.9
1948–49	59	401	127	.317	240	161	.671	143	415	7.0
1949–50	56	167	55	.329	134	96	.716	78	206	3.7
Totals	175	794	242	.305	511	342	.669	256	826	4.7

Playoffs

	G	FGA	FGM	Pct.	FTA	FTM	Pct.	A	Pts	Avg.
1946–47	5	32	7	.219	13	7	.538	4	21	4.2
1947–48	3	16	6	.375	14	10	.714	2	22	7.3
1948–49	6	40	15	.375	23	19	.826	7	49	8.2
1949–50	1	0	0	.000	0	0	.000	0	0	0.0
Totals	15	88	28	.318	50	36	.720	13	92	6.1

Acquired: Signed February 1947
Departed: Retired prior to 1950-51 season
(reprinted from "New York Knicks Fans Ultimate Fact Book")

---

fense, boxing out for rebounds, and setting up picks on offense. "That's what I was . . . a slob!" What a player did without the ball mattered most to VBK.

Butch was a star lecturer for the Knicks, conducting several clinics before youth groups in the summer. The Department of Parks in New York City frequently rounded up dozens of teenagers and brought them to the local "Y" where Butch explained and then demonstrated the fundamentals of basketball. The desire to teach and share his thoughts on the game of basketball surfaced as an early part of his personality.

In many respects, Butch van Breda Kolff was a basketball junkie. He also played for the Verona Inn, a tavern

Butch as Knick Lecturer. Credit: VBK private collection

located on Bloomfield Avenue near the Verona-Montclair border. Richie Tarrant, who coached for twelve years at Richmond University while accumulating an impressive record of 239-126 (including five NCAA appearances), was a member of the VI team. Tarrant coached the 1991 Spiders, who were the first number 15 seed to defeat a number two seed in NCAA tournament history. At any rate, when Butch was quizzed about the Verona Inn, he claimed to be the group's coach, appearing in a suit and tie in the squad's official team photograph.

After the war, Butch also played sporadically for the Montclair Athletic Club whose season extended well beyond the normal basketball months of November through April. Butch's high school chum Ted Winpenny also played for the MAC, which reeled off a 48-2 record for the 1946–47 season. The first loss came at the hands of the Jewish American Club of Newark, whose gymnasium was shaped more like a maze than a rectangle. The second de-

Butch exhibited teaching and lecturing skills early in his athletic career. While playing for the NY Knicks, Butch frequently spoke about the fundamentals of basketball before youth groups in New York City. Credit: VBK private collection

feat was to the Seton Hall University freshman and their young star Pep Saul.

In addition to playing for the Knicks, the MAC, and the Verona Inn, Butch also played for the Wilkes Barre

Butch (upper right) joins the other NY Knicks in Old Timers Day game in early 1950's. Credit: VBK private collection

Barons and the Reading Rangers of the Eastern League in order to help supplement his income. When questioned by the media as to why the duplication, Butch generally replied that he was "on loan" from the Knicks as a part of his scouting and assistant coaching responsibilities. The constantly negative media hoped to accuse VBK of moonlighting or indicate he had been cut by the New York franchise.

Soon the regional landscape of college and professional basketball altered dramatically. Butch van Breda Kolff was beginning his basketball life at the dawn of the expansion era in professional sports in general and basketball in particular.

Knicks Coach Joe Lapchick was one of the most respected and knowledgeable mentors of the era. While the Knicks struggled in second place behind Red Auerbach's Washington Capitols, Lapchick praised the play of Butch van Breda Kolff as the spark plug of his team. Lapchick preached defense and VBK was his man. In a key matchup

The Formative Years: Circa 1922–1951   29

with the Philadelphia Warriors, Butch was assigned to cover the NBA's leading scorer, Joe Fulks. Butch "held" Joe to a mere thirty-three points! As far as offense was concerned, Lapchick said "We just played. The offense took care of itself." Lapchick recognized that Butch's abilities transcended that of a player, and soon Lapchick had him scouting college players and functioning as assistant coach. Then Lapchick laid it on the line, telling Butch, "It's high time you started to concentrate on coaching as a career. You're the perfect type."

According to Effrat of the *Times,* only Lou Rossini had received comparable advice from the soft-spoken Lapchick. Rossini went on to a highly successful coaching career at Columbia University.

Someday, the transition to a head coaching position would be an easy one for the young VBK. He had the experience. He knew the game thoroughly. He had the passion. All he needed was the opportunity.

Butch's best friend in the military was fellow-hitchhiker Lafayette King. Before enlisting in the Marine Corps, King had been a running back for Georgia University. King was a proud Marine. "I am King" was how he introduced himself. His girlfriend was Martha Pylka from Pawtucket, Rhode Island. Martha's best friend was Florence Smith, and so Lafayette and Martha were instrumental in setting up a double date with Butch and Florence while they all were serving in the Marine Corps in Cherry Point.

Florence Smith was a Marine from Collingswood, New Jersey. She graduated from Mary Washington College (then the women's division of the University of Virginia). Butch and Florence both attained the rank of sergeant around the same time.

After a brief courtship, Butch and Florence were married in 1945, and they settled into a carriage house in Montclair. They would produce four offspring. Naming the children was distinctly a Dutch process.

First came the twins and their names were Karen and Kristina. Their only son Jan was born in 1952 and he recently was named head basketball coach of St. Bonaventure University in Olean, New York. Their youngest child Kaatje became one of his staunchest supporters at the nadir of Butch's career in the mid-1970s.

In 1964, Butch and Florence invested in their summer cottage at Harvey Cedars on Long Beach Island in New Jersey. The salty setting and extensive beaches afforded Butch a chance to relax and clear his head from the turbulent world of coaching, especially coaching in the NBA.

He particularly enjoyed taking three- to four-mile walks along the beach. Harvey Cedars also helped keep the somewhat far-flung family together. Whenever Butch suggested selling the property, he was met by firm disapproval from the rest of the family.

Florence likes to stress the mellower side of Butch's personality. In a *Sports Illustrated* article by Jack Olsen written in 1969, Florence mentioned Butch had "a heart of whipped cream." "He might hurt a fly, but he'd worry about it for weeks. He went hunting once in his life, and he shot a squirrel, and then he practically broke a leg rushing it to the vet!"

Florence has been very conscientious about keeping meticulous scrapbooks about Butch's coaching experiences through the years. The books teem with newspaper articles and photographs, letters, and magazine articles about Butch's past. Recently, an old friend of Butch's visited him in his Sun City Center Florida residence, and started to look through the scrapbooks. Several hours later, both men were totally wrapped up in the long and varied history of Butch's career. Butch admitted it was the first time he had looked at the books. They probably had been sitting on the coffee table for five years or so! At age seventy-eight, a little nostalgia was creeping into his soul. Butch had always lived in the present, with a modest emphasis on the immediate future. He rarely looked back to take credit for previous successes. He rarely apologized for past mistakes, nor did he make excuses for any miscues. Above all, he lived for the game of the day, the season, and the team.

After putting the scrapbooks back in their assigned location, and wanting to shift the attention from his own background, Butch asked his friend who he thought was the best player of all time. "Wilt the Stilt," his friend responded, knowing that would stir up some historic juices within VBK. "No," responded VBK. "It was Bill Russell! He was the greatest rebounder and defensive player I ever saw." He continued on, "And to think the Celtics traded away Cliff Hagen and Easy Ed MacCauley to get his services. Had to be the trade of the century!" Undoubtedly, the Stilt was aware of Butch's reverence for Bill Russell, which only tended to widen the rift between the two professionals. Then his friend reminded him of the trade whereby the Knicks obtained Dave DeBusschere from the Detroit Pistons in exchange for Howie Komives and Walt Bellamy. "I had to live with that one . . . It happened just before I arrived in Detroit," Butch said.

For the twins, they greatly enjoyed monitoring their father's career. They competed for who would be first to post a "W" or "L" mark on the schedule taped to their refrigerator. Karen eventually graduated from Centenary College in Hackettstown, New Jersey, and for fifteen years has been a vice president with the Chase Bank. She is in charge of the human resources department of the bank's Cleveland operation. Kristina graduated from Wheaton College in Norton, MA. Kristina is a teacher in the biology lab of a community college in Spokane, Washington.

For the younger two children in particular, they grew up constantly changing addresses. Once VBK hit the NBA in 1967, he moved from LA to Detroit to Phoenix to Memphis and finally to New Orleans. Jan and Kaatje were the equivalent of Army brats!

Several grandchildren fill out the family tree. Butch won't let Karen's son Willem call him "grandfather."

Willem and the other grandchildren are instructed to call him "Uncle Butch." He used to say, "I'll never be fifty," but he gave up on that claim long ago.

When Willem was in grammar school—he now is seventeen years old—his teachers would ask him the name of his grandfather. Properly drilled, he would always respond "Uncle Butch." The teacher would repeat the question, stating that his grandfather couldn't be his uncle. But Willem persisted, and the teacher became concerned that he might have some sort of learning or memory disability. Upon calling Willem's mother Karen, the teacher was updated on the fact that his grandfather was indeed "Uncle Butch"!

The family always enjoyed an element of "friendly competition" at its family reunions. All the van Breda Kolffs were fond of meat loaf sandwiches, and there was a sharp disagreement as to who made the best meat loaf sandwich. And so, it was decided to have a "Bake Off" to determine just who in the family *did make* the best meat loaf sandwich.

Butch went down to the local butcher and bought enough ground beef to feed several basketball teams. Upon returning from the store, the ground rules were established. For example, each family participant would have to spend a minimum of one hour in the kitchen.

The Bake Off began. Everyone worked frantically at his or her finished product. Butch, at the last minute, slipped a banana into his version. As impartial observers, Uncle Brick and Aunt Moo—the assistant coach of Hofstra's track squad and his wife—were designated referees. To Butch's dismay, his daughter Karen was declared the winner.

"Hopefully, at least one of the grand children will go to Princeton!" Butch recently remarked.

"I'm obviously not in it for the money. Just look at the clothes I wear," was Butch's reply to the media who sought the rationale for his resignation from the coaching job with the Detroit Pistons. Butch is much more comfortable in sweats than in a business suit.

Dr. George Borzelli, an avid Lafayette College basketball fan and prominent Philadelphia area dentist, says that he wishes he had Butch as a patient years ago. "I would love to have straightened out Butch's crooked teeth," noted George as he watched the replay of the Notre Dame-Lafayette game of 1988 in the lobby of the school's new sports facility. Many feel that Butch, with his piercing huge brown eyes and jagged teeth, has the look of a mad scientist when he confronts a referee or a player who has violated one of his sacred tenets. His animated antics and aggressive gum chewing mannerisms aggravate this appearance. Members of his family, the players under his coaching influence, and close friends know Butch to be a reasonable man of extremely high principles.

Often in his life, Butch used the expression, "Oh, what the hell."

This was Butch the fatalist talking.

His became a life of games, most noticeably basketball. Playing the game to perfection, or in his own words *"playing the game right,"* became his passion. Power, money, prestige—all of these were secondary or not important at all. The beauty of the perfect basketball game was an end unto itself. He really didn't care if he upset his superiors. The allure of climbing the "corporate ladder" just wasn't for him.

He was like an artist painting a picture.

"When basketball is played right, I don't know if the right word is most beautiful, but that's the kind of game it is—a blend of individual skills, of team skills, of thinking man's game, of physical game."[2]

---

[2]Newark Star Ledger, April 1984. "Lafayette's Stroke of Genius" by Mark LaRose.

Lafayette College was founded in 1826 as a private institution with a token affiliation with the Presbyterian Church. The college sits on a prominent hill overlooking the Delaware River and the small city of Easton, Pennsylvania. In 1951, the enrollment of the all-male school was approximately 1500. At the time, the college attracted most of its students from the tri-state area of New York, New Jersey, and Pennsylvania. Most students lived on campus, with roughly 65 percent living in fraternity houses. The main fields of study were liberal arts, engineering and business administration. Athletic success was evident in all major sports—football, basketball, and baseball.

While scouting players in the Eastern Basketball League for the New York Knicks, Butch became familiar with the topography of Northeastern Pennsylvania. He needed no introduction to the attributes of Lafayette College in Easton. Following the 1950–51 basketball season, a vacancy at Lafayette gave young Willem Hendrik van Breda Kolff the chance to display his credentials as a collegiate basketball coach. He jumped at the opportunity.

Chapter 2

The Early Lafayette Years 1951–1955

> *"I can honestly say Butch was one of the most influential people in my life and has my utmost respect as both a person and a coach. On a personal level, he had the unique ability of being a friend to the players without losing their respect as a coach. As a coach in 1952, he was well ahead of his time.*
>
> Edward D. Knapp, Lafayette '56

Affectionately known as "the Big Dance," the NCAA college basketball tournament was a mere sampling of the collegiate universe when it was originally set up in 1938. In sharp contrast to the existing structure of sixty-five entrees, the founding tournament committee invited only eight teams, usually consisting of six representatives from the major conferences from around the country plus two independents. At the time, the National Invitational Tournament seemed to draw more attention with its discreet selection of six qualified teams competing for the entire tournament at New York's Madison Square Garden. With TV and mass media yet to play a role in sports promotion, major market cities such as New York City and Philadelphia were where "March Madness" took place.

In 1939, Oregon University won the first NCAA tournament. In the 1940s, coaching greats Branch McCracken of Indiana, Hank Iba of Oklahoma A&M, and Adolpf Rupp of Kentucky guided their teams to the NCAA title. Holy Cross was a smaller independent which snared the crown in 1947. In 1950, the City College of New York, coached by the legendary Nat Holman, won both the NCAA and the NIT tournament in the same year. Oddly enough, Bradley University was their victim in both finals of this the only "slam" in college basketball history.

At the conclusion of the 1950 season, the NCAA voted to expand its field to sixteen teams. Under the new format, Kentucky University captured the national title for the 1951 season. The Wildcats featured future NBA stars Frank Ramsey and Cliff Hagen as well as 7-foot center Bill Spivey. Meanwhile, Brigham Young University rolled through the NIT field, besting the upstart Dayton University Flyers in the finals. Following the season, a broad-based point shaving scandal rocked the programs of CCNY, Long Island University, and as many as twenty other colleges.

Aside from basketball, Bobby Thomson's home run, which snatched the National League pennant for the New York Giants from the Brooklyn Dodgers, was probably the most memorable sporting event of the year.

In April 1951, President Harry S. Truman fired General Douglas MacArthur as commander of U.S. troops when he threatened to escalate the Korean War into an invasion of mainland China.

Meanwhile, in Easton, Pennsylvania, where Route 22 crosses the Delaware River, the saga of a new coaching legend was just beginning. In April of 1951, at the tender age of twenty-eight, Willem van Breda Kolff launched his head coaching career at Lafayette College. Fresh from playing four years with the original New York Knickerbockers, van Breda Kolff could draw on his scouting and assistant coaching experience accomplished under Joe Lapchick. Lapchick and Ken Fairman, the athletic director for Princeton University, were both strong supporters of VBK's candidacy when Lafayette's Athletic Director Bill Anderson was in the market for a new coach.

In the postwar period, Lafayette had experienced seven consecutive winning seasons. Veteran coach and athletic director Bill Anderson led the 1948–49 squad to

The Early Lafayette Years: 1951–1955   37

the first twenty win season in the school's history and the 1949–50 team went 18-6. The high scorer for those teams was Marty Zippel, who became only the second player in the school's history to pass the 1000-point milestone. A charter member of the Lafayette Hall of Fame, Zippel continues on to this day as an active supporter of the Leopard basketball program. One of his biggest thrills was in March of 2000 when the young Lafayette players invited him to join in the ceremonial cutting down of the net to acknowledge their Patriot League championship.

Back in 1946, Muhlenberg College of Allentown, Pennsylvania, was an Eastern powerhouse. In early March, they accepted a bid to the NIT before the end of the regular season based on their probable first place finish in the Middle Atlantic Conference. Their final opponent was Lafayette. Zippel, who had returned from five years with the Army Air Corps just weeks before, scored twenty-two points as the Leopards upset the Mules 59-58, backed into the MAC title, and totally embarrassed the NIT selection committee with a 17-3 record. Nowadays, the NCAA and the NIT await the decision of all conference championships before extending postseason bids.

Although the 1950–51 Leopards slipped to a somewhat unexciting 14-11 mark, the season was certainly not a disaster. George Davidson led the team in scoring. Nonetheless, two-year coach Ray Stanley stepped down to pursue other interests, thus creating the coaching vacancy VBK coveted. In short, Butch van Breda Kolff inherited a winning tradition and a veteran lineup in his first season as a head coach. His job was not only to win, but also to take Lafayette to a higher level.

As a neophyte coach, VBK eased his way into his relationship with his players. As such, he initially sought to diplomatically phase his coaching principles into the Lafayette program. He politely corrected his players when they made court mistakes, and encouraged them to try harder the next go-round. "Please" and "Thank you" were an integral part of his vocabulary. Butch suppressed any outward and visible signs of pent-up emotion, and the players reacted accordingly. Mr. van Breda Kolff was a "gentleman" coach after all.

Then one practice session, he got extremely upset over a poorly thrown pass by one of his younger players. As the ball rolled to his feet, Butch scooped up the ball and booted it skyward onto the track that encircled Lafayette's gym. The entire team trembled as VBK screamed at the player responsible for the errant pass. The real Butch van Breda Kolff had shown his colors, and he never reverted back to "player diplomacy." The blunt, irascible style of VBK had made its debut and would be on stage for over forty years. The Lafayette cagers of the 1950s respected him for his actions and became better players as a result.

In his relationships with his players, Coach VBK walked the fine line of simultaneously being a disciplinarian and a good friend. He was very open as to who made the team and who did not. Hustle and defense were attributes he admired most.

When Butch took a look at his original Lafayette roster, he noted that some sixteen players were carried on the squad, many of whom were on scholarships valued at $1500 each. Butch wasn't as drastic as Cappy Cappon, but he generally speaking liked playing with seven or eight players. In recruiting his potential players, Butch liked to emphasize that the athlete would receive a lot of playing time at Lafayette. He needed at least ten players to have effective scrimmages, and so he opted for a traveling squad of twelve men. He eventually whittled the size of the team down more to his way of coaching.

Leadership would not be a problem for the 1951–52 Lafayette team. At a meeting of the basketball team in October of 1951, senior Pete Carril was elected captain of Lafayette. Although his Delta Tau Delta brothers tabbed him the "quiet man" at their fraternity house, Pete was a very vocal, conspicuous leader on the basketball floor. At 150 pounds and 5'6 3/4", Pete was the smallest man on the Lafayette team, but nonetheless was consistently among the high scorers for the Pards averaging close to thirteen points per game. His season high of twenty-nine points was registered against local nemesis Muhlenberg College.

Scoring statistics aside, Pete was the perfect VBK protégé. Relentless drive and outstanding hustle characterized his game. He was constant motion, with or without the ball. Some say he was "wired" from drinking so many Cokes during practice sessions. The hometown Lafayette crowds were captivated by his fancy dribbling and ball hawking. At the end of the season, Pete was named to the "Little All-American" team for 1952. Pete Carril was the quintessential overachiever.

Captain Pete Carril of the 1951–52 Lafayette Leopards, the first team which Butch coached upon leaving the Knicks. Credit: Madison Square Garden program

Van Breda Kolff and Carril. Bill taught Pete to drink beer and Pete got Bill into cigars. Thus, almost a half a century ago, two of the greatest basketball minds in the history of the sport converged at a relatively small all-male college in Easton, Pennsylvania.

Another built-in advantage was available to VBK. Lafayette played its home games at Alumni Memorial Gymnasium, an on-campus facility, which listed a maximum capacity of 2000. It seemed that only the home team players could thread their shots from the corners so as to avoid striking the overhead track. If you got to the game early, you sat within inches of the basketball court. As roll-out stands, the seats had no comfortable backs. Fans literally sat on the edge of their seats. The proximity of the highly partisan local fans indeed gave the home Pards an advantage over their opponents. During VBK's first four years at Lafayette, his teams were 37-9 at Alumni Gym for a winning percentage of .822. The building wreaked of perspiration.

Opposing coaches detested playing at Alumni Gym. Jack Ramsey of St. Joe's used to say, "Alumni Hall is the only gym where you can take pictures and develop them at the same time." Corky Galtere, rebounding forward on the '54–55 team, recalled the first time they turned on the new lighting system, the entire team laid down on the floor, raised their practice shirts and pretended to get a sun tan!

As the early '50s evolved, the Middle Atlantic Conference became more and more competitive. Temple boasted one of the nations high scorers in All-American Bill Mlkvy, who won notoriety as the "Owl without a Vowel." At the time, Mlkvy held the single game college scoring record of 73 points versus Wilkes College. Rumor has it that Temple Coach Harry Litwack supposedly waited outside Butch's locker room to see if he could discern any strategy moves. LaSalle's glory years were about to surface. St. Joseph's was always competitive. For van Breda Kolff, the challenge of attaining either the NCAA or the NIT was indeed formidable.

For Butch's coaching debut, Lafayette started the 1951–52 season with a murmur as it went 4-4 in the first eight games. One of the team's early losses was a 62-52 defeat to then ninth ranked LaSalle University. Pete Carril scored seventeen points against the much taller Explorers, whose starting five averaged 6'4"—not exceedingly tall by today standards, but large by comparison with most college fives at the time. The lack of rebounding surfaced as an early Achilles heal for VBK.

Then on January 5, 1952, van Breda Kolff took his Leopards to Madison Square Garden to play New York University. At the time, NYU was ranked sixth in the nation and was just coming off a victory over Arizona University in which they scored 103 points to set the MSG record. Not to be intimidated, Lafayette employed a tight man-to-man defense and slowed down the Violet scoring machine and gave the locals fits throughout the evening. In the second half, Cary Ahl came off the bench to score six straight points which closed the Pards to within five. Pete Carril registered fifteen points as his team ultimately lost to NYU by a 59-49 margin. Taking minimal solace in the team's strong defensive showing, Coach van Breda Kolff publicly expressed displeasure for his team's poor foul shooting under pressure. Otherwise, Lafayette might have recorded a major upset.

While at the Garden, Lafayette was cheered on by a contingent of VBK's former Knick teammates. Carl Braun, Bud Palmer, Harry Galatin, Ernie Vandeweigh, Sweetwater Clifton, Dick and Al Maguire, and Max Zaslofski came not only to the NYU contest but all the others involving Butch and the prominent New York facility. According to Cary Ahl, "They went out with some of us after the games to have a beer or two. There was a real bond between them and Bill." Also, Butch used to take some of his Lafayette players to the Knickerbocker games and they all would go to the locker room either at the half or the end of the game. This surely was a real treat for the young Lafayette athletes.

The NYU game was somewhat of a watershed for Lafayette, as the Leopard players gained confidence knowing that they could stay with a nationally ranked team. The game turned the corner for Lafayette, as the team won its next nine games and eleven of its last thirteen contests. VBK's first season as head coach produced a respectable 15-9 record.

In 1952, Jan van Breda Kolff was born. Eighteen years later, he would become the Southeast Conference "Player of the Year" at Vanderbilt University. Subsequently, he coached at Vanderbilt and currently is head coach at St. Bonaventure University. More on Jan later.

The Role of Pete Carril

As a senior, the 1952 season marked the end of the collegiate playing career of Pete Carril. It would be the only year that Carril and VBK worked together "as a team." Nonetheless, the similarities in their coaching philosophies—as well as their proximity in age—acted as a bond and they remain close friends to this day.

In his book entitled *The Smart Take from the Strong,* Pete had the following comments about Butch van Breda Kolff:

> "He was something special. He was not yet the great coach he was going to be, but he was very wise. He taught me how to be organized, how to evaluate things, how to know what was important, and what was not, and most of all, how to see the game differently from the way I had."

Also, he wrote,

> "He was the biggest influence on my playing and coaching career. He is a born coach. He taught me how to think. I wasn't that smart a player. In fact, I was kind of dumb. But I was a hard worker. The only time he yelled was when you didn't try."

In the dedication of his book, Carril singles out three personalities: his high school coach (Joseph Preletz), his college coach (Bill van Breda Kolff), and his best friend

The Early Lafayette Years: 1951–1955   43

(Rocco Calvo). In his dedication, he said "Two coaches and a friend without whom I never would have had my turn at bat." Pete openly regarded Butch as his "mentor."

In 1967, when Butch van Breda Kolff left Princeton University to coach the Los Angeles Lakers, Pete Carril took over his slot as the Tiger basketball coach. Carril left his post at Lehigh—where he had coached for only one year—to snare the prestigious Ivy League job.

Carril was an immediate success, as he sustained the winning tradition of the Bradley-VBK era for close to thirty years. Pete's college coaching record includes the following achievements: winningest coach in Ivy League history (525), thirteen Ivy League Titles, eleven NCAA appearances, and an NIT championship for the 1975 season. No previous Ivy school had ever won the NIT, and Carril's charges beat Holy Cross, South Carolina, Oregon, and Providence to take the championship. In the 1996 NCAA Tournament, Pete climaxed his final season as head coach of Princeton with a remarkable upset of defending champion UCLA, 43-41. Carril acknowledges that their coaching methods were not entirely alike. In analyzing this difference, Carril remarked. "His goal was to take things as they are and build around them. I take things and if they aren't right for me I try to change them."

In 1980, Carril was elected to the Lafayette Hall of Fame and the National Basketball Hall of Fame in Springfield, Massachusetts in 1997. As of this writing, he is an assistant coach for the Sacramento Kings in the NBA.

In January 1952, the Lafayette freshmen played a game against the Willow Grove Naval Air Station, and one of the Navy stars was George Young. After the game, Butch introduced himself and Bill Anderson, the athletic director. Impressed with his style of play, they informed George that if he could produce high school graduation information and pass a college entrance exam, they could arrange a scholarship at Lafayette.

But Butch was unaware that George had never graduated from high school, even though he starred at Olney High School in Philadelphia for three years. "The offer of a scholarship and a chance to play college ball motivated me in a way I never experienced before and I managed to complete a year and a half of high school in the next seven months and pass the entrance exam for Lafayette," George Young explained. "The opportunity given me by Butch was the catalyst. No member of my family ever went to college and there certainly wasn't enough money to make it happen any other way. I don't think he knows how his offer to come to Lafayette really changed my whole life."

In 1952–53, van Breda Kolff's charges posted a 13-12 record—which was his weakest showing in his first stint at Lafayette. But the Leopards continued to offer stiff opposition to the tougher teams on their schedule. In February of 1953, LaSalle University was ranked fourth in the country when it invaded Lafayette's somewhat obsolete basketball facility. LaSalle was the defending NIT champion from the 1952 season and was led by consensus All-American Tom Gola.

The graceful Gola was the complete basketball player. At 6'7", he was a prolific scorer, a pure passer, a solid rebounder, and great defender. During the 1954 season, he almost single-handedly carried his team to the NCAA title. LaSalle struggled throughout the contest, but prevailed by a 56-50 margin. Gola was flawless as he scored twenty-five points, enabling him to hit 1000 points in just two seasons of collegiate competition. LaSalle plays its home games now out of The Tom Gola Arena featuring a seating capacity of 4000. "They should," remarked VBK when he heard that Gola had been so honored. Butch felt they should have named a soda after the Explorer great. "*GolaCola*' would have been a big seller in Philadelphia," he projected.

In the off-season, Butch spawned a "three-on-three" league as a means of encouraging esprit de corps and conditioning among his players. All the participants would throw in a few dollars to hold a party in honor of the mini-season champions. Butch played on one of the teams and he always gave 100 percent. He greatly enjoyed bonding with his players.

Right out of the gate, VBK started his third season with a major challenge. The Leopards opened the 1953–54 campaign with the Redmen of St. John's University who were coached by Dusty DeStefanno. Despite a strike at all the New York City newspapers, a near-capacity crowd of 15,000 was on hand at the old Madison Square Garden, located at 50th Street and 8th Avenue. The first game of the doubleheader featured scoring sensation Bevo Francis from tiny Rio Grande College (Ohio) versus Adelphi College. In his freshman year at Rio Grande, Bevo had averaged 50.1 points per game against some very small colleges and universities (i.e., Hillsdale, Alliance, and Bluffton). The Adelphi cagers "held" Bevo to a mere thirty-two points while posting a fifteen point victory, and the myth of Bevo Francis faded as the season progressed.

In the second game, the youthful Lafayette Leopards were probably somewhat awed by the presence of Madison Square Garden. In the pre-game warm-ups, sophomore Eddy Knapp was introduced to Ned Irish, managing director of the facility. Never at a loss for words, Eddy mentioned to Irish, "Mr. Irish, I like your garden but where are the flowers?"

The "Garden Jitters," a common visitors syndrome, quickly infected the Lafayette team and they fell behind by 17-4 in the first quarter. But Lafayette settled down and outplayed the Johnies for the balance of the game, actually closing the gap to two points with a minute to go. The Redmen refused to panic, however, and clutch foul shooting enabled the heavily favored SJU to carve out a 66-61 victory.

At this early point in VBKs coaching career, "moral victories" seemed to outnumber "real victories." However, the concept of playing a strong schedule soon produced constructive results and the "W" column started to fill in.

The captain of the 1953–54 team was John Alviggi, who at 5'11" was all of four inches taller than Carril. Alviggi—who frequently shot the two-handed set shot—established the Lafayette single game scoring record of thirty-six points in a victory over CCNY, thus breaking the previous record of thirty-four jointly held by Carril and George Davidson. Butch liked to go to his best shooters, and John was his man for his third season at Lafayette.

Princeton University was always an early challenge on the Lafayette schedule, but sophomore forward George Young was oblivious to the "Tiger Hex" as he delivered twenty-four points to lead the Pards to their third straight win of the season. The play of sophomore guards Eddie Knapp and Ernie Peters along with Alviggi's thirteen points also were vital in the victory. Leon Miller at center provided the rebounding chores.

One of Lafayette's historical challenges had always been winning in Philadelphia. In a key early season game against St. Joseph's, Peters was quite concerned about his showing because he had encouraged some thirty fans from his home area of Delaware County to make the trip to the Hawks home gym to witness the game. Midway through the second half, Peters hadn't scored a point. Desperate, he launched a bomb from today's NBA three-point range. The shot clanged off the rim. Peters recalls what happened afterward. "During the next time-out Butch bellowed at me, 'Who's the shooter on this team?' I meekly replied 'John (Alviggi).' To which Butch barked, 'Well, Goddammit, pass him the ball!" Alviggi scored 20 points, Peters none, and the Pards lost 59-57.

The Pards later avenged the loss at St. Joe's with a convincing win at Alumni Gym. In the season's finale, a victory over Rutgers brought the Pards to a final 17-10 mark, the best thus far for the young VBK. Yet another sophomore, Todd Walker, a 6'6" forward, was critical in both wins. In hindsight, two tough losses to nearby rival

Muhlenberg were particularly painful. Nonetheless, Butch's embryonic coaching philosophy was taking hold. He preached Defense, Hustle, and Rebounding as the critical aspects to winning basketball. A player could have reason for an off night with his shot, but there was no excuse for not playing aggressive defense, boxing out on rebounds, or all-around hustle.

According to Knapp, "The hallmark of his philosophy was defense and having his athletes in top physical condition."

During the course of the '53–54 season, four of the sophomores—Peters, Knapp, Young, and Walker—bought some beer and visited Butch at his house. With Peters as their spokesman, the group essentially told Butch that they were better than the players who started ahead of them. They exhorted Butch to start themselves plus John Alviggi and they would win more games. Peters said, "Butch allowed us to get things off our chest. The end result was that he said he was the coach and he appreciated how we felt, but he was going to go with what he felt was best for the team."

The sophomore-led group did ultimately get more playing time, although the first time Butch accommodated them, they immediately fell behind to Gettysburg by fifteen points and eventually lost by twelve.

An annual pilgrimage to Buffalo to play the University of Buffalo was a social and athletic highlight for the Lafayette team. The night preceding the game, the team usually stayed at the hotel where the local burlesque queen (and her two poodles) was in residence. According to Cary Ahl, "She was fun. We would joke around with her a lot!"

After topping the U of B by 76-63, several of the players went to a nearby pub to celebrate the victory. But soon, the owner of the pub asked the well-behaved youths to leave. Apparently, a large portion of the pub's client base was derived from Canadian Indian traffic. The Indians couldn't drink in Canada, and so they crossed the border to New York. The owner said they were frightened by seeing so many tall people and he was afraid of what they might do. The Indians bought beer by the case, put it in the middle of the table, and when the Lafayette players left there was a stack two high! On the train-ride home to Easton, the Lafayette players consumed a case of beer with the referees.

During VBK's initial coaching years, Lafayette did not fall under the NCAA guidelines permitting freshmen to play varsity basketball, unlike some other schools on its schedule (i.e., LaSalle, Muhlenberg, and Albright). But VBK's recruiting class, represented by the 1953–54 freshmen team, showed a lot of promise in posting a 12-5 mark. Most talented among the frosh were rebounding phenom Jim Radcliff and sharp-shooting Stu Murray.

Prior to attending Lafayette, Radcliff starred for the Hill School basketball team. A hard-fought scrimmage against the Lafayette freshmen led to the players bringing Jim to VBK's attention. After Butch made a special recruiting trip to Pottstown, Jim was so impressed that he immediately phoned his father at his automobile agency to say that he had decided on Lafayette instead of Penn State.

In recollecting his playing years at Lafayette, Radcliff talked about the intensity of the team workouts. Radcliff recalled the classic VBK drill which entailed four players passing the ball back and forth going down the court. The ball *could not touch the floor.* You had to make the basket at one end of the floor and come back to make the basket at the other end. Any mistakes, and you had to do it again ("and one") and again ("and two") and on *ad infinitum.* The drill taught ball-handling skills without dribbling and made the players focus on making layups. Dunking was not permitted, as it disrupted the fluidity of the activity. Down and back. Back and forth. The drill was a great vehicle for conditioning as well. The players soon tabbed him "Big Hearted Coach." "Do it again" was his response.

Butch initially classified the drill as "and ones" and "and twos," which stood for the number of layups required. He expanded the drill to be labeled "and threes" and "and fours." Eventually, his players figured out a way of "beating the system" in which two or three of the players would "dog it" while one player would go full tilt. He then modified the drill to include all players touching the end line at the completion of each rotation.

At 6'6", the athletic Radcliff filled a long-standing void of VBK's first three Lafayette teams. Radcliff became an "instant starter" as a sophomore and soon became the master of the "double-double," averaging over sixteen rebounds and sixteen points per game. In retrospect, he was like a smaller version of Bill Walton. The pure-shooting Murray, the brother of Philadelphia Warrior star Ken Murray, had pumped in thirty-six points against the Rutgers freshmen and soon became a critical member of the varsity lineup.

1954–1955: The Near Perfect Season

As the 1954–55 hoop season got underway, optimism was at a feverish pitch. Early season victories over Princeton and Delaware fed the frenzy. In the Delaware game, the impact of VBK's coaching was apparent as Young scored thirty-three points, most of which were scored on the end of fast breaks as perfected in Butch's patented layup drill. The momentum for a great season was intensifying.

VBK used a squad consisting mostly of juniors and sophomores, thus highlighting the talents of Radcliff and Murray. Todd Walker, Corky Galtere, and Davey Jones also gave the Pards more muscle under the boards. Rebounding soon became an asset rather than a liability to the Leopards. Coupled with the radar style shooting of Murray and George Young, Lafayette possessed a powerful inside-outside combination.

Eddie Knapp provided the team with a rallying cry. Nicknamed "Dward," Eddie made a fist with his knuckles raised, palm downward, while making a pumping motion from the waist. It became Ed's trademark and soon all the players adopted the motion, not unlike the high fives and knuckle wraps we know today.

In the early Fifties, the social scene at Lafayette centered around the fraternity system. Lafayette was renowned for its weekend party atmosphere. Intra-Fraternity Weekends (which the students dubbed as I-F) in the spring and the fall featured renowned "big bands" such as Stan Kenton and Count Basie. Young women were imported from Cedar Crest, Centenary College, and from spots all over the eastern seaboard. During the week, however, many students ventured their way down the steep hill leading from the well-defined campus into the back streets of Easton where a plethora of bars subsisted. On many occasions during the off-season, members of the basketball team strolled to the base of College Hill to get a few beers. At the Paradise Inn (a.k.a. "The PD"), the favorite order of all was Cold Gold at ten cents a pop. A favored form of entertainment was Capt. Ernie Peters' rendition of "Stranger in Paradise."

As a younger coach, Butch enjoyed socializing with his players. On many occasions, during the off season, he invited members of the basketball team to his home at 227 McCartney Street just one block from the Alumni Gym. Beer was served and Butch relished the gatherings. As Coach Butch perhaps overindulged more than his players, he frequently dozed off at these little parties. The next day, the coach awakened to find small signs pinned to his shirt or sitting in the refrigerator. The signs read, "The Coach can't take it!" The parties continued and so did the signs.

The nation's leading scorer was Frank Selvy of Furman University, who averaged 41.7 points per game. Selvy bulged his statistics when on February 13, 1954, he scored 100 points against Newberry College (non-Division I) to shatter Mlkvy's record of seventy-three registered against Wilkes.

A firm believer in "hands on" management, Butch frequently scrimmaged with his team in the off-season. The ultimate gym rat, Butch was in excellent physical condition and was only about ten years older, more or less, than most of his players. In his early coaching years, these workouts helped Butch set the example of how to play an aggressive man-to-man defense. Likewise, whenever he would catch one of his players "turning his head on defense," he would immediately cut for the basket setting up an easy back-door lay-up. *"Never turn your head on defense"* was a cry frequently heard during Pard practice sessions. On offense, his strategy was focused on motion, picks, cuts and getting free for an easy lay-up. The "slob" skills which he perfected as a member of the New York Knickerbockers were soon transferred to the playing styles of the Lafayette cagers.

Recruiting was one of Bill's greatest talents. His strengths included his physical presence, his history as an athlete, and his enormous charisma. He could go to any level to secure a prospect. As a recruiter, Butch found fertile territory in Essex County, New Jersey, taking advantage of the concentration of talent that participated in the County's tournament each February. VBK lined up Stu Murray (West Orange), Tipsy Werner and Corky Galtere (Belleville), Tony Mack (Bloomfield), Davey Jones (East Orange), and Ed Knapp (Irvington). Niagara's Jim McConnell (Belleville) was one player who slipped away and came back to haunt the Leopards.

Coach VBK, given his own Princeton undergraduate experience, knew how important it was for his players to stay on top of their academic game. Corky Galtere was having a big problem with biology, and Butch's wife Florence had been a biology major in college. So Butch volunteered her services for tutoring. Galtere felt like he was intruding, since the only free time Flo had was when the young children were taking their naps. "She deserves the Congressional Medal of Honor for just trying to teach me," Galtere remarked.

As expected, on December 11, 1955, Lafayette lost to NCAA champion LaSalle. Chalk up thirty-five points for Tom Gola! One week later, Lafayette traveled to New Rochelle, New York, to meet Iona University. The Gaels showed no ill effects from the graduation of future Knick star Richie Guerin and thoroughly embarrassed Lafayette by 100-68. The thirty-two point loss was VBK's worst defeat and represented the only game in which his team allowed 100 points or more. Forty-five years after the game, VBK shuddered when reminded of the defeat. "They killed us!" he remarked while shaking his head in disgust. Galtere mentioned that the White Plains floor was like a skating rink. Iona handled the surface without a problem.

The loss to Iona acted as a classic wake-up call to van Breda Kolff and his young team. The 1954–55 Leopards then reeled off twenty consecutive victories, the longest ever recorded in the school's history.

The twenty-three wins turned out to be the most wins ever accomplished by a Lafayette team, and the 23-2 regular season record was the best percentage season ever. The twenty-three outright wins withstood the test of time until March 2000 when Coach Fran O'Hanlon won twenty-four games in a season.

Much of the success of the 1954–55 team can be attributed to the play of "The Red Caps," a spirited collection of substitutes which brought a fierce level of competition to Leopard practices. According to Radcliff, "they literally beat the crap out of us every day, many times scoring more in the scrimmages than the starters did." Named after "Carling's Red Cap Ale," a popular brew in the '50s, the press caught wind of the groups importance to the team and sought the derivation of their nickname. In the interest of propriety, Coach VBK told the sports writers that they were called "Red Caps" because they wore red vests during scrimmages.

The ring leader of the Red Caps was Jimbo Powers, who was called "Chief" by the other members of this team-within-a-team. At first, VBK had his doubts about having a subsidiary division within his master plan, but after witnessing the furor the Red Caps generated in practice, he relented and worked with the "Chief." Mack, Werner, Lloyd Zachery, Jones, and Galtere were the mainstays of the Red Caps "wrecking crew." The only senior on the

The Early Lafayette Years: 1951–1955   53

team, Powers died in a car crash shortly after graduation from Lafayette.

Actually, VBK effectively used Stu Murray as the sixth man on the team. Greek mythology was popular at Lafayette and so Stu's nickname was Cyclops, or "Cye the Eye." Over his three year varsity career at Lafayette, Murray scored 1,177 points to rank seventeenth in the school's history. Unfortunately for Stu, he was born a little too soon as most of his field goals would have counted as three pointers in today's game. At the point of his graduation, Murray ranked second on the list of all-time scorers. He was inducted into the Lafayette Hall of Fame in 1989.

Murray went on to be a history teacher and coach at Shawnee High School in Medford, New Jersey. He later wrote, "I still think that was the best team Lafayette's ever had . . . He assembled that team through his personality and ability to recruit ball players."

One of the highs along the extended ride of the 1954–55 season was the Hofstra Christmas Invitational Basketball Tourney held between Christmas and New Year's. Lafayette swept the field, including wins over St. Peters, Marietta, and host Hofstra. George Young, reflecting on the influence of the tourney some forty-five years later, said:

> "At Hofstra, we not only played and practiced together but we also went out together as a group. We ate together, even slept as a group in a large barracks-like room during the tournament. It was what you would call today, a bonding experience. During the games we seemed to work better together, as if we finally realized each other's strengths and weaknesses and played together by using that knowledge. That carried over for the rest of the season."

Peters confirmed Young's thesis about the tourney. "After we beat a good Hofstra team, we were off to the races."

At the conclusion of the season, Hofstra star Bill Thieben received the coveted Haggerty Award recognizing the outstanding player in the Metropolitan New York area. During the Hofstra holiday tournament, Thieben was practically unstoppable but Lafayette prevailed in the final game to win 75-72. At the time, he "did not like the coach from Easton," but he admired him because he was a winner. In about a year, Thieben would get to know VBK a lot better.

In his fourth year as head of Lafayette basketball, VBK had already set some astonishing records. For his coaching achievements, Bill van Breda Kolff was named "Coach of the Year" by the Metropolitan Writers Association. At the tender age of thirty-one, he was the youngest ever to receive the award.

In addition, the coach and the team were also honored by the Philadelphia Sportswriters as the most outstanding visiting team to play in Philadelphia during the 1954–55 season.

The sportswriters of Philadelphia, however, were unaware of the escapades of "The Lafayette Hotel Felons." The evening started at the Civic Center with Lafayette's bizarre victory over St. Joe's by a 69-62 margin. Lafayette went to the foul line fifty-seven times and converted on forty-one of those opportunities. Otherwise, they were outscored from the floor by 50-28. After the game, six of the Lafayette players wanted to catch the final quarter of the Villanova-Seton Hall game at the Palestra across town on the Penn campus. Coach VBK granted permission to the Jimbo Powers-led group to go see the end of the game, provided that they were back to the bus by 10:30 p.m. The game went into overtime, and suddenly the Lafayette players had missed their curfew. They dashed back to the rendez-vous area for the bus, and it was gone. They all laughed and figured that the Coach was trying to teach them a lesson. For sure, they thought, the bus was located just around the corner.

The Lafayette players searched the entire one block area and there was no bus to be found. After taking an inventory of their lean financial resources, the players adjourned to a nearby tap room to discuss their strategy. By then, the group had picked up two more Lafayette students. The decision was made to check into a nearby hotel and take the train back to Easton the next day. Jimbo Powers and Corky Galtere secured the room, and one by one, six Lafayette players plus two of their pals made their way up to the room. Eight guys in two beds or anyplace you could find to sleep! The next morning, each player left the hotel separately, not carrying any team bags (which included the Lafayette uniform). Last to leave was Jimbo Powers who toted at least six bags. As he approached the lobby, an employee of the hotel ordered him to stop. He kept on moving, and just outside the hotel, he tossed the bags along to the various players. The group hurried to the train station thinking for sure Philadelphia police would be on their case. The police never showed. The bill for their accommodations was never paid.

At practice the following Monday, nothing was said about the incident. The players, however, thenceforth adopted the nickname "Big Hearted Coach" for VBK. The players never missed another curfew.

In reviewing the fabulous season with Butch, he dwelled on the Pards victory over the then-powerful New York Athletic Club team. The contest was viewed as an "exhibition game" in the eyes of the NCAA since the NYAC was obviously not a college or university. Still, the game was hard-fought, as the NYAC contingent suffered its only loss for the season at the hands of Lafayette. The Pard victory was accomplished at the awkward NYAC facility, no less, which added credence to the young team's capabilities. Butch liked to think his team was 24-2, perhaps with a little footnote or asterisk in the record book.

Toward the end of the regular season, Marquette University boasted the longest winning streak in the country at twenty-two games. When they lost to Notre Dame, Lafayette at twenty games moved into first place as the team with the longest winning streak by routing St. Joseph's University by a 83-67 margin. Jim Radcliff scored twenty-one points and five of his teammates scored in double figures. Lafayette College, one of the smallest representatives in Division I basketball, suddenly vaulted into the national limelight.

Lafayette Jim Radcliff (14) jumps center against St. Peters University early in the 1954 season. Lafayette defeated the Peacocks 78-54 and started the longest winning streak in the school's history (20) and earned the Leopards a berth in the NIT. Credit: VBK private collection

Arch rival Lehigh came ever so close to spoiling Lafayette's dream season. Over a span of twelve years, Lafayette had chalked up twenty-four straight wins over the Engineers, including an early season 61-45 romp in Easton. However, the rematch at Grace Hall in Bethlehem was a different matter. In fact, Lehigh led the Pards with twenty-three seconds to go by 48-47. In their excitement, the Engineers fouled Stu Murray, Lafayette's best foul shooter, who calmly sank two free throws, and the Leopards secured a 49-48 victory. Otherwise, the spectacular streak would have ended, as well as any chances of an NIT bid. Coach VBK noted after the game, "God was with us."

Unlike today, the college teams of the mid-1950s had their choice of playing in the NCAA or the NIT tournament. The NCAA, given its regional bias, immediately ran into a problem when the two strongest teams in the New England District—Holy Cross and the University of Connecticut—opted to play in the NIT. For its New England District representative, the NCAA settled for Williams College, a school better known for its academic than athletic achievement. The Williams College Ephs (so nicknamed in honor of its founder Ephrain Williams) had a respectable record of 14-6.

Seeking some better-known names elsewhere, the NCAA selection committee tapped Middle Atlantic Conference Champion LaSalle even though the Explorers had outwardly expressed interest in returning to the NIT.

Paul Horowitz, the highly respected sports writer for the *Newark Evening News,* did some strong lobbying with the NIT committee membership and supported his convictions in articles about Lafayette's outstanding team. He stressed the fact that the team had averaged 82.7 points per game to rank nineteenth in the country. Three times they had passed the 100 mark during the season. He kept posing the question in his column, "How long will it take the NIT selections committee to get around to picking Lafayette as one of its twelve entries?"

VBK always used to criticize the NIT for being overweighted with Catholic institutions. At one point, he advocated the NIT be called the CIT instead (i.e., Catholic Invitational Tournament). Indeed, from 1952 through 1955, in the four seasons when Butch coached at Lafayette, fourteen of the sixteen final four participants in the NIT were from Catholic colleges. He frequently thought Lafayette would have been selected more readily if its name were Saint Lafayette!

Horowitz was well aware of the driving force behind the Lafayette attack. So often Radcliff and Walker got the rebounds and started a fast break, threw the outlet pass to Peters or Knapp, and then a pass to Young for the simple layup. The drills, the teamwork, the perfection demanded of VBK helped George Young finish tenth in the nation in field goal percentage and produced a roster with six players averaging in double figures. The NIT could have a scoring machine at its disposal!

Actually, Murray averaged 9.9 points per game. Butch and the entire team made a special effort to get that extra point, but Stu just fell short!

Soon the NIT responded with a bid—it was delighted to include Lafayette in its twelve team field. Not only had VBK compiled the best statistical record in the schools history, but also he had achieved Lafayette's first ever postseason birth.

The 1955 NIT Tournament

Lafayette entered the NIT as a relatively obscure selection although their record of 23-2 was the best in the field. (See chart.) Other than St. Francis of Loreto, the balance of the NIT field had participated regularly in NITs and Holiday Festival Tourneys for several years. Athough Lafayette was prepared to play anyone, its first round opponent would be a tough one. Lafayette soon discovered its first round foe would be the Purple Eagles from Niagara University.

Niagara had achieved quite a record during the 1954–55 season, posting a 19-5 mark and leading the nation in rebounding. An impressive victory over Holy Cross, the defending NIT champions, highlighted the Eagles' season. Niagara's star was Ed Fleming, a 6'3" center with amazing leaping ability. Fleming held the NCAA record for most minutes played in one ball game when in 1953 he played all seventy minutes of a six-overtime win over Siena. He wore number 70 to acknowledge the achievement.

Niagara also featured stars Charley Hoxie, Hubie Brown, and Jim McConnell. They were loaded! Niagara's coach was the veteran Taps Gallagher, who was in his twenty-first season at the helm of the New York college. The Lafayette rooting session at the Garden certainly made its presence known as 1500 fans and students—virtually the size of the total enrollment of the school—were bused in from the Easton environs. The Leopards entered the contest without the full services of Stu Murray, who sustained an ankle injury against NYU. Key rebounder Todd Walker was also sidelined with "water on the knee." The "Garden Jitters" arrow favored Niagara, which was appearing at MSG for the fifth time in 1954–1955, and had competed in NIT in four of the last five years. For Lafayette, it was the first visit of the season and its first NIT ever.

Despite the efforts of Radcliff and Galtere, the Eagles out-rebounded Lafayette by an overwhelming 79-42 margin. VBK indicated that the Niagara front court literally played volleyball off the offensive boards. Nonetheless, the Pards stayed within five points most of the game as the hot hand of George Young (thirty-one points) kept them in the game. "George had the game of his life!" Butch noted. But Fleming's twenty-eight points, mostly from inside, proved insurmountable and Lafayette eventually lost 83-70. Jimmy McConnell, the lad from Essex County who got away, registered twenty-five points.

The power rating of the NIT field in the early- to mid-1950s was easily on a par with the rival NCAA tourney, and many would contend that the NIT was even a stronger event. In 1953, for example, Seton Hall University was ranked third in the Nation and boasted a 28-2 record. Behind stars Walter Dukes and Richie Regan, the Pirates swept the NIT field. In 1954, Holy Cross (23-2) ranked eighth nationally and took the NIT championship. The field included Duquesne (number 3 and 24-2) and Western Kentucky (number 4 and 28-1).

Maurice Stokes of St. Francis of Loretto (Pa) was named the MVP, even though the event was won by Duquesne and its superstar combination of Sihugo Green and Dick Ricketts. Stokes scored 124 points in four games to set the NIT record at the time. Stokes' performance in an overtime loss to number 9 Dayton University, whose line-up included 7-footer Bill Uhl and superstar John Horan, is one of the most memorable in Garden history. Holy Cross was paced by Tom Heinsohn. These were indeed the glory years of the NIT.

The 1954–55 Lafayette team stands out in the annals of the school's basketball history as one of its best, but for Butch—more than their record—they *played the game right.* From this viewpoint, he frequenetly referred to this team as the finest he ever coached.

Some six weeks after losing to Niagara and four weeks after receiving his "Best Coach" award, Butch van Breda Kolff abruptly submitted his resignation as the coach of Lafayette. He had assumed the head coaching position at Hofstra College in Hempstead, New York. Lafayette athletic director Bill Anderson was shocked by the move as the college had supposedly extended a substantial raise to VBK. But Hofstra's offer must have been fairly generous, as VBK stated publicly he was leaving for "personal and financial reasons." Radcliff and most of the other players expressed extreme disappointment in Butch's decision.

One of the factors influencing Butch's decision was that his Lafayette contract required him to coach lacrosse in the spring in addition to soccer in the fall. Although Butch's athletic background included just about every sport possible, Butch had never coached lacrosse before, and in fact had never even seen a game. His first coaching effort resulted in a 0-9 record. When interviewed about his prospects for his second season as lacrosse coach, he responded, "Look at the record. We can't do any worse." Unknown to Butch, Athletic Director Anderson had lined up a ten game schedule and sure enough the Pard stickmen went 0-10. In his third year, however, the lacrosse team broke the ice and won its opener versus Adelphi. Butch recalls the gala celebration that ensued after the victory.

The Early Lafayette Years: 1951–1955   **61**

Bobby Geer was one of Butch's star soccer players. In a closely contested game against CCNY, Geer broke away for an apparent uncontested open shot versus the Beaver goalie. Geer booted the ball toward the net, and it found its target to give the Pards a 2-1 victory. However, the CCNY goalie—as he lunged to block the ball—landed on Geer's kicking leg after he had let fly with the winning shot. The goalie crushed Geer's leg and he was taken to the hospital. Geer had a broken leg and would miss the balance of the season. Several years later, Geer's daughter would marry baseball star Cal Ripken Jr. of the Baltimore Orioles, the man who broke Lou Gehrig's iron man streak of most played consecutive games.

The normally talkative van Breda Kolff turns very reticent when asked why he left the Lafayette program. But Eddie Knapp, former president of the First Fidelity

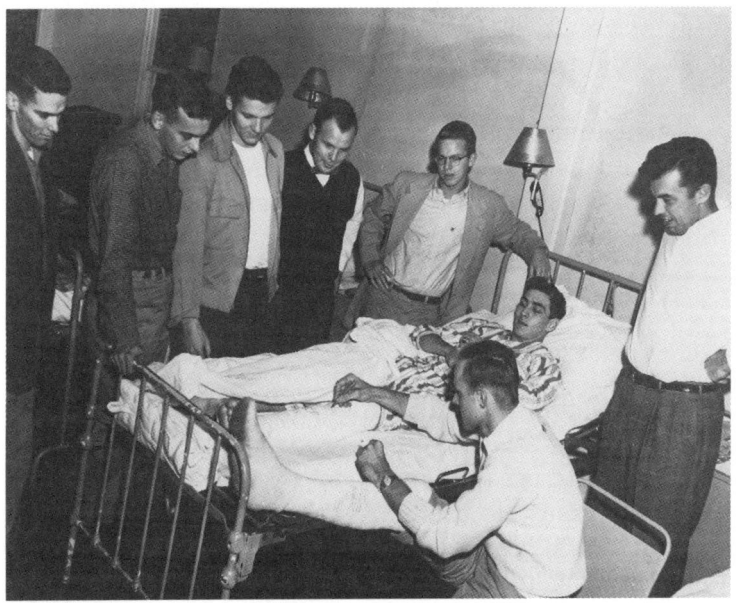

Bobby Geer, one of Butch's star soccer players at Lafayette College, lies in a hospital bed in Easton PA after simultaneously scoring the winning goal and breaking his leg against CCNY in 1954. Later on in life, Geer's daughter married Cal Ripken Jr., legendary iron man of the Baltimores Orioles. Credit: VBK private collection

Bancorp, directly addressed the question from the financial standpoint: "He was married, had a child, and was earning $5,000 per year. Based on his performance as a coach, he requested a $500 raise and was turned down by the Athletic Director (Anderson). In my opinion, the 1955–56 team would have been even stronger than the 1954–55 team if he would have remained the coach."

VBK's legacy continued at Lafayette as the nucleus of his NIT team returned for two more seasons. Although VBK recommended Pete Carril as his replacement, athletic director Bill Anderson selected George Davidson, star of the 1951 team, to be the coach. Employing VBK-recruited personnel, including three graduates from the freshman squad—Bob Mantz, Joe Sterlein, and Tom Brett—Davidson immediately took the Leopards to a second NIT appearance in 1956.

The Pards were eliminated in the first round by St. Francis (New York) by a score of 85-74.

In 1957, Davidson led Lafayette to a 23-5 record and its first ever trip to the NCAA. Despite Murray's thirty point performance, Lafayette's bid for its first postseason tournament win fell short before Syracuse University by a 75-71 difference. Davidson was elected to the Lafayette Hall of Fame for his achievements.

In the 1957 tourney, Wilt "The Stilt" Chamberlain burst onto the collegiate basketball scene as a star for Kansas University. He led the Jayhawks all the way to the final game only to lose to the University of North Carolina by one point 54-53. The famed "underground railroad," which siphoned off many of New York City's finest basketball players in the direction of Chapel Hill, North Carolina, paid its way as the victory for UNC sealed a perfect undefeated season of 32-0 for the amazing Tar Heels. Some twelve years later, "the Stilt" would appear in the NBA Finals and have as his coach none other than Butch van Breda Kolff.

The Early Lafayette Years: 1951–1955

☆ ☆ ☆

Nonetheless, the era of 1950–1957 was a successful one for little Lafayette College. Three post-season appearances in three years were indeed marvelous achievements.

In 1958, the Board of Trustees of Lafayette College voted to eliminate athletic scholarships. Athletes seeking financial aid were required to qualify on a "need" basis.

In 1970, Lafayette College elected to go coeducational and expand its enrollment to approximately 2,000 students.

In 1978, Jim Radcliff became the first VBK recruit to be inducted into the Lafayette Hall of Fame. The two-time All-American still holds the College career rebounding record of 1,148 and ranks twenty-seventh on the list of all-time scorers. He later played four years in the Eastern Basketball League. Radcliff called VBK "The best coach I ever played for."

By 1984, Interstate Highway 78 connected Easton, Pennsylvania, to the rest of civilization, essentially replacing the albatross of Route 22. In the spring of 1984, Butch van Breda Kolff drove his Mazda pickup truck from Mississippi to Pennsylvania and again took over the head coaching job at Lafayette. A lot happened in the personal and basketball life of VBK in those intervening twenty-nine years.

THE LOG OF LAFAYETTE COLLEGE'S 23-3 SEASON (1954–55)

Date	Opponent	Score	W-L
12/4/54	Swathmore	91-54	W
12/8	Princeton Univ.	85-74	W
12/11	Delaware Univ.	86-62	W
12/15	LaSalle	60-76	L
12/18	Iona	68-101	L
12/22	St Peters College*	78-54	W
12/29	Marietta*	90-61	W
12/30	Hofstra College*	75-72	W
1/5/55	Moravian	90-61	W
1/8	Wilkes College	104-63	W
1/12	Lehigh	61-45	W
1/15	Bucknell	117-93	W
1/19	Muhlenberg	84-70	W
1/22	St. Joseph's	69-62	W
1/29	Albright	88-71	W
2/3	Rider	81-49	W
2/7	Scranton	70-54	W
2/9	Bucknell	81-72	W
2/12	Rutgers	93-75	W
2/16	Muhlenberg	81-70	W
2/19	N Y U	99-71	W
2/23	Lehigh	49-48	W
2/26	Gettysburg	94-74	W
3/2	Rutgers	101-69	W
3/5	St. Joseph's	83-67	W
	N.I.T.		
3/12	Niagara #	70-83	L

*Hofstra Invitational at Hempstead, New York
at Madison Square Garden

THE 1955 NATIONAL INVITATIONAL TOURNAMENT ("THE NIT")

Entrees	Regular Season Record	Percentage
Lafayette College	23-2	.920
*Dayton University	22-3 (9)	.880
Connecticut University	20-4	.833
*Duquesne University	18-4 (6)	.814
*Manhattan College	17-4	.810
*Niagara University	19-5	.792
*St. Francis (Loretto, Penn.)	18-5	.783
Cincinnati University	19-6	.760
*Holy Cross College	18-6	.760
*Saint Louis University	19-7 (20)	.731
Louisville University	18-7	.720
*Seton Hall University	17-8	.680

*Indicates Catholic college or university
Figures in parentheses: National Ranking in Final AP Poll

BOX SCORE, LAFAYETTE COLLEGE VERSUS NIAGARA UNIVERSITY MARCH 1955

LAFAYETTE COLLEGE

Player	Goals	FTs	Fouls	Total
Young	12	7	4	31
Radcliff	4	2	2	10
Mack	0	1	0	1
Knapp	3	2	1	8
Murray	0	0	0	0
Werner	0	0	0	0
Galtere	2	1	3	5
Peters	4	7	0	15
Totals	25	20	10	70

NIAGARA UNIVERSITY

Player	Goals	FTs	Fouls	Total
Hoxie	6	0	2	12
McDonald	0	0	0	0
Brown	1	2	1	4
McConnell	11	3	4	25
Osa	0	0	0	0
Donohue	0	0	0	0
Hemans	4	1	3	9
Worosz	2	1	3	5
Prechtl	0	0	0	0
Flemming	12	4	2	28
Totals	36	11	15	83

Chapter 3

The Early Hofstra College Years 1955–1962

"They [the members of the 23-1 Hofstra basketball team] remember how they loved playing for Butch van Breda Kolff, who later would bark at Bill Bradley and Wilt Chamberlain the same way he barked at them."

George Vecsey, *NY Times* Columnist

When Butch van Breda Kolff took over as head basketball coach of Hofstra College in 1955, he had a built-in franchise in Bill Thieben. About to enter his senior year, Thieben had dominated the rebounding and scoring statistics for the Flying Dutchmen during his sophomore and junior seasons. His spectacular numbers for those two seasons are outlined in the box at the top of page 68.

Over his career, he had a shooting percentage of .498. He once pulled down forty-three boards in a game against Springfield College. Included in his scoring figures was a forty-eight-point outburst against Wilkes College, which still stands as the most points ever scored by a Hofstra player.

Whereas at Lafayette he had six players who averaged in double figures, Butch would have to alter his strategy to accommodate such an outstanding athlete. VBK regretted that he would have but one season with the talented Thieben, and immediately set out to capitalize on his ability.

Season	Rebounds	Rebounds/ Game	Points	Points/ Game
1953–54	620	25.8	589	24.6
1954–55	627	24.4	760	29.2

Forty-four years later, when asked to describe his first year at Hofstra, Butch simply replied "I had Bill Thieben."

Originally, Thieben was upset by the departure of his mentor Frank Reilly. "A great coach and motivater, he recruited me. I was heartbroken. And now my new coach was my arch enemy from Easton. Now what?"

Slowly, however, Thieben warmed up to the VBK methodology. First, there was the team meeting called in the fall of 1955. Recalling Butch's pep talk to the team, Thieben remembered the coach saying:

> "I am a winner. I like winning games. I want all you guys to come over to my house, meet my family, and we will get to know one another."

Before long, Butch, Hofstra, and Thieben were in harmony. After conquering Fairfield in the season's opener,

Thieben in College. From *Hofstra Media Guide*

The Early Hofstra College Years: 1955–1962

Bill Thieben was VBK's franchise player at Hofstra for the 1955–56 season. Forty-five years later, the two remain friends and meet regularly to rehash old times. Credit: Thieben

Hofstra traveled to Princeton to play Cappy Cappon's Tigers. For Butch, this was his fifth game against his former college coach. While at Lafayette, he had split four games with Cappy. Butch definitely wanted to maintain the edge in the "series." For the Hofstra players, this was one of the bigger name schools on their schedule.

Midway through the game, Hofstra fell behind by fifteen points, and Butch made a few adjustments at the half, but didn't get his troops overly aroused. "Not a good day at the beach" about summarized his thoughts concerning the deficit facing his team. The second half was all Dutchmen as they outscored Princeton by twenty-four points and won 69-60.

Hofstra added ten more wins as they blitzed through their early schedule to start the season at 12-0. Winning their own Christmas Tourney added satisfaction to the streak. Following a home-court loss to Maryland State, another eight-game win skein brought the Flying Dutchmen to 20-1. Late season losses to St. Johns and Manhattan brought their overall record to 22-4.

Nicknamed "The Babe," Thieben adapted to the VBK coaching style as he continued to rebound and score at the same phenomenal pace. His final career rebounding average per game was 24.2 and points per game were 26.9. Both marks still stand as the best ever recorded at Hofstra.

For his accomplishments, Thieben received the coveted Haggerty Award, which is annually given to the outstanding player in the metropolitan New York area as determined by the Metropolitan Basketball Writers Association. The award, subsequently dubbed the NIT/Haggerty Award, has been presented since 1936, and three times has been won by Hofstra players: Thieben (1956), Richie Laurel (1977), and "Speedy" Claxton (2000). Butch felt that one of his recruits—Steve Nisenson—was deserving of the award during the 1962–65 period. Nisenson broke Thieben's career scoring record for total number of points (Thieben's average is slightly higher) and still ranks as Hofstra's all-time leader. His efforts were overshadowed by Barry Kramer (NYU), Nick Werkman (Seton Hall), and Warren Isaac (Iona).

The Early Hofstra College Years: 1955–1962

Part of Thieben's responsibilities was driving the team around Pennsylvania. "The coach knew every gin mill in Pennsylvania. So when we were on the road coming back from Lycoming, Muhlenberg, Sranton, Albright, etc., we hit them all. I remember doing a lot of driving myself." Later on in life, Butch challenged Thieben's recollection. "He did it once!"

Upon graduation, Thieben continued to exhibit his talents in the NBA and enjoyed six successful seasons with the Ft. Wayne Pistons. He is a history professor at St. Joseph's College (New York) at the school's Patchogue campus. Thieben writes of his friendship with Coach VBK:

"I have been an educator for forty-four years, and with any luck will drop dead in front of a classroom. As Robert Frost said, 'I am not a teacher but an awakener.' I am very good at what I do and that is in large part because my mentor was an awakener and/or motivator. I learned from the best. He taught basketball and I teach history."

To this day, he remains a close friend of Butch's.

Founded in 1935, Hofstra College was a relatively young institution when Butch van Breda Kolff took over as head basketball coach in 1955. After completing his one and only coaching experience in lacrosse, Butch made his way from Easton, Pennsylvania to Hempstead, New York in 1955, taking Route 22 in New Jersey, the Holland Tunnel through New York City, and the infamous Long Island Expressway for roughly twenty-five miles to the fifteen-acre Hofstra campus.

Hofstra is a family Dutch name which literally translated from the Frisian dialect means "from the courtyard or farm." Hofstrans migrated from the Province of Friesland in Holland to the United States around the middle of the eighteenth century, and one of their descendants—William Sake Hofstra—started the Nassau Lumber Company in Hempstead. William S. Hofstra fared well financially, and his mansion (which he named "The

Netherlands") ultimately evolved into the epicenter of the Hofstra University campus. Currently known as "Hofstra Hall," the historic mansion is the seat of the school's president and other top officials. The Dutch influence is also exhibited in the school's alma mater, which essentially is the Dutch national anthem (entitled "The Netherlands") featuring lyrics written by a Hofstra University faculty member.

Hofstra has always shown pride in its Dutch heritage. Until late in 2000 when school officials adopted the transparent sobriquet of "The Pride," the nickname for its sports teams had always been "The Flying Dutchmen." Every spring, the Dutch Festival highlights 100,000 tulips and traditional Dutch food and beverages. A Volks Parade featuring Dutch costumes and a Dutch Burgher Guard are among the activities. Van Bourgondien's, one of the nation's leading tulip importers and distributors since 1919, advertises in the College's athletic game programs.

Hofstra was one of the early colleges to host a holiday tournament at its own campus. The primary objective of the tourney was to provide competition during the normally lean period experienced by smaller colleges during the Christmas recess. The tourney's founding fathers were by no means interested in colleges specializing in the "production of high powered basketball squads" which demand big money guarantees. According to the Hofstra mission statement about the tourney, "this was strictly a tournament for colleges and universities whose main desire is for a sound basketball program that is just one segment of an equally sound overall program of intercollegiate athletics."

As mentioned in the previous chapter, while at Lafayette, Butch successfully swept the eight-team field and upended Hofstra in the tournament finals of the 1954 event. In his first season at Hofstra, Butch roared by Bucknell, Wagner, and Muhlenberg to take the tourney for the hosts. In effect, he won the tourney two years in a row—but for two different colleges!

To supplement his income, Butch frequently worked nights at either Roosevelt or Yonkers Racetracks. He

The Early Hofstra College Years: 1955–1962   73

rarely gambled on the races, but worked some nights until eleven P.M. when not otherwise engaged coaching the Dutchmen. Occasionally, he would hit the daily double "big time" and immediately spread the wealth by buying drinks for all within the Hofstra athletic community. In short, Butch van Breda Kolff always felt right at home in the Hofstra environment, and may partially explain his thirteen year record at Hofstra, easily the longest in his well-traveled career. In addition to coaching the basketball team, Butch was the freshman soccer coach. He traveled extensively with the varsity and drove one of the vehicles on many a road trip. John Uustol, a member of the Hofstra soccer team from 1959–62, speculated that Butch might have opted for a career in soccer if there had been more lucrative career opportunities in the sport at the time. "Relatively speaking, Butch was a much better soccer player than a basketball player." Basketball definitely had the monetary edge, the more visible financial future. Uustol also mentioned that Butch was "everyone's friend" on the trips. "He loved to party," he added.

In the mid-'50s, Hofstra was almost exclusively a commuter college, relying on local students to fill its classrooms. Huge parking lots dotted the otherwise attractive campus. A series of quonset huts functioned as dorms. Students from beyond the commuting range lived either in these huts or with local families who would rent out living space. After class, there was little interaction between professors and students, coaches and athletes. After a certain hour, everyone just dispersed. Basketball recruiting was confined almost exclusively to the Long Island environs.

Hofstra initially played in the small college division (Division II) of the NCAA and was eligible for the "little dance" or small college division year end tourney. They upgraded to Division I as the enrollment and reputation of the school's sports program mounted. In the mid-'70s, they made back-to-back appearances in the "big dance" but lost to UConn by 80-78 (1976) and Notre Dame 90-83 (1977), overriding outstanding performances by Richie Laurel.

Despite their banner record of 22-4, the Thieben-led Dutchmen saw no post-season action. While Lafayette College was playing in its second straight NIT under VBK's successor coach George Davidson, Hofstra and its Division II classification just didn't fit the guidelines of the tournament. Butch resurrected his theory that the NIT favored Catholic institutions. He frequently dubbed the tourney the CIT, i.e., "Catholic Invitational Tourney." He sincerely thought the NIT missed the boat by not having a showcase player like Thieben. Thieben was easily to Hofstra what Maurice Stokes had been for St. Francis of Loretto in the 1955 tourney.

The "Makeshift" 11-15 Season

With Thieben graduated, Butch had to face the 1956–57 season with an entirely new coaching strategy or focus. When he received his eligibility reports from the Hofstra administration, he discovered that four of his expected returning starters were scholastically ineligible. Butch was frantic! He scouted the intramural touch football league and landed Bob Burness. Soon he recruited John Baldwin from the varsity football team. Baldwin stood an unimpressive 5'9" but had the aggressive skills that Butch looked for in his players. Lance Blackshaw was a walk-on transfer from Princeton who made the team.

Butch put together a team of eight athletic players. Improvising the fact they didn't have the minimum number of players to have effective intra-squad scrimmages, Coach VBK and his assistants doubled as players in the practices. Regardless, the team received a course in fundamental basketball. They hustled, they played good defense, and compiled a 11-15 record. The displaced Hofstrans scored a respectable average of roughly sixty-five points per game, but the opposition scored more (seventy-one points per game).

Ray Cunneen, who averaged twelve points per game, was the team's leading scorer. Because of he was twenty-seven years old, his teammates called him "father time." What Cunneen lacked in speed, he made up with shooting accuracy. In the front court, there was Henry Schwab at 6'6" tall and weighing all of 175 pounds. Butch recalls him as being "78 inches of stalk" with an exaggerated Adam's apple. When he got mad, about the worst profanity he could muster was "Oh fiddlesticks!" One game, after Schwab had zero rebounds in the first half, Butch yelled at Henry so harshly that he intimidated him into scoffing ten boards in the second half and led Hofstra to victory. Though constantly facing bulkier centers from other teams, he improved his game and managed to average 9.4 rebounds per game to lead the team in that category. The highlight of the season was a late season victory over MAC small college division rival Wagner, 63-61. A loss to Wagner the previous year had probably kept Hofstra from postseason play.

Although this was Butch's first losing season in six years of coaching, it may stand as one of his outstanding achievements given the lack of talent "on hand" at the beginning of the season.

The principles which Butch used to develop his "makeshift" team of 1956–57 were essentially those that stayed with him throughout his career. In seeking his "instant recruits," Butch sought athletes who played their respective sports with enthusiasm and intensity. Hustle was an overriding characteristic. He frequently said to his team, "Play hard and I'll teach you how to win!" In the same vein, he stressed the importance of a strong defense. His main style of defense was "man-to-man" and this defense relied on players who gave their all. Butch only occasionally employed a zone defense. When asked on the issue, he said, "If the other team is tearing you apart, you have to go to a zone."

Butch taught his neophyte Hofstra players that the object of defense—zone or man-to-man—was to make the other team take bad shots. Then the emphasis shifts to rebounds and quickly moving the ball down court. With hustling players, rebounds and fast breaks fall into place. Butch preferred the motion game to that of "grinding it out with an inside game."

VBK continued to stress the importance of conditioning and instituted his patented "and two" layup drills at Hofstra.

VBK often felt his offensive style resembled "organized confusion." His lesson to the young Flying Dutchmen and all players that he coached thereafter was *learn to figure out what the defense gives you*. Butch stressed moving and cutting, passing, picks and rolls; he seldom employed "set plays" feeling that if the play failed, the team would be left "flat-footed." "That's why a team loses momentum. The whole team just stands around!" His offense was conceptual, not patterned.

As far as playing against a zone defense, Butch inserted his two best shooters and continually ran them through the zone trying to run off someone to get an open shot. Many coaches say that slick passing is the way to beat a zone. Butch saw the value in passing, but also stressed the value of motion without the ball as a means of freeing his best shooters.

For 1957–58, Butch got his record back on track as the Flying Dutchmen went 15-8, and his record for 1958–59 improved to 20-7 and a Middle Atlantic Conference (Division II) championship. Sophomore Ted Jackson, an eventual member of Hofstra's 1000 point club, was the team's leading scorer (17.3 points per game average) while Schwab continued as a reliable rebounder averaging 8.7 per game.

From 1959–62, Steve Balber played for Coach van Breda Kolff, and he emphatically states that the coach had a

The Early Hofstra College Years: 1955–1962

strong impact on his life, as he did many of the other players he coached. As a sophomore, Steve liked to smoke cigarettes when he played at Hofstra even though his scholarship was predicated on his not smoking or drinking. Prior to a regular season game at Cortland State, Coach VBK passed Steve's locker and discerned a bulge in his jacket pocket. He patted the bulge and out popped a pack of *Lucky Strikes*. Steve was absolutely petrified! Butch gave Steve a stern look then, without hesitation, kicked the pack under the locker and never said a word to anyone.

As far as drinking was concerned, Butch controlled the situation by inviting the players to his home.

Butch was a thorough disciplinarian as far as the business of basketball was concerned. High scorer Ted Jackson was late for a practice and Butch suspended him from the team until he came before the team and apologized to the group. Butch had no tolerance for prima donnas. He was a purist of the game.

Teaming up with Balber in the backcourt for the 1958–59 season was Stevie "Radar" Dunn. According to Balber, "he was the best pure shooter we ever had." He was selected all-conference and received many honors. Subsequently, he became a great poet. His poem entitled *"Losing Steps"* depicting the aging process on the occasion of the fortieth anniversary of the 1959–60 team appeared in the *New York Times*.

After four seasons at Hofstra, as winners of the MAC title, Butch's Flying Dutchmen made their first ever postseason appearance. In their first round game, the Dutchmen routed Weslyan by 76-48. Then came the American University game. Hofstra played without the services of Don Laux, who had a broken wrist. Laux later returned to Hofstra after graduation to be a volunteer assistant coach for Butch. Ted Jackson scored over half his team's points (forty-two). The Dutchmen held the ball for a last second shot, as Steve Balber tried to get the ball to the red-hot Jackson. "But 'Attitude' Jackson just disappeared on me!" Balber recalled. "I had to take the last shot. It double rimmed. I still think about it." "The ball just didn't go in!" repeated VBK several times when recalling the game. And so, by the narrowest of margins, Hofstra lost a real heartbreaker by 66-65, and its season ended abruptly. Basketball's version of "sudden death" became a reality to the young Hofstrans.

Hofstra's Best Season Ever: 23-1

Butch's next season was a great one, in many respects the best in Hofstra history. The Flying Dutchmen went 23-1 and featured a ten-game winning streak to open the season and thirteen-game streak to wind up the regular season. Hofstra ranked fifth in the nation among Division II schools at the end of the season, and ranked first among teams in the East. The team was "vintage" van Breda Kolff. "The boys fight hard for the ball," Butch said of his team. At 6'3", Stan Einbender was the tallest man on the squad and he hustled his way to the team rebounding title. Nicknamed "The Bender," his "buzzer beater" provided a major win over Army early in the season. Dr. Einbender is now a dentist who specializes in root canals! Ted Jackson continued to lead a well-balanced free-lance scoring attack. Butch tried to isolate Jackson in one-on-one situations to take advantage of his great ability to penetrate for driving lay-ups. The Dutchmen were perpetual motion.

Ironically, Coach VBK replaced veteran Stevie Dunn with sophomore Richie Swartz, a.k.a. "The Jaw" or "The Pelican" (he had two nicknames). Richie's brother was captain of a strong Providence College team. According to Balber, "It was hard to believe that a player as great as Radar was benched. Vintage Butch!" Following graduation in 1962, Richie had a try-out with the New York Knicks. Steve Balber was captain of the team as a junior.

The Early Hofstra College Years: 1955–1962   79

A ferocious defense limited foes to just 56.4 points per game. In practices, a spirited "second crew" gave the starters all they could handle and provided excellent preparation for Hofstra's games. In games where the Dutchmen had secure leads, Butch installed the second team as a unit. The first team then exhorted their replacements with a standard cheer, "Keep 'em under fifty."

But the one defeat of the 1959–60 season was a crucial one. Their only loss came at the hands of Wagner by 50-48 on the last shot of the game. Wagner's Harry Orlando, though closely guarded by Balber and Swartz, managed to fling a pass to teammate Bob Larsen. Hofstra's Brent Alyea tried to distract Larsen rather than foul him, but the Seahawk center sank the winning shot as time expired. Although Wagner's overall record was 16-8, the Seahawks had claim to the Middle Atlantic Conference title by virtue of the win over Hofstra, and thus they went to the small college NCAA. At the time, only one college per conference was invited to the "little dance." There were no runner-up slots available, even for a 23-1 team. The NIT took a hard look at the Dutchmen, but decided on Detroit University (another Catholic institution!) and its superstar Dave DeBuscherre. "I'd have whipped his butt," Einberger speculated some forty years later. As he thought at Lafayette, Butch wondered if he should rename the school St. Hofstra!

On the occasion of the fortieth reunion of the Hofstra-Wagner game, George Vecsey in his "Sports of The Times" column wrote in the February 6, 2000, edition of the *New York Times:*

> "They remember how they loved playing for Butch van Breda Kolff, who would later bark at Bill Bradley and Wilt Chamberlain the same way he barked at them.... In that long ago time, they enjoyed the best of college sports—fun and respect as competitive as the games. They won 23 and lost only one. Not a bad ratio at all."

Butch van Breda Kolff, the master at assigning nicknames to his players, assigned the name "Grantland" to

George Spencer Vecsey. He always showed the utmost respect for the scribe.

Following an impressive road victory over Scranton University, Butch and his team stayed at a hotel in Scranton, Pennsylvania. Sensing that the bars would be closed in this remote city, Butch had purchased a six-pack for con-

THE LOG OF HOFSTRA'S 23-1 SEASON (1959–60)

Opponent	Score	W-L
Long Island Univ.	68-61	W
Washington	79-54	W
Army	58-56	W
Loyola (Balt)	72-70	W
Delaware Univ.	58-41	W
Upsala	77-55	W
USMMA	75-59	W
Lehigh Univ.*	78-58	W
Adelphi*	82-56	W
Rutgers Univ.*	59-52	W
Wagner	48-50	L
Albright College	76-65	W
Manhattan	67-57	W
Wilkes College	81-52	W
Williams	82-62	W
Farleigh Dickinson	61-47	W
Susquehanna	70-60	W
Lycoming	85-67	W
LIU/CW Post	85-55	W
Moravian	85-63	W
West Chester St	57-52	W
Scranton Univ.	81-58	W
Lebanon Valley	60-42	W
Gettysburg	92-66	W

* Long Island Invitational Tournament at Hofstra

The Early Hofstra College Years: 1955–1962   81

sumption after the game. To keep the beer cold, he placed the six-pack out on the window ledge of his hotel room. To his surprise, when he went out to quench his thirst after the game, he found the beer had been pilfered by a daredevil player—Zeke Gadzinski—who had crawled out on the ledge. An incredible roar emitted from Butch's room when he found the beer missing.

Butch followed up with yet another twenty-win season for 1960–61, as his troops produced a 21-4 record. Garribrant Ryerson Alyea ("Brant" for short) was the high scorer on the squad. Brant also was a power hitter on the Dutchmen's baseball team and played over 300 major league games with the Minnesota Twins and other franchises. In 1970, he batted .291 and hit sixteen homers for the Twins.

The culprit in the MAC switched from Wagner to Albright College, which had a sharp shooting guard in Tom Piersall. Albright went on to beat Hofstra on two occasions. Three of the year's four losses came by a total of six points, including a 3-point overtime loss to Army. Again, the Dutchmen ended their season without a postseason bid. When asked about the possibility of an NIT bid, Butch simply stated, "Forget it!"

Butch's seventh season at Hofstra was a coach's dream as his team went 24-4 and reversed the dual losses at the hands of Albright. The NCAA small college tourney awaited, and the Flying Dutchmen squeaked by LIU/CW Post 56-55 in the first round. Mount St. Mary's was too strong for the Hofstra cagers in the second round, and Hofstra's bid for further glory ended. In his eighth season at Mount St. Mary's, Coach Jim Phelon eventually racked up over 800 wins in forty-six years at the college.

On March 3, 1962, Wilt "The Stilt" scored 100 points in a regular season game against the New York Knickerbockers in Hershey, Pennsylvania.

Butch, Florence, and the children enjoyed their life on Long Island. They lived in a beautiful three-story house located at 119 Harrison Street in Baldwin. Most enjoyable for the family were the frequent summer cook-outs at nearby Jones Beach. The van Breda Kolffs loaded up the Chevrolet station wagon with blankets, towels, toys, and all the equipment imaginable for a cook-out. More often then not, they were joined by the Hofstra assistant coaches and their respective families. Butch loved the beach, his family and friends, and the entire Hofstra scene.

In seven years at Hofstra, Butch had achieved the following:

- 136 wins, forty-three losses .760 pct.
- five twenty-win seasons
- Best single season percentage in school's history (23-1) .958 pct
- Two postseason appearances in NCAA Division II Tourney

In the fall of 1961, Bill Mazeroski's home run in the bottom of the ninth with the score tied at 9-9 lifted the Pittsburgh Pirates to a 4-3 game victory over the New York Yankees in one of the most thrilling World Series ever.

In the middle of the 1960-61 season, Cappy Cappon of Princeton suffered a fatal heart attack. After finishing the season and a half with interim coach J. L. McCandless, the Tigers were in market for a high profile basketball coach. They couldn't ignore VBK's record. Butch loved his years at Hofstra, but undoubtedly was ready for a new challenge. The Ivy League, Division I basketball, soon provided a new venue for his coaching abilities.

Chapter 4

The Princeton Years 1962–1967

"He (VBK) is an Abstract Expressionist of basketball. Other coaches have difficulty scouting his teams, because he doesn't believe in a set offense. He likes his offense free-form."

John McPhee, *A Sense of Where You Are*

Over the final days of 1964, while the bright sparkling lights on the marquee advertised the Broadway debut of the movie *Goldfinger,* nearby Madison Square Garden had a show of its own to compete with the infamous James Bond (a.k.a. Agent 007). The dramatic soundtrack from the classic film easily could have been played as a backdrop to the confrontations forthcoming at the Garden's Holiday Festival college basketball tournament. The tournament soon provided the avid New York basketball fan with wall-to-wall excitement over a five day period.

The Holiday Festival was the creation of the Eastern College Athletic Conference (ECAC) and for over twenty years brought national and local powers to the Garden the week between Christmas and New Year's. Usually eight teams competed for the title in a series of day-night double-headers. At the time, the festival truly reigned as the premier event of the early season in college basketball.

The 1964 festival field was especially attractive. The number one ranked team in the nation—Michigan University—headed the list of entries. The Wolverines were led by their All-American candidate Cazzie Russell.

Princeton University, which was making its first trip ever to the event, had an All-American of its own in Bill Bradley, ranked by many as the outstanding player in the nation. Others in the field included LaSalle, Cincinnati, Syracuse, St. John's, Temple, and Manhattan. Tickets were at a premium as basketball fans packed the old Garden as never before in the history of the tourney. Early on, the crowds fell in love with Bill Bradley and the underdog Tigers.

The showcase matchup of the tournament occurred in the semifinals when heavily favored Michigan from the powerful Big 10 Conference faced Princeton, the defending Ivy League champion. The Wolverines had disposed of Manhattan College in the first round, highlighted by a thirty-six point performance from Cazzie Russell. The physical presence of Michigan's front court highlighting Oliver Darden and Bill Bunting wore down the undersized Jaspers. Meanwhile, Princeton had advanced by ousting Syracuse by a 79-69 margin. Bradley netted thirty-six points to outshine David Bing (twenty-eight points) of the Orangemen. Jim Boeheim, who in the 2000–01 season celebrated his twenty-fifth year as head coach of Syracuse, had ten points in the loss.

Officially, 18,499 fans shoe-horned their way into the old Madison Square Garden on the evening of December 30, 1964. While coaches David Strack of Michigan and Butch van Breda Kolff of Princeton exchanged pre-game handshakes, the excitement of a Russell-Bradley matchup spread throughout the crowd. You hardly felt like sitting down after the organist Gladys Gooding finished playing the *Star Spangled Banner.* Soon, the center jump took place and the action rolled into full swing.

Bradley entirely dominated the first half as he poured in twenty-three points including a streak of twelve straight points to end the session. Princeton led by a narrow 39-37 margin, as the crowd became increasingly infatuated with the possibility of an upset of the number one team. When the Tigers exited their locker room and came onto the court to start the second half, the Garden crowd roared with approval and threw its collective vocal capacity behind the Tigers.

"Lets Go Tigers," was chanted by genuine Princeton supporters and newly adopted fans as well.

A faint display of polite applause from alumni and friends greeted the Wolverines when they reentered the arena. The "sixth man" feature of crowd support had overwhelmingly swung over to the Princeton camp. Butch van Breda Kolff had either played in or coached a gazillion games before this point in his career. The magnetism, the mystique, and the atmosphere at Madison Square Garden were like no other in his vast experience. The stage was set for a dramatic second half.

VBK's strategy of a tight man-to-man defense had indeed been effective in the first half. Butch had assigned his ace defensive man Dick Rodenbach to guard Cazzie during the first half, and the pesky guard was able to limit the Michigan star to just six points in the period.

Offensively, the Tigers and Bradley continued to roll. Bradley's artistry was classic. Michigan collapsed its entire defense to try and stop his moves—all to no avail. Bradley's spinning jump shots with either hand dazzled Michigan. He rebounded, he brought the ball up against the Wolverine press, created turnovers and ultimately took over the defensive effort against Russell. Up to that moment, Bradley had held his defensive assignment—Oliver Darden—to just one point.

As Bradley expended so much energy, his physical exhaustion became quite visible. Ted Winpenny, a spectator at the game, recalls Bradley uncharacteristically missing two foul shots in a row. As he staggered back to pick up his defensive assignment, he accidentally bumped into a Michigan player and Referee Steve Honzo whistled Bradley for his fourth personal. Bradley's fifth personal foul followed shortly thereafter, as he grabbed Darden's arm when the large Michigan forward drove the basket. With 4:28 left in the game, Bradley was forced to leave the game.

As Bill Bradley jogged off the court, his team leading by thirteen points, the capacity Garden crowd stood united while applauding the unbelievable performance of the Man from Missouri. His statistics read as follows: forty-one points, nine rebounds, four assists, four steals. As the referees tried to finish the game, the roar of the crowd, the emotion of van Breda Kolff hugging his star player, this—perhaps the biggest single moment in Garden history—took priority. The refs let the fans acknowledge Bill Bradley for a while longer.

The glow of Bradley's performance sustained Princeton for only a few more minutes. Soon the talented Michigan team fiercely pressed the leaderless Tigers, and with two minutes left and the score stood at 78-70 in Princeton's favor. Tiger sub Bill Koch filled in for Bradley and was responsible for guarding Russell, who kept scoring. "God, I wish Bradley were still in here," he thought as the seconds ticked away. Four straight baskets by Michigan quickly knotted the score at seventy-eight each. Fifty-one seconds remained on the clock.

The no-name Princeton offense had a shot at the winning basket but turned the ball over to Michigan. The slick Wolverines, finally showing their number one stuff, moved the ball and set up their main man Cazzie for a jump shot form the corner. With three seconds left, Russell nailed the jumper, lifting Michigan to an 80-78 victory. The crowd, totally drained, was silent.

After the game, Coach Dave Strack of Michigan said of Bradley's performance, "I never thought one player could do as much for his team as Bradley did tonight. That was the greatest performance I've ever seen."

Immediately after the game, Coach van Breda Kolff barred the press from the MSG locker room. Although this was Bradley's finest hour, VBK was aware of how miserable the team felt in its failure to protect the thirteen point lead which prevailed when Bradley departed the game. VBK wanted to console his team, even take responsibility for the loss. He felt he had probably left Bradley in too long following his third or fourth foul. He was also upset at Referee Steve Honzo's call which produced Bradley's fourth personal. Regardless, the press could wait.

The other game of the double-header featured heavily favored Cincinnati University against St. John's. The Redmen (subsequently re-nicknamed "The Red Storm") salved the appetite of the local fans and upset the Bearcats by a 66-64 margin. For a little more than four hours, the Holiday Festival conceivably provided two of the greatest college basketball games in the history of the sport.

Coaching St. John's was Joe Lapchick, who was van Breda Kolff's coach in 1947 when VBK was a member of the original Knickerbockers. Following a twenty-year stint, Lapchick was in his final season as coach of the Redmen and his team responded later in the week with an upset victory over Michigan to garner the festival title. Lapchick and his team, Bradley and VBK, Cazzie and the Wolverines had given the New York basketball fans a real show. The attendance for the five nights registered 73,250, which represented the Festival record until the opening of the new and larger Madison Square Garden in 1968. VBK said that Bradley could have attracted 73,000 fans on his own—if only the arena had been large enough!

Both of Princeton's 1950 and 1951 football teams rolled through their respective schedules with back-to-back undefeated 9-0 records, finishing sixth in the nation's Associated Press polls for both years. Spearheading the Tigers was their outstanding single-wing tailback, Dick Kazmaier, who was the overwhelming 1951 winner of the prestigious Heisman Trophy annually awarded by the Downtown Athletic Club of New York to the best college football player in the nation. Kazmaier wore jersey number 42.

Fourteen years later, the outstanding player in college basketball was generally recognized to be Bill Bradley of Princeton University for the 1964–65 season. At the end of the season, he received numerous "Player of the Year" awards from such organizations as the United Press International and the U.S. Basketball Writers Association. If the Downtown Athletic Club had presented the Heisman Trophy for the best college *basketball* player, Bill Bradley probably would have been the recipient. Bradley wore number 42 while playing for Princeton.

Since the end of World War II, such awards have been unusual, almost unprecedented, for representatives from the scholastically inclined Ivy League. In 1971, Ed Marinaro of Cornell narrowly missed winning the Heisman Trophy. Otherwise, Kazmaier is the only Ivy League Heisman winner since the 1930s. And in basketball, Columbia's Chet Forte—who won the UPI award in 1957—is the only Ivy Leaguer to be named Player of the Year other than Bradley.

Of the approximately 145 players in the NBA when Bradley entered the twelve team league in 1967, only one held his degree from an Ivy League institution. Rudy LaRusso, who graduated from Dartmouth in 1959, was a three-time All-Star and was renowned for his rugged rebounding style while averaging roughly twelve points per game for the San Francisco Warriors. The pattern continues to this date as documented in the *Street & Smith* basketball magazine for the 2000–2001 season. The preliminary rosters for the twenty-nine NBA franchises indicate 464 players are on board for the season. Only three of those players (Chris Dudley of Yale, Matt Maloney and Ira Bowman of Penn) are of Ivy League extraction, virtually the same ratio that prevailed when Bradley went pro.

Down through the years, the consistently high academic standards of the Ivy League have limited the number of potential athletes seeking application to the eight member schools. Harvard, Yale, Princeton, et al. are above all academic institutions. At the risk of oversimplification, let it be said that most applicants to Ivy League colleges have long-term objectives that transcend the world of athletics. Prior to Bradley's career at Princeton, the Ivy League had not had an entry in the Final Four of the NCAA since 1944 when Dartmouth finished second behind Utah University. After Princeton's effort in 1965, Penn achieved the Final Four in the 1979 tourney featuring the Indiana State (with Larry Bird)—Michigan State (with "Magic" Johnson) matchup.

As a heralded high school basketball star from Crystal City, Missouri, Bill Bradley was intensely pursued by a multitude of colleges and universities. Bradley's high intellectual standards, especially his goal of becoming a Rhodes Scholar, helped him narrow the potential field of colleges. Duke University was initially at the top of his list, in recognition of the school's academic and athletic record. However, Bradley apparently determined that the pipeline to Oxford was more efficient from Princeton University than through Duke, and so he settled on Princeton as his choice for his undergraduate college years. Despite his high school basketball achievements, he would not be entitled to a basketball scholarship because of his father's relatively high income level as president of Crystal City State Bank. Only need-based scholarships were available at Princeton. Given the dramatic escalation of tuition costs as a percentage of personal income gains since 1961, the question arises whether or not Bradley might have considered a scholarship inclined institution if he had to make the choice today.

When Bradley arrived at Princeton in the fall of 1961, freshmen were precluded from playing varsity sports. The varsity coach was Jake McCandless, who had replaced the venerable Franklin "Cappy" Cappon midway through the 1960–61 season. Following a practice session, Cappy collapsed in the Dillon Gym shower and died of a heart attack shortly thereafter. McCandless finished out the season with an 8-8 record on his own and the following year coached the varsity to a 13-10 mark. Meanwhile, Bradley toiled on the freshman team and the Princeton athletic department searched for a permanent coach.

After a thorough study, Princeton announced that its new coach, effective for the 1962–63 season, was Butch van Breda Kolff. At the relatively young age of thirty-nine, van Breda Kolff had compiled an impressive record at Lafayette College and Hofstra College. Over eleven seasons, his record stood at 204 wins and seventy-seven losses for a winning percentage of 72.8 per cent. His 1954–55 mark at Lafayette (23-3) was in the history books as the best ever recorded at the College. The same was true for his 1959–60 season at Hofstra (23-1), where he had just produced four twenty-win seasons in a row. Butch van Breda Kolff was a proven winner. By inheriting Bradley's talents as a sophomore, VBK was virtually guaranteed three more years of successful and exciting basketball.

The question was, how far could Princeton go with Bradley on the court and VBK on the sidelines?

Few members of the Princeton athletic staff remained from the mid-1940s when van Breda Kolff was an undergraduate. Veteran trainer Timmy Sullivan, who taped Butch's ankles when he was a player, was pleased to have VBK back at Princeton. "He has a lifelong job here," commented Sullivan when he heard Butch was returning. Butch's response to the comment was: "I don't plan my life. I just see what happens." To VBK, life was a continuous "ad hoc" reaction to given situations. Life was a continuous coin flip.

When Butch van Breda Kolff took over the reigns of Princeton in the fall of 1962, his coaching resume highlighted his emphasis on team defense. With the talents of an offensive threat such as Bradley at his fingertips, Butch changed his focus to a more-or-less 50-50 allocation between offensive and defensive concentration. Part of Butch's strategy entailed getting more production out of captain Art Hyland, who had an excellent shooting eye in his own right. During this period, the game of basketball was revolutionized by the jump shot, and soon Butch incorporated an offensive strategy freeing Bradley and Hyland for open jumpers. VBK's new offense was more fluid, downplayed the weave, and relied more on the fast break.

In a TV interview with ESPN's Dick Schaap, Bradley described the VBK style as "freelance on the court in an intelligent way." As such, the offense bore little resemblance to the deliberate tactics of the late Cappy Cappon. Under Cappon, Bradley might have led a more inhibited basketball life than under the motion oriented VBK.

Preseason scrimmages between rival colleges and universities have been discontinued, but in the early 1960s they were a regular part of the team's preparation for the regular season. Nowadays, NCAA members scrimmage the likes of foreign all-star teams in exhibition games. One of the first tests for the 1962–63 Princeton Tigers was a scrimmage against Seton Hall University, which then featured Nick Werkman—who went on to lead the nation with a 29.3 average. The Pirates completely outplayed Princeton, and Coach van Breda Kolff was absolutely livid with his team's performance. After the scrimmage, VBK went into a tirade criticizing virtually every member of the team, with the possible exception of Bill Bradley. He saved the harshest remark until the end. Directing his remarks at Art Hyland, he screamed, "And how can you expect to win any games with a *'fat ass captain?'*" Shocked and embarrassed, Hyland didn't eat a meal for two weeks. He lost ten pounds and became a more effective player thereafter. Hyland went on to become one of Princeton's 1000-point scorers and ranks twentieth on the all-time list in points scored. Hyland and VBK became very close during the season, and later Hyland returned to be his assistant coach for two seasons (1966–67).

Hyland recalls how Butch trained his team to focus on foul shooting. At the end of most practice sessions, VBK would divide the squad into two separate foul shooting units. Each player would shoot a "one and one" from the foul line, with a maximum of two shots per player. No one could leave the gym until both teams had made eleven foul shots in a row. Butch believed in the theory that a team prospered and suffered together.

On this one November Saturday, Princeton had a home football game scheduled against Harvard, and many of the basketball players had out-of-town dates in for the game. As usual, basketball practice took place early that Saturday morning. As expected, VBK congregated his players for the foul shooting drill as a finishing touch to the practice session. The teams struggled with the eleven-shot requirement, and the practice which should have ended by noon was still in session at 2 P.M.— well beyond the appointed time for the football game kickoff. Princeton became a very strong foul shooting team during the regular season.

By the time Bradley was a senior, the Tigers had won two Ivy League titles and had made back-to-back NCAA appearances. In the 1963 tournament, they were eliminated by then powerful St. Joseph's (Pennsylvania) 82-81 despite Bradley's forty points and sixteen rebounds. In the 1964 event, they routed Virginia Military Institute representing the Southern Conference by 86-60 to advance to the second round. For both Bradley and van Breda Kolff, this marked their first "big dance" post-season victory ever. In the second round, they suffered a tough 52-50 defeat at the hands of the University of Connecticut. Bradley's twenty-two points again led the Tigers.

Venturing to Tokyo in 1964, William Warren Bradley was the youngest and only college junior to play on the victorious U.S. Olympic basketball team. For sure, he was instrumental in the United States bringing home the gold.

Following the excitement of the Holiday Festival, the balance of the regular season consisted mostly of going about the working project of wrapping up the Ivy League title and securing a berth in the NCAA tourney. Their only Ivy loss of the season was sustained at Cornell on a last-second shot. The Tigers later avenged the defeat with a resounding 107-84 win at home.

Although Bradley was far and away the dominant player for Princeton, VBK gave extensive credit to his supporting cast of players. Taking their clue from Bradley's flawless passing, his teammates moved fluidly without the ball and reciprocated with outstanding passing of their own. The Tigers of the Bradley era *played the game right!* The Ivies usually scheduled their league games on Friday and Saturday nights, thus freeing the balance of the week for academic pursuits. Princeton cruised through the fourteen game schedule with only the one loss, although Yale and Brown almost caught them looking ahead in the final games of the season. The first half of the Brown game was cause for a VBK eruption during the intermission. John McPhee's account from his book *A Sense of Where You Are (Bill Bradley at Princeton)* recaptures the moment:

> Van Breda Kolff walked into the locker room during the half, picked up a piece of chalk and threw it against the blackboard so hard that it disintegrated into a puff of dust. He was violently sucking air into his mouth and breathing it out in what might have been a flame. He picked up another piece of chalk and wrote at the top of the blackboard in huge letters: FOOD, SLEEP, GIRLS, STUDIES. Far down the blackboard, in extremely small letters, he wrote "Basketball"...Then he wrote in even smaller letters, "winning." "Nobody wants to win!" he bellowed.

Princeton went on to earn a narrow victory over the Bruins. All in all, it had been a fabulous regular season. For Bradley, the accolades were endless. For VBK, the challenge of the NCAA loomed ahead.

The 1965 NCAA Basketball Tournament

In the first round of the 1965 NCAA Tourney, Princeton drew Penn State University—an at large representative from the Middle Atlantic region. Contemporary sports writers termed it an "ugly game" as neither team played very well. As the clock worked its way down, Princeton dodged the bullet and edged The Nittany Lions by 60-58. Bradley's twenty-two points led all scorers.

Princeton's second-round foe was North Carolina State, who was representing the Atlantic Coast Conference. NC State was coached by Press Maravich (father of the infamous "Pistol Pete" Maravich, who was then a high school senior) who had guided the Wolfpack to a 20-5 record and successive wins over Maryland, Virginia, and Duke in the ACC year-end tournament. Princeton easily disposed of the Wolfpack as Bradley scored twenty-seven points.

The Tigers then had to face Providence College, one of the top-ranked teams in the nation. The Friars were led by All-American guard Jimmy Walker and were clear favorites to eliminate the Tigers. Coached by veteran Joe Mullaney, the Friars started out defensively in a matchup zone which failed to contain the Tiger offense. Following an early time-out, Providence then shifted to a man-to-man defense, which was certainly to VBK's liking. "The matchup zone might have given us problems eventually," he speculated. Princeton's offense caught fire instantly and never was challenged as they won by an unexpectedly easy 109-69 margin. Without a doubt, Princeton made its strongest showing of the season. Bradley's forty points easily overshadowed Walker's twenty-seven as Princeton packed momentum marching into its first ever visit to the Final Four. The Tigers were on their way to Portland, Oregon along with Wichita State, UCLA and Michigan. Princeton University, Bill Bradley, and Butch van Breda Kolff needed only two more wins to secure the national title. Given their performance against Providence and their near upset of Michigan in the Holiday Festival, the Tigers certainly had reason to be confident.

Most pundits favored UCLA. They were coached by the legendary John Wooden, who was in pursuit of his second straight National Championship. His star was Gail Goodrich, but included other notables such as Walt Hazzard, Keith Ericson, Ed Lacey, and Kenny Washington. The free-wheeling Bruins had scored over 100 points in ousting both BYU and San Francisco University from the tourney. Michigan, on the other hand, had just slipped by

The Princeton Years: 1962–1967 95

Vanderbilt by an 87-85 margin to earn its trip to the Final Four. In its Regional Final, Wichita State used only six players in a defensive struggle with Oklahoma State, prevailing ultimately by 54-46.

In the first semi-final game, UCLA again rolled past the century mark as they easily eliminated the Wichita Shockers by a 108-89 margin. The Bruins led 65-38 at halftime as the outcome was never in doubt.

The second semifinal game featured the rematch of Princeton and Michigan. Fans everywhere yearned to see the Holiday Festival duel of Cazzie Russell and Bill Bradley. Princeton played a tough first half, and only trailed the Wolverines by 40-36, but the physically stronger Big 10 reps wore down the Ivy Leaguers. Bill Bunting, a massive 6'7" power forward, controlled the backboards and scored twenty-two points. Princeton's aggressive defense caused the Tigers to send the Wolverines to the foul line twenty-four times. Princeton was fouled only fourteen times. Again, Bradley fouled out with roughly five minutes remaining and Michigan capitalized to win by a 93-78 margin.

Although Bradley outscored Russell by 29-28, he was most disappointed in his performance. "I failed as captain of the team. We weren't ready for that game mentally. The real place was at halftime. I should have had something to say. I sat there. I said something, but it wasn'much."

In the NCAA championship game, the high-scoring UCLA machine made Michigan its final victim, 91-80, and John Wooden had won his second straight national title. Thus, one of the classic dynasties in sports history was in its early stages. After Wooden's team failed to qualify for the 1966 event, UCLA then reeled off eight national titles in nine years to totally dominate the college scene for the decade.

A regular diet of mostly meaningless consolation games cluttered the NCAA tourney for most of its basketball history. A notable exception to this pattern took place in the 1965 game for third place between Wichita State and Princeton University. Playing in his final collegiate game, the normally unselfish Bradley was encouraged by his teammates to shoot-shoot-shoot. Forever the team player, Bradley passed the ball back to his teammates. Soon he got his marching orders from VBK, "For crissake, Bill. Everyone up there's here to see what you can do. For once in your life, just shoot the goddam ball."

And shoot he did. Bradley's repertoire included hook shots, twisting layups, long one-handers, as he gunned away. Thinking that his fellow players were aiming at the team single game record, Bradley accommodated them by making twenty-two of twenty-nine from the field and fourteen of fifteen from the foul-line. His sum total of fifty-eight points set the individual record. VBK felt he could have easily scored 100 points had he not passed off so much! Regardless, his record held up until Notre Dame's Austin Carr pumped in sixty-one points in the 1970 Tourney.

By the way, Princeton beat Wichita State 118-82. The NCAA discontinued the practice of consolation games in 1982.

In the aforementioned interview with ESPN's Dick Schaap, the veteran sports announcer asked Bradley if the Wichita State game represented "The *real* Bill Bradley." Reflecting back in time, Bradley modestly responded, "Not really."

When the Princeton Tigers returned to New Jersey, they were greeted by a huge crowd of their supporters. Bradley attempted to apologize for the Michigan defeat, but his efforts were soon drowned out by the appreciative assemblage.

At the close of the 1964–65 season, Bradley was named the MVP of the NCAA Tourney and van Breda Kolff was named "Coach of the Year" by the US Basketball Writers Association. Despite the notable awards, and there were many others, the most memorable moment of the year was that point in time when Bradley fouled out of the Holiday Festival game and was hugged by Coach VBK as 18,499 fans voiced their appreciation. You had to be there to believe it!

The Princeton Years: 1962–1967   97

John Wooden and his UCLA Bruins were at the forefront of a dynasty which methodically dominated the college scene for ten years. As the championships piled up for UCLA, fans craved the return of a team possessing the charisma of the 1965 Princeton Tigers, Bill Bradley, and Butch van Breda Kolff.

☆ ☆ ☆

As a journeyman basketball coach, Butch van Breda Kolff greatly enjoyed his personal life while living near the Princeton University campus. Butch felt like he was back in college again as he relived many of his undergraduate experiences. His wife Florence was convinced that the Princeton environment, with its cultural and intellectual emphasis, was the best possible location to raise their four children.

Enhancing the quality of life was the fact that Butch had the additional responsibility of coaching the freshman golf team. The job was tantamount to having a country club membership for VBK. He had unlimited use of the beautiful Princeton University course. While Lafayette conscripted Butch to coach soccer and lacrosse in the off-season, Princeton afforded him the opportunity to hit the links almost any time he wanted to play.

Butch van Breda Kolff even adopted a gentlemanly quality while coaching at Princeton. In the *Princeton Press,* he advocated that the hometown Tiger fans abstain from yelling while the visiting teams attempted their foul shots. With the great majority of Ivy League games being played on Friday and Saturday nights, students were in effect liberated from the confines of Princeton Library. Watching Bradley play, cheering on the Tigers, jeering the other Ivies, was a great way to let off steam for the undergraduates. Like Alumni Gym at Lafayette, Dillon Gym with its roll-out seats and 2,700 capacity provided a built-in advantage for VBK.

Princeton's accessibility to the New Jersey shore was another attraction of his most recent assignment. The family invested in a small summer home in Harvey Cedars Township on Long Beach Island. To this day, Butch and his family have enjoyed the facility immensely since acquiring the property during the Princeton years.

The Ivy League dress code just didn't fit the personality of Butch van Breda Kolff. Harris tweed jackets, button down collared shirts, and felt-brim hats were just not his style.

Butch and Cary Ahl—one of his Lafayette lifetime buddies and a former player—had planned to get together in conjunction with a Leopard-Princeton game at Dillon Gym. The day before the game and following a light practice session, Butch invited Cary to join him for a couple of beers before he headed off to northern New Jersey on a recruiting mission. When Cary picked up his complimentary tickets at the "will call" window the next evening, there was a personal note from Butch attached. The note read: "If you see Florence tell her you were with me until very late." When Cary turned around to see who else was on line, there was Florence van Breda Kolff right behind him, "nose-to-nose." Following instructions, Cary apologized for keeping Butch out so late. "We hadn't seen each other in a long time." She looked straight through Cary's words and said "Better you than someone else!"

During the summers of 1963 and 1964, Butch was an active part of the coaching staff of a basketball camp in Brookville, Long Island. Also on the "faculty" were coaches Lou Carnesecca (St John's), Frank Leyden (Utah Jazz), and Dick Schultz (Iowa). Among the 100 high school players were Julius Erving, Rick Pitino, and Billy Donovan. Butch invited Artie Hyland, captain of the '62-63 Princeton team, to participate as "demonstrator." One of Butch's favorite players at the camp was Chris Thomforde, who eventually went on to star for the 1966–67 Princeton Tigers.

Thomforde recalls the camp as being extremely meaningful in his development as a player and as a human be-

Joe Lapchick (left), Butch's coach on the original New York Knickerbockers, receives "Sportsman" award while VBK (center) earns "Coach of the Year" and Bill Bradley (right) is named "Player of the Year" by the Philadelphia Sportswriters Association in 1965. Credit: VBK private collection

ing. He noted that Butch had the unusual quality of instilling intensity and focus in his players without losing sight of the fact that basketball was a game of *fun*.

Thomforde greatly enjoyed the lunchtime games when he teamed up with VBK and played other groups in games of "three on three." Chris says he learned more about basketball in those lunch-hour games than in the camp's formal sessions, perhaps in his entire coaching experience. Then at dinner, Butch formed a team which played in the Rockville Center League. Butch, Chris plus Jim Schultz, Jim Kisssane (Boston College), and Rudy Waterman (Dayton University) teamed up to win the RC League championship.

Generally speaking, Butch cited Princeton as being one of the "best" of all his "stops." Life was a series of "stops."

At the conclusion of the 1966–67 NBA season, the Philadelphia 76ers won the League Championship behind the MVP performance of Wilt "The Stilt" Chamberlain.

In many respects, VBK's coaching capability was overshadowed by Bill Bradley during the All-American's three years of varsity play. Surely, many fans and scribes felt that Bradley made VBK rather than vice versa. With Bradley on the court, coaching was like playing the game on permanent "automatic pilot." Anyone familiar with Butch van Breda Kolff knew he would "actively coach" the team. The drills, the emphasis on teamwork, *playing the game right,* business as usual prevailed during the Bradley years.

Butch van Breda Kolff hated to see "Dollar Bill" leave, but was above all interested in coaching. He took particular pride in the 1966–67 Princeton University team, a team 100 percent recruited under his watch. One of his significant newcomers was guard Gary Walters, from Reading, Pennsylvania. Gary's high school coach was Pete Carril, and his talents were sought by many basketball powers from around the country. Maryland University was particularly interested in his credentials. But at the behest of Carril, Butch van Breda Kolff made a special visit to see Walters play against Central Dauphin High School in Harrisburg.

Butch brought along Art Hyland, captain from the '62–63 squad. Walters was the point guard for Carril's team, and he was a superb dribbler. On one offensive sequence, Walters started to penetrate the middle, dribbling from right to left, and he became concerned that he would have his dribble stolen away. Without hesitation, Gary instinctively put the ball behind his back and broke free for a sensational layup. The crowd went crazy! Butch quickly indicated to Hyland, "We gotta get that guy!"

After the game, Coach Carril accused Walters of "hot dogging" with his Cousy-like stunt. Walters explained his move was born out of necessity rather than any inclination at showboating. Out of the corner of his eye, Walters could see VBK smiling in the background. Butch liked the assertiveness of the kid from Reading. The leader for the 1966–67 team was right before his eyes.

Up front, the post-Bradley team was led by 6'9" Chris Thomforde, VBK's playing partner from the Long Island basketball camp. An unselfish performer, Chris usually played the entire game while constantly working inside and outside to help free his teammates for easy baskets. For three seasons, Thomforde averaged fourteen points per game and ranked fourteenth among the school's all-time highest. He is one of twenty-four Tigers to score more than 1000 points during his career. Additionally, he was an excellent foul shooter, posting a career average of .830.

During the summer of 1966, Chris was conscripted by Coach VBK to assist him in a series of lectures to basketball camps in Northern New Jersey and the Catskills. Butch was the speaker and Chris was the demonstrator model. Chris greatly enjoyed driving around the Northeast with Butch. He joked a lot and he had many serious stories such as his experiences in the Marines. At night, Chris joined Butch in his visits to the local bars, where Butch always excelled as the life of the party. Butch was well aware that Chris was preparing for the Lutheran ministry. Not to be diverted, Chris graduated from Yale Divinity School and currently is president of Bethany College in Kansas.

Further strength in the forecourt was provided by Ed Hummer, captain, and John Haarlow. The team definitely had better height and balance than the Bradley-led teams. Thomforde-Haarlow-Hummer respectfully stood as the school's fifth, seventh, and tenth rebounders in the school's history.

Alongside Walters at point guard was Joe Heiser, who led the well-balanced scoring attack with a 15.1 point average. The aggressiveness of Walters and Heiser was key to the success of the tenacious Tiger man-to-man defense. Along with Thomforde, both were selected to the All-Ivy team for 1967, with Heiser getting the nod as an All-East selection as well. Both guards received the coveted B.F. Bunn Trophy, awarded to "a member of the varsity basketball team who through sportsmanship, play, and influence has contributed most to the sport at Princeton." There was not a weak link in the starting five of the 1966–67 Tigers.

Heiser is in the Princeton record book as the school's all-time best foul shooter. He holds the season mark of .900 and the career record of .888. Almost all the other statistical scoring records at Princeton are held by Bill Bradley!

Walters is the current director of athletics at Princeton University. Following graduation from Princeton, Walters became the youngest varsity college coach on record when he took over the top post at Middlebury College at age twenty-three. He then moved on to Union College, where he coached the Tiger mentor Bill Carmody. In the summer of 2000, Carmody announced he was leaving Princeton to accept the head coaching job at Northwestern University, members of the Big 10 Conference. The terms of his contract with Northwestern reportedly included a seven-year deal worth $3.5 million.

Butch also had two future NBA stars recruited for the freshman team: Geoff Petrie and John Hummer, Ed's brother. Yet another Princeton powerhouse was in the making. *Sports Illustrated* referred to Princeton's program as a "basketball dynasty." Butch called his squad "a small-time outfit trying to get along."

The 1966–67 Tigers roared through the early stages of their schedule, and ranked fifth in the nation on the strength of their 18-1 record in mid-January. Only powerful Louisville—whose lineup included All-Americans Wes Unseld and Butch Beard—had beaten the surprisingly strong Ivy Leaguers. Ed Hummer was ill and unable to play in the ten-point loss to the Cardinals.

On New Year's Eve, the Princeton Tigers were scheduled to fly from Philadelphia to Raleigh-Durham to take on the number three ranked University of North Carolina Tar Heels, who were coached by the legendary Dean Smith. However, their flight was canceled because of fog, and so the Tigers took the train instead. The train took forever into the night, but failed to impede the Princeton cagers. The next day, Princeton beat UNC by a 91-81 margin. Within a few weeks, *Sports Illustrated* highlighted the Princeton successes with Walters and Thomforde appearing on the cover of its February 27 edition. When Butch was asked what he thought of his team's number five ranking, he replied: "My wife can't spend the press clippings at the A&P!"

Inwardly, Butch must have felt very gratified by the Princeton performance. Many major college programs packed their rosters with the equivalent of paid entertainers. Statistics such as graduation rates or grade point averages were rarely publicized at the nationally ranked schools. For so many of these players, college basketball was a transition phase between high school and the NBA. Butch's star players at Princeton were real scholar athletes destined for careers outside the world of sports. They played as a team. They played old-fashioned pure basketball, although Thomforde likened it more to *jazz* than *Mozart*. And they finished the regular season ranked number five in the country!

"It is not surprising that in the same year Princeton produced twice as many Rhodes Scholars as any other university in the country it should also produce one of the nation's best college basketball teams," wrote Christopher D. Jones '67 in the *Princeton Alumni Weekly*.

Several years later, Bobby Knight was quoted in the January 26, 1981 edition of *Sports Illustrated* as saying that Butch van Breda Kolff was the "best college coach I ever saw." Knight went on to describe his own offensive style as being an "amalgam of the freelancing style used at Princeton in the early '60s by Butch van Breda Kolff intertwined with the passing game that the venerable Hank Iba employed at Oklahoma State."

Sifted in with victories over the national elite was a near clean sweep of the Ivy League. Cornell upset the Tigers by a 62-56 margin in Ithaca.

Then a road trip the last week of the season almost resulted in a dual loss at both Brown and Yale. Butch somehow brought home narrow victories, however. In the Yale game, Butch blamed himself for sticking with an experimental zone defense too long in the game, and the highly favored Tigers barely escaped with an 81-80 win. When confronted by some alumni on the streets of Princeton town, the elder statesmen grumbled about the narrow margin of victory. At 23-2 Butch felt no compulsion to

ASSOCIATED PRESS 1967 FINAL POLLS

Team	Coach	Final Record
1. UCLA	John Wooden	30-0
2. Louisville	Paul Hickman	23-5
3. Kansas	Ted Owens	23-4
4. North Carolina	Dean Smith	26-6
5. Princeton	B. van Breda Kolff	25-3
6. Western Ky.	Johnny Oldham	23-3
7. Houston	Guy Lewis	27-4
8. Tennessee	Ray Mears	21-7
9. Boston College	Bob Cousy	21-3
10. Texas Western	Don Haskins	22-6

apologize for a "W." In the Ivy League, often the Tigers played to the level of the competition. At the season's end, a narrow victory or sometimes a loss reminded a team not to enter the post season with over-confidence. Coaches like to see how their teams react to adversity in a meaningless game as a preparation for a bigger test later on. Butch saw the therapeutic value in the Yale game. He also felt the Ivy League was severely underrated by the media. But the Alumni wanted blood versus their Ivy rivals. Butch felt unappreciated.

The rematch with Cornell was marked by intense preparation. Butch looked to snap his team out of a complacency that had somehow affected its style of play in the second half of the Ivy season. On Thursday night, he held an extra scrimmage between the first and second teams. The second team won by five baskets, and VBK stormed off the court. He showered and left the arena without speaking to the team. The wake-up call worked, as Princeton handily disposed of Cornell by 81-66. John Haarlow starred with twenty-five points while wearing a face mask to protect his fractured nose. Hopefully, the Tigers had recaptured some early season form.

Soon the NCAA tourney was at hand, and the Tigers opening round foe was West Virginia University. The game resembled a home tilt for the Mountaineers, as the site of the game was Blacksburg, Virginia on the Virginia Tech campus. Turnovers and nervousness were evident on both sides. Notwithstanding, Princeton disposed of WVU by a 68-57 margin. Foul shooting was key as the victors hit eighteen out of twenty-one from the stripe.

Next on the agenda was the University of North Carolina, a previous conquest for the Tigers. Playing without John Haarlow, the game was close throughout, with UNC leading by one at the half, and the score being knotted at sixty-three at the end of regulation. But the foul shooting that carried them in the first round disappeared in the second as the Tigers hit but ten of twenty-one. Meanwhile, the Tar Heals pumped in thirty-two of forty-three at the line while VBK's charges were reduced to subs in the OT as three of his starters fouled out of the game. Aggressive defense had its price afterall, and Princeton fell 78-70 to the ACC champs. The quest of Butch van Breda Kolff had ended. The long-shot hope of confronting John Wooden and Lew Alcindor in the finals was now nothing but a dream unfulfilled.

While all eyes were on the battle between Houston University and UCLA, Dayton University—the surprise member of the Final Four—upset UNC by 76-62. The Flyers were led by Donnie May, who scored thirty-four points. After easily beating the Houston Cougars and its star Elvin Hayes, UCLA prevailed in the finals against Dayton and finished the season with a perfect 30-0 record. The Bruins' margin of victory in four games of the 1967 tourney was 23.75 points. Lew Alcindor, a 7'1" sophomore, was the Player of the Year among collegians. Coach John Wooden had won his third title in four years. With Alcindor on the team, he was a shoo-in for two more.

At the time, the NCAA continued to dilute its tournament schedule with consolation games, even at the regional level. Thus, Princeton ended its 1966–67 season with a consolation game versus St. John's University, who had lost a heartbreaker to Boston College 63-62 in the first round. Butch decided to start five seniors, three of whom were subs, in recognition of the upperclassmen's contribution to the team for three years. The final score, though not meaningful, saw Princeton wallop the Redmen by a 78-58 margin. When challenged by the press as to his starting five, Butch replied: "Basketball is a game of fun. I don't make enough money to make it a business."

The 1966–67 Tigers indeed had a lot of fun while compiling a 25-3 record, Butch's finest while coaching at Princeton. During practices, the members of the team shot set shots for money. If a player lost a shoot-out, he paid $5 into the "kitty." Other revenue sources were also available. Haarlow busted the rim in the Harvard game and had to donate $5. Adler wore the wrong uniform to the Cornell game and was docked $5. Each time that Butch had a technical called on him, he contributed $5. No wonder the cup "ranneth" over! The investment purpose of the fund? To finance a season-end party, of course! In coaching fifteen seasons of college hoops, Butch van Breda Kolff at age forty-five had amassed over 300 wins and had a winning percentage of almost seventy-five percent. At the time, he was the third most successful among active coaches ranking behind Adolph Rupp of Kentucky and John Wooden of UCLA. However, feeling so comfortable at Princeton made VBK feel uncomfortable. The alumni lack of appreciation for his coaching style gnawed at his soul. The potential mechanical dominance of John Wooden, UCLA, and Lew Alcindor over the next two seasons took a lot of the luster out of the college scene.

Butch's annual salary at Princeton was $12,000, and he was assured of a $1000 raise for the 1968 season. Five years at Princeton, despite all its amenities, left him craving for new challenge.

That challenge was soon forthcoming. From halfway across the planet, the Los Angeles Lakers came knocking at his door. The feisty owner of the Lakers—Jack Kent Cooke—admired Butch's record and offered him a solid three-year contract, and VBK decided to make the move. Soon he was singing Al Jolson's tune, "California, Here I Come."

Partially in response to Butch's recommendation, Princeton named Pete Carril as head basketball coach for the following season. Pete remained at Princeton until his retirement from college coaching in 1996. Exclusive of the World War II years and McCandless' interim stint, Cappy Cappon, Butch van Breda Kolff, and Pete Carril—just three coaches—represented the Tigers on the sidelines for a total of 54 years.

Furthermore, Princeton proved to be fertile territory for young assistant coaches looking to assume head coaching positions. Jan van Breda Kolff (Pepperdine), Bill Carmody (Northwestern), Armond Hill (Columbia), and

Joe Scott (Air Force Academy) advanced to their current positions via the Princeton stepladder.

Butch always felt the Ivy League was underrated, and the years following his top five ranking tended to confirm his feelings.

The unusual ranking of Princeton in the top ten in 1967 was followed up by Ivy League partner Columbia University in 1968. Spearheaded by All-Americans Jim McMillian and Heyward Dotson, the Lions won the Ivy crown with a 12-1 mark, captured the Holiday Festival Tourney, and finished the season ranked number seven in the Associated Press poll. Coached by Jack Rohan, their final record was 23-5 and included victories over Boston College and St. Bonaventure in the NCAA tourney.

The next Ivy League team to crack the top ten was the University of Pennsylvania in 1972. Penn was coached by Chuck Daly, who went on to the NBA where he guided the Detroit Pistons to back-to-back Championships in 1989 and 1990. The '72 Quakers finished third in the AP polls with a 28-1 record and a 26-0 regular season mark. Under coach Bob Weinhauer, Penn made it to the Final Four of the 1979 NCAA before running into Michigan State and Magic Johnson. The Quakers were ousted by 101-67.

More recently, Bill Carmody in his first year as Princeton coach, took the Tigers to a 27-2 mark and a number eight ranking in the polls.

Thesis: Possible Interaction of VBK with Bradley's Political Career

After Princeton, Bill Bradley completed his studies for his Rhodes Scholarship in England, spent six months on active duty in the Army, and went on to star for the New York Knickerbockers of the NBA. Indeed, Bradley was a key member of the well-rounded Knicks, which won the NBA titles in 1970 and 1973.

In 1977, after ten successful seasons, Bill Bradley retired from the Knicks. When veteran Republican New Jersey Senator Clifford Case announced he would not seek reelection in 1978, Bill Bradley decided to make a run for the open United States Senate slot on the Democratic ticket. He soundly defeated Republican Jeff Bell in the election. He was reelected to the Senate in 1984 and 1990. His victory in 1990 was by the narrowest of margins, as Christie Todd Whitman gave him the battle of his political life.

Near the end of his third term, Bradley announced he would not seek re-election to the U.S. Senate. In mid-1999, he announced his intentions to run for president in 2000, essentially challenging Vice President Al Gore for the nomination. Karen van Breda Kolff was slated to be a delegate to the Democratic convention in Los Angeles had Bradley generated more support. Her twin sister Kristina was working for the Bradley campaign in Spokane, Washington and was photographed with Bill's wife Ernestine in the local press. Art Hyland worked on the Bradley campaign. Hyland never had been involved with politics before.

Apparently, many Republicans registered as Democrats in order to vote for Bradley in their state's primary elections.

However, the traditional Democratic organization gave Bradley little or no support. Eventually, Gore's well-oiled machine brought home several early primary victories and Bradley dropped out of the race. Bradley's efforts were possibly impaired by his irregular heartbeat problem.

Many of the players formerly coached by Butch van Breda Kolff have volunteered how important an influence he was on their lives. When Butch first encountered Bill Bradley, the young star had already set his sights on a Rhodes Scholarship. Bradley even had his thesis topic picked out ("The 1940 Senatorial Campaign in Missouri"). While at Princeton University, Bill Bradley loved to study; he was the consummate student. After a hard-fought home game, Bill hit the showers and was on the way to the library. Coach van Breda Kolff was essentially a social person, who after the game was likely to stop at his favorite pub.

Butch was a proactive coach wherever he went. In Bradley's case, however, he rarely tried to impose his coaching philosophy on the young scholar. He encouraged him to shoot more, he urged him to develop a left-handed hook shot, and Bill responded by shooting a little bit more and by developing a flawless lefty hook. VBK knew natural ability when he saw it. Butch molded his team around Bradley's talents and the results were outstanding.

Butch's coaching entailed a subtle emphasis on equality. Whenever his teammates would criticize one another, he would restrain them from making further comments. Frequently, he was urged to write his memoirs about all the stories of his life, but he hesitated for fear he might embarrass some of his friends. According to Thomforde, Butch was a sincere man in the traditional sense. In Latin, *sincere* means "without varnish." Butch was definitely a man "without varnish."

Butch never liked politics, feeling that most politicians were corrupt and dishonest. His impact on Bradley's political philosophy probably related to his talking "common sense" on very general issues rather than any structured social-political theory. Both Butch and Bill Bradley grew up in "financially oriented" homes, with Butch's father being a stock broker at Goldman Sachs and Bradley's father being a bank president from Missouri. Both fathers weathered the economic storm of the Great Depression. Neither VBK nor Bradley sought to pursue their careers in the financial universe. VBK was a hands-on coach who greatly enjoyed "fraternizing with the enlisted men." He probably enjoyed playing "three on three" at lunch time more than he did coaching the NBA finals! As a moderate-liberal Democrat, the politician Senator Bill Bradley favored the "little guy" in most of his legislative proposals. In Bradley's brief presidential run in 2000, he seemed to identify with the populace as the candidate who was "believable."

Underneath it all, Butch van Breda Kolff conceivably was a role model to Bill Bradley.

KEY BOX SCORES

National Third Place, March 1965
Princeton 118, Wichita State 82

Princeton	fg-fga	ft-fta	rb	pf	tp
Haarlow	4-7	2-3	0	3	10
Bradley	22-29	14-15	17	4	58
Brown	3-5	1-1	11	4	7
Rodenbach	7-14	2-2	1	2	16
Walters	3-5	0-0	3	1	6
Hummer	3-4	3-3	4	3	9
Kingston	0-1	0-1	1	1	0
Shank	1-2	0-0	2	0	2
Koch	5-6	0-3	3	1	10
Neimann	0-1	0-0	1	2	0
Roth	0-0	0-0	2	0	0
Adler	0-1	0-0	0	0	0
Team Totals	48-75	22-28	49	21	118

Wichita St.	fg-fga	ft-fta	rb	pf	tp
Smith	3-6	7-9	5	4	13
Thompson	6-15	6-7	3	4	18
Leach	5-10	0-0	2	5	10
Pete	6-11	9-13	8	2	21
Criss	5-9	0-0	1	5	10
Nosich	1-3	2-2	1	0	4
Davis	1-4	0-1	0	0	2
Zafinos	0-1	0-0	0	0	0
Troppe	0-0	0-0	0	0	0
Reimond	0-0	0-0	0	0	0
Team Totals	29-66	24-32	32	21	82

Half time: Princeton 53-39. Officials: Korte and Magnuson

COLLEGE COACHING RECORD
"Phase I" Butch van Breda Kolff

Lafayette College (Division I)

1951–1952	15-9
1952–1953	13-12
1953–1954	17-10
1954–1955	23-3

4 Year Totals 68-34

Hofstra College (Division II)

1955-1956	24-4
1956–1957	11-15
1957–1958	15-8
1958–1959	20-7
1959–1960	23-1
1960–1961	21-4
1961–1962	24-4

7 Year Totals 138-43

Princeton University (Division I)

1962–1963	19-6
1963–1964	20-9
1964–1965	23-6
1965–1966	16-7
1966–1967	25-3

5 Year Totals 103-31

Totals for 16 Years of College Coaching

1951–1967   Won 307   Lost 108   .739%

Chapter 5

The NBA Years: The Lakers 1967–1969

"'Hard-Headed Dutchman?' I admit it! I am stubborn but I refuse to compromise on what I think is right. Sorry, but that is the way I am."

Butch van Breda Kolff

Normally, ex-Marine Corps sergeants don't cry, but Florence van Breda Kolff, a retired Marine Corps sergeant, cried all the way on the drive from Princeton to Los Angeles. She really had hoped for a longer tenure in Princeton, especially with Butch placing a team in the top five in the national rankings. Why leave?

At 15, their son Jan was likewise upset about the fact of leaving behind so many friends. He was just getting the hang of playing high school basketball. Their daughter Kaatje, a bright spot on the trip, looked forward to being so close to Hollywood. The twins were off to College in New Jersey and Massachusetts, and would visit when the family was settled.

As the van Breda Kolff family drove the 3,000 mile journey cross country, Butch thought of UCLA walking away with the national collegiate title while their crosstown professional counterparts—the Los Angeles Lakers—were posting an uninspiring 36-45 losing record for the 1966–67 season, finishing third out of five teams in the Western Division of the NBA. Indicative of the expansion of the NBA, the Western Conference currently has fourteen member teams. But back in 1967, three straight playoff losses to the San Francisco Warriors had quickly ended the Laker season. As he drove the highways on the long trip West, Butch tried to envision how he would turn this Laker team into a League Champion. There was so much talent at his fingertips. All they had to do was play as a team, he mused.

In the season prior to Butch's arrival in Los Angeles, the Lakers seemed to sleepwalk their way through the schedule despite the presence of a star-studded lineup, which included Jerry West and Elgin Baylor, two of the greatest players to ever play the game. The coach of the Lakers was mild mannered Fred Schaus, who had coached West at West Virginia University and even in high school. Schaus' approach to coaching was similar to many of the coaches in the league. He basically tried to keep his stable of super-egos in harmony and hoped they would produce more wins than losses.

Schaus' best years as a professional coach were 1965 and 1966, when he took the Lakers to the NBA championship finals against the Celtics. In the 1966 series, he narrowly lost in the seventh and final game. However, as his career evolved, he became less of a "hands-on" manager. He seemed to rationalize that his players were grown men requiring little if any proactive coaching. Regardless, someone had to take the blame for the Lakers' mediocre season during 1966–67. As is the case with most professional sports, the coach or the manager is the scapegoat for a team's poor performance. Schaus' time had come and he was ideally suited for a shift to an upper management position of an NBA team.

When Butch van Breda Kolff arrived on the Los Angeles scene, he observed that the Laker fans and their polite applause reminded him of a "theatre crowd." The Lakers seemed to exhibit an air of complacency as the players focused more on their individual statistics rather than on succeeding as a team. The Lakers needed someone to stir up the crowd, inspire the players, and above all play as a unit rather than as a collection of prima donnas. The situation was custom made for Butch van Breda Kolff's personality and coaching ability. He was convinced—the Lakers needed to be shown how to *play the game right!*

When Jack Kent Cooke, the president and principal owner of the Lakers franchise, hired Butch van Breda Kolff, he simultaneously moved taciturn Fred Schaus into the general manager's slot. The fiery Cooke wanted an inspirational force on the floor to lift his Laker team to its fullest potential.

As a showman, Cooke anxiously awaited the Lakers' performance in their new 17,095-seat home facility. Named "The Forum," the structure was the first privately funded indoor arena in the United States. Literally a "seating palace," "The Forum" was a self-erected monument designed by Cooke to acknowledge his own presidency. Cooke was impressed with VBK's collegiate record, especially his most recent season at Princeton where he led the Ivy League champions without Bill Bradley to the number five spot in the country. With Butch heralded as an "offensive genius," Cooke drooled as he envisioned what VBK could do with the likes of Baylor, West & Company.

"The Legends"

By way of background: Elgin Baylor graduated in 1958 from Seattle University, where he led his team all the way to the NCAA championship game, only to lose to Kentucky by 84-72. In his rookie NBA year in 1959, he was the co-MVP of the All-Star game with veteran Bob Pettit of the St. Louis Hawks. At the age of thirty-three, Elgin was entering his tenth season in the pros and was ranked fourth among the all-time scorers, setting the then single-game record of seventy-one points against the Knicks.

Baylor was a classic power forward. A fierce driver in a one-on-one situation, Baylor had a deadly shot from the outside as well. For the 1966–67 season, Baylor averaged 26.6 points per game. No doubt about it, Baylor was a living legend.

Jerry West graduated from West Virginia University in 1960. Like Baylor, West led the Mountaineers to a second place finish in the 1959 NCAA where his team lost to California by 71-70. At age twenty-nine, West was starting his eighth season in the NBA and ranked as the fourth leading scorer among active players and ninth all-time. For the season just prior to VBK's arrival in Los Angeles, West had averaged 28.7 points per game. Injuries, however, restricted his playing time to sixty-six of the Lakers' eighty-one contests. Butch was impressed with West's profile as a "team player," as evidenced by his team leading 447 assists (6.8 average) which featured a career high of sixteen. West also was a living legend.

Both Baylor and West were in the prime of their playing careers. Both were to be later named to the list of players honored as the 50 Greatest Players in NBA history when the League commemorated its fiftieth anniversary in 1996.

Two other Lakers—Gail Goodrich (UCLA '65) and Darrall Imhoff (California '60)—had led their college teams to NCAA championships before joining the pros. Tom Hawkins (Notre Dame '59) added to the list of heralded college players available to VBK.

Following a very successful rookie year, Archie Clark (Minnesota '66) was fast developing as one of the top point guards in the league and worked smoothly in tandem with West, a shooting guard. Clark was the master of the crossover dribble. Clark and Hawkins were the type of players which typified a successful van Breda Kolff team. They were excellent passers, showed great hustle, and moved well without the ball.

Butch was the first and only coach in NBA history to come directly from an Ivy League school to become head coach of a professional franchise. Chuck Daly, who coached the Penn Quakers to four titles in six years in the 1971–77 period, came to the NBA as an assistant for the 76ers and did not take a head coaching slot until the 1981 season. Daly got off to a 9-32 start with the Cleveland Cavaliers and was fired before the end of the season. Ultimately elected to the Hall of Fame, Daly's career took off with the Detroit Pistons and he led them to two NBA titles, 1989 and 1990.

Butch immediately set the record straight as to how he was going to lead the Lakers. He was not going to change his coaching style in the pros. Early on, he established his *modus operandi*—-he was determined to get more out of his players. He knew they had the potential, and he knew he could convert that potential to winning basketball games.

"The idea of the game, on any level, is to score. You don't have to worry much about teaching a player to shoot; that's the one thing he has worked on since he owned his first basketball. Getting the shot; that's something else . . . The things we have to work the hardest on with college players are getting open, making the percentage pass, moving without the ball. And I find that the pros need to be taught the very same things."

That was Butch's credo. *The pros needed to be taught!* Butch was intent on returning to the fundamentals of team basketball. He was going to install his style of basketball even if it meant roughing up some egos. Marine Corps drill sergeant van Breda Kolff had reported for duty and was in total command of his troops.

Seventeen years separated Butch's experience as a player for the NY Knickerbockers from that as a coach of the Los Angeles Lakers. The style of NBA coaching that prevailed in 1967–68 changed dramatically over that time span. Teaching coaches such as Joe Lapchick by and large disappeared in favor of former players. In VBK's first year of coaching in the NBA, former players Gene Shue, Bill Russell, John Kerr, Richie Guerin, Bill Sharman, and Al Bianchi reigned as coaches without any collegiate coaching experience. Essentially, they took a group of proven athletes, many of them former All-Americans, and tried to create a harmonious atmosphere in which these high-priced stars could play together.

Butch, on the other hand, was the consummate coach. His team was not a "democracy." His team was not ruled by the "invisible hand." Any form of "diplomacy" had disappeared in his first few months at Lafayette. Undeterred by the high salaries that his superstars commanded, Butch represented "authority" and he sought to impose his total basketball philosophy on the Lakers and future NBA teams. To that extent, Butch was an aberration in the NBA. He would be the subject of unending controversy over the next ten years.

Another culture shock for VBK occurred with respect to NBA club owners. Collectively, they sought to not only win basketball games but also to provide entertainment. They wanted their superstars to roll up the statistics. The subtlety of whether or not the game was *played right* disappeared beneath their radar screen. The owners liked their "big bullies" and paid dearly to keep them happy. In contrast, in his Hofstra years, Butch recommended that the press omit box scores and instead list team scores only. Basketball was a team game. Butch, it seems, was constantly at odds with the system.

As a crossword puzzle addict, one of Butch's favorite vocabulary words is "sycophant." Given the clue of "sycophant" and six-letters to fill in, the correct answer might be "yes-man," or possibly "fawner." VBK as a college coach and immediately as a professional coach was nobody's sycophant. With the Lakers, he set out to alter the proven individual styles of Baylor and West so as to make them both more effective team players. Butch was less than diplomatic as he volleyed many a verbal barrage at his legends and their teammates. He wanted the Lakers to hustle more, box out, set picks, get back on defense, move without the ball, pass to the open man. Veterans and rookies alike were subject to his wrath.

Initially, Jerry West was skeptical about VBK's approach and constantly whispered "that SOB" under his breath when subjected to one of Butch's tirades. Soon, aware of the complacency engendered by Shaus' methodology, Jerry altered his thoughts about VBK and said "SOB" in a different tone of voice. After practice, Jerry would interpret his initials to stand for "Sweet Old Bill."

Like Jekyll and Hyde, the double meaning of "SOB" became a rallying cry for the team's understanding of Butch's coaching strategy. He was a real "SOB" when he chewed you out for missing a rebound box-out, but he was just "Sweet Old Bill" after the game was over and he had a chance to review the situation with you. Over a beer or two of course.

Just as he had openly embarrassed his Princeton captain Art Hyland with his *"fat ass captain"* remark, Butch seemed determined to motivate his Laker leader Elgin Baylor as well. During the course of a regularly scheduled game, Butch conspicuously yelled at Elgin for throwing an errant pass, and referred to him in terms which implied the legendary forward was "stupid". A fire burned within Baylor as he conjured up the "evil" "SOB" image of his drill sergeant coach. Butch, however, sensing that he might have been a bit harsh, met with Baylor later on that evening to discuss the incident. After a long discussion, the two were on the same page. Baylor's self respect had been restored, and he became one of the strongest forces in unifying the Laker team behind Butch.

Elsewhere around the NBA, the team to beat was the Philadelphia 76ers. For 1966–67, the Sixers recorded a spectacular 68-13 (.840 pct.) mark during the regular season and subsequently defeated the Cincinnati Royals, the Boston Celtics, and the San Francisco Warriors to capture the NBA title. While working their way toward the championship, the Sixers ended the Celtics streak of eight straight titles. Wilt "The Stilt" Chamberlain paced the Sixers while leading the team in scoring (24.1), field goal percentage (.683), rebounds (24.2 average), and assists (7.8 average). His supporting cast included Hal Greer, Chet Walker, and Billy Cunningham. He was selected as the league's MVP in 1960, 1966, and 1967. His most memorable statistic was the record 100 points he scored against the Knicks on March 3, 1962, in a regular season game played in Hershey, Pennsylvania. Some say Wilt was the best to ever play the game.

The Boston Celtics finished second in the Eastern Division in 1966–67. Their player-coach was rebounding great Bill Russell. His balanced lineup included Sam Jones, Bailey Howell, Tom Sanders, Don Nelson, and probably the best sixth man in basketball history, John Havlicek. Prior to the 76ers title run of the 1966–67 season, the Celtics—a veritable dynasty—had dominated the NBA from 1958–66. Pervasive to the Celtics dominance was the influence of Red Auerbach. He coached the Boston franchise up to 1965–66 when Bill Russell took over. He retained an authoritative role as general manager, and the Celtics continued their dynasty for two of the next three seasons.

Exuding confidence, Butch van Breda Kolff announced preseason that he expected to be playing for the league championship in April. He forecast that the San Francisco Warriors were the main challenge in the West, despite the retirement of the league's leading scorer Rick Barry (35.6 points per game). He looked forward to the November 1 game versus the New York Knicks at the Forum when Bill Bradley was scheduled to come to town. He speculated how strange it would be to see Bradley and Cazzie Russell playing on the same team together!

The van Breda Kolff system took hold and by season's end the Lakers had achieved a 52-30 record. The "new team" which featured the same players from the previous season had not only won sixteen more games but also progressed through the playoffs where they were pitted against the Boston Celtics in the finals. For Butch van Breda Kolff, an NBA title in his rookie season was just four victories away.

The 1968 NBA Championship Series: Lakers vs Celtics

Defying all odds, the Boston Celtics were a most unexpected representative of the Eastern Division in the finals of the 1968 Championship Series of the NBA. Continuously on the brink in their series with the Philadelphia 76ers, the Celts rallied from a 3-1 deficit to defeat Wilt Chamberlain & Co. by four games to three. The Lakers, on the other hand, swept the San Francisco Warriors with relative ease.

While the Celtics played all week with their backs to the wall, the Lakers enjoyed a week-long respite from the wars of the NBA.

In the series opener, the well-rested Lakers pulled out to a 61-48 halftime lead and were on top by 78-63 midway through the third quarter. Then the Lakers turned ice cold, and by the end of the quarter the score stood at 85-81. The Lakers never could find the mark, as their shooting percentage for the day registered 36.8—well below their league leading average of 47.8. West and Baylor shot three for seventeen in the final stanza while six Celtics scored in double figures. Russell dominated with twenty-five rebounds, as the Celts triumphed 107-101 to take a 1-0 advantage in the series.

Three nights later, the Lakers legendary duo of West and Baylor scored thirty-five and twenty-three points respectively, and the Lakers held on to win 123-113 and tie the series at 1-1. VBK was hit with a technical foul after Baylor drew his fifth personal foul with 4:02 left in the third quarter. The teams essentially traded baskets in the fourth quarter, and soon the second battle between the two top teams was history.

In game number three, the Celtics dominated behind the play of Russell and in game number four the West-Baylor show combined for sixty-eight points to enable the Lakers to tie the series at 2-2. While the Lakers cruised to a relatively smooth 118-105 win, Butch "blew his cool" (the words chosen by Bill Becker of the *New York Times*) resulting in two technicals and his ultimate ejection from the contest.

In the case of the second technical, the entire Laker bench rose to protest a call by one of the referees. Butch, in attempting to prevent a "team technical," put his back to the refs and waved his arms wildly, barking at his team to sit down. The refs thought VBK was imitating them or mocking them, and so called a technical on the coach. In the end, the Lakers were able to win without Butch on the floor, although he thought that he would have removed the slightly injured Jerry West from the game once it was under control. The pivotal game of the 1968 series was game number five at the Boston Garden. The contest involved many lead changes and saw the Celtics squander a 108-104 lead and the ball in the front court with only forty-four seconds left in the game. A pair of steals by the Lakers resulted in two quick layup baskets and the score was suddenly tied. Then Bill Russell traveled and the turnover gave the Lakers a chance to win the game in regulation. But Baylor's desperation shot at the buzzer bounced off the rim and the two teams were headed for overtime.

The overtime belonged to the Celts. Substitute Don Nelson had never scored more than twenty-five points in a game, but in the game number five he tallied twenty-six clutch points, including four in the overtime period. His defense against Elgin Baylor was key. Nelson's final second foul shot led to a 120-117 win for the Celts.

The Celtics now needed but one victory to secure another championship, their ninth in ten years. The well-balanced Celts got top performances from Bailey Howell (thirty points) and John Havilicek (forty points, twelve for twelve from the foul line) whereas the Lakers' Jerry West was hampered by a twisted ankle and was below average with twenty-two points. Player-coach Bill Russell, sensing the title, blocked innumerable shots in the fourth quarter to thwart any possibility of a Laker rally. Mel Counts was a bright spot for the Lakers with twenty-five rebounds, but the Celtics were just too sharp. The 1968 title belonged to Boston as they breezed by Los Angeles by a 124-109 margin.

Excluding exhibition games and the postseason playoffs, the pro game in the late '60s entailed an eighty-one game schedule in comparison to the average of twenty-five to thirty games played at the college level. For Butch van Breda Kolff, this was a major adjustment. Butch was a perfectionist of the game and he built himself up mentally and emotionally before every contest, often working himself into a veritable frenzy. Combined with the evolving media blitz of professional sports, the October through May aspect of the NBA seemed to frazzle the hyper inner nature of VBK. At the college level, he had an opportunity to have a few beers with his friends after the game. At Lafayette and Hofstra, the local press was not always in in his face seeking comments. At Princeton, he could break away to Harvey Cedars. In the pros, it was off for the next stop on the schedule.

There were no "breathers" in the NBA. The league had just expanded to twelve teams and was packed with superstars. Although van Breda Kolff had vocalized with the referees in his college days, his exchanges with the professional refs seemed to intensify as the pressures of the long season took its toll. Before long, Butch began ringing up technical fouls as the refs just wouldn't tolerate his courtside antics. In one season alone, he logged in forty technicals, supposedly an NBA record.

Butch also felt that the press, in its constant quest for the sensational news, grossly exaggerated the facts of a story. They thrived on VBK's expressiveness. To emphasize their independence, he continually referred to the press as the *fourth estate,* the "untouchable" faction evolving out of the French Revolution. Even so, Butch had many allies among the sports writers nationwide, including George Vecsey (*New York Times*), Paul Horowitz (*Newark Evening News*) and John Hall (*Los Angeles Times*).

Photographs of VBK thumbing his nose with his other four fingers in the air hit all the major press services. Butch humorously explained he was just calling for the "number five" play, but the refs thought otherwise. Other photos accentuated VBK's crooked teeth and huge disclike eyeballs. Indeed, the press had a field day with the animated expressiveness of Butch van Breda Kolff.

Additionally, Butch soon started pontificating on his theories about the NBA with the press. One of his pet subjects was the roll of the "big bullies" in the NBA and how the referees allowed the big-name superstars sporting huge physiques to back their way in, charge, walk, or camp in the three-second lane at will. The game was just too physical. The refs were instructed, he intimated, to encourage more scoring by the name players in order to attract more fans. Every player had to be another Dr. J! He even suggested high school kids play soccer instead! Coaches and players worried more about their contracts and sneaker endorsements than playing the game properly. Such comments invoked the wrath of Walter Kennedy, the president of the National Basketball Association. Coach van Breda Kolff was fined $250 and received a strong letter from Kennedy in the wake of his "big bullies" remarks.

The impact of all these theatrics was probably detrimental to his relationship with owner Jack Kent Cooke. To begin with, Cooke dressed the role of the multimillionaire that he was. He dreaded Butch's appearance in his stylish executive offices when the coach appeared in T-shirt, cut-offs, sneakers, and a cigar in his mouth. The owner preferred a more formal approach and cringed when Butch referred to him as "Cooker." Without doubt, Butch's reputation as a showman began to overshadow his great accomplishments as a coach, his passion for the game, and the fond appreciation of his team. Butch had amassed 307 wins in fifteen years of college coaching and in his first season as a pro he had turned in a 52-30 record. He was destined for immortality. But pitfalls such as flunking out of Princeton and his exchanges with Walter Kennedy would make that road quite a bit bumpier.

Unhappiness was brewing in Philadelphia. The 76ers and their superstar Wilt Chamberlain were disgusted after the team had blown a 3-1 lead in the 1968 semifinals versus the Celtics. Alex Hannum, the only coach to break the ten-season (1959-1969) championship winning streak of the Celtics, resigned. For his new coach, Wilt demanded

The NBA Years: The Lakers 1967–1969

NATIONAL BASKETBALL ASSOCIATION
5317 EMPIRE STATE BUILDING
NEW YORK, N. Y. 10001
BRYANT 9-1535

OFFICE OF THE PRESIDENT

October 23, 1967

Mr. Bill van Breda Kolff
Los Angeles Lakers
3939 S. Figueroa
Los Angeles, Calif.

Dear Bill:

From time to time I have read with much interest - and some concern - statements and quotes from you in various newspapers around the country. Because you are a new coach in a new role in professional basketball, I felt that you needed a short period of time to get adjusted to your new environment. For that reason, I refrained from fining you for issuing statements that were detrimental to the NBA, as noted in my recent letter.

However, your outrageous statements to Robert Markus appearing in the Chicago Tribune of October 19, 1967, are so detrimental to the best interests of basketball and to the NBA, that I am hereby fining you $250, payable within ten days. Any continuation of such public statements will result in a stiffer fine.

Basketball has been good to you - both as a player in college, as a player in the NBA, as a college coach, and now as a professional coach. No matter what your personal feelings about the professional sport at this time, it would seem that your good judgment would dictate that you should keep these opinions to yourself, or discuss them with me personally, on your trips to New York.

I believe that I am quite reasonable in the administration of my duties as Commissioner. However, one thing that I will not tolerate is public criticism of the Association and/or its officials.

Please make the check payable to the National Basketball Association.

Cordially,

Walter Kennedy

WK:ba

Exhibit B: Letter from Walter Kennedy to VBK

the 76ers hire Frank McGuire or Bill Sharman. He even alluded to becoming a player-coach like his counter-part in Boston. He was cited in the *New York Times* as saying, "Rather than have some stumblebum on the bench, I would consider coaching. No one knows player Wilt better than Wilt."

Meanwhile in Los Angeles, owner Jack Kent Cooke was determined to "buy himself" a championship. He was convinced he needed a big-time center to counter the impact of Bill Russell, just in case the Celtics were the Lakers' opponent for yet another championship run. In July, before the start of the 1968–69 season, Cooke orchestrated one of the blockbuster trades of the century with the Philadelphia 76ers. With VBK's approval, in exchange for Darrall Imhoff, Archie Clark, and Jerry Chambers, the Los Angeles Lakers received Wilt "The Stilt" Chamberlain. Cooke was sure that Chamberlain, with Baylor and West by his side, could neutralize the Celtics or any other representative from the Eastern Division.

"The Big Dipper," Elgin Baylor, and Jerry West. Three legends. What a combination, especially given the proven coaching techniques of Butch van Breda Kolff. The Lakers immediately were labeled the pre-season favorite for the NBA title.

VBK quickly adapted his game plan to reflect the addition of Wilt. He planned to place a stronger emphasis on defense in order to exploit "The Stilt's" height and talents. Likewise, he contemplated a more deliberate offense in which the team moved the ball into Wilt's hands.

Although Baylor and West had adjusted their games and their lives to incorporate the coaching style of Butch van Breda Kolff, Wilt never thoroughly committed his psyche to the VBK philosophy. Wilt was not going to listen to any coach from Lafayette, Hofstra, and Princeton tell him how to play the game. Wilt was above discipline. In his own mind, he was "The Greatest." He only had to walk onto the court, wield his 7'1" body into action, and the wins would roll in. In practice, he mainly worked on his career-long problem, i.e., foul shooting. Wilt preferred a coach like Fred Shaus who—like the psychiatrist—let his patient on the couch do all the talking. Otherwise, coaches were "stumblebums."

The press—in its endless pursuit of controversy—found fertile material in the relationship between Butch van Breda Kolff and Wilt Chamberlain. Surely, with three legends on the court at once, someone's statistics would have to suffer. There just weren't enough basketballs to go around! Wilt was concerned that the coach and the rest of the team had overlooked his league-leading assist mark from the previous season. Wilt felt he was indeed a team player. In his book entitled *A View from Above,* Wilt suggested that Butch initiated the anxiety between the two with his remark, "He'll play it my way or not at all." Thenceforth, Wilt was negative about the likelihood of his working with Butch. In his words, the "unavoidable clash" was in the works. Later in his same book, Wilt accused Butch of "bigotry."

But Butch, being Butch, persisted. He tried to get Wilt to focus on defense. He yelled at Wilt for blocking shots out of bounds rather than into the hands of his teammates. "They get the ball back," he screamed at Wilt. "What good is that?" He further antagonized Wilt by comparing his play to that of his professional adversary Bill Russell. "Russell always blocked the shots in the direction of his teammates," Butch stressed to the flabbergasted Wilt.

The comparison between Wilt and Bill Russell was well-documented. Robert Lipsyte of the *New York Times* wrote in his column "Sports of the Times" about their different styles:[1]

> They are very different on the court. Chamberlain moves almost stiffly, as if afraid his nearly 300 pounds will crush someone, and there is no second effort in him. His lips are moving, making excuses in advance. He plays episodically: A spurt of action, a look around, a rest, then kick over the engine and start again. There seems little pleasure in it for him.
>
> Russell, his sly, wise face impassive, is always moving, loping, strutting up and down the court, his long arms beating like wings hooking over his head for a shot, wiping a ball out of Wilt's hands, or sweeping little Johnny Egan off his feet.

In fourteen years in the NBA, Wilt Chamberlain never fouled out of a game. Intuitively, VBK interpreted the statistic to imply that Wilt was less than aggressive in his defensive efforts.

---

[1] Robert Lipsyte, "The Titans," *New York Times,* April 30, 1969, p. 49.

Indeed, the friction between Wilt and Butch began to magnify. In a midseason game, the Lakers were trailing the underdog Sonics by a sizable margin at halftime. On the way to the locker room, in the corridor of the Seattle Coliseum, Butch started screaming at Wilt. In an instant, Wilt and Butch were in each other's face, and an all-out fight seemed imminent.

Team captain Elgin Baylor and half the Laker team broke up the altercation between the two professionals.

Despite their differences, Wilt and Butch and the Lakers compiled a 55-27 regular season record, the best in the club's history. "Big Deal! We won three more games and I lost a half a head of hair," Butch reflected.

The 1969 NBA Championship Series: Celtics vs Lakers

The Lakers finished first in their division and were impressive in their early victories of the 1969 playoffs. After dropping two straight to the San Francisco Warriors, the Lakers caught fire and reeled off four in a row. Then they faced the Atlanta Hawks, and emerged victorious in winning four out of six. The Hawks were coached by former Iona College and New York Knicks star Richie Guerin. Johnny Egan, one time Providence College star and a new addition to the Laker lineup, was a key factor in the Hawks series. With virtually no time left in game two against the Hawks, Egan drove the length of the court and sank a layup to ice the victory 104-102.

Following their fourth place finish in the regular season, the Celtics amazing run in the playoffs during the previous ten years was perceived to be at an end. Sam Jones and Bill Russell were both thirty-five, and the playoffs were infinitely more draining than the freewheeling regular season. However, the old Celtic pride surfaced shortly after the opening tip of the "second season." Boston easily disposed of the Philadelphia 76ers, winning four out of five. Next, the Celts faced the New York Knicks in the Eastern Finals. After several bruising contests, the Celts ousted the New Yorkers 4-2 and made it to their twelfth championship series in thirteen years. The stage was set. The 1969 NBA Champion would be determined in a best of seven series between the Los Angeles Lakers and the Boston Celtics. The matchup between Bill Russell and Wilt Chamberlain, anticipated by owner Jack Kent Cooke when he traded for the Stilt, would soon become a reality.

The Celtics were known for their outstanding team play, strong defense, and unlimited hustle. Compared to the regular season, the Celts played a different game during the "crunch time" of the playoffs. They were consistent winners throughout the history of the NBA, but were especially strong in the '60s when Bill Russell, John Havlicek, Sam Jones, and Bailey Howell led the way. Their home court—The Boston Garden—featured a magnificent parquet floor, which symbolized their perfection.

In the opening game of the 1969 championship series, Jerry West was unstoppable as he scored fifty-three points. Celtic Coach Bill Russell tried several different defenders to try and limit West, but to no avail. West's fifty-second and fifty-third points gave the Lakers a 119-116 lead which they never relinquished.

In game number two, the Lakers continued on with West registering forty-one points. Newcomer Johnny Egan at 5'11" scored twenty-six points from long range and set up several lob layups to the dismay of Bill Russell. Chamberlain and Russell played the entire game, and effectively neutralized each other. Chamberlain had one of his best defensive games as he made the center lane "a virtual no man's land for the Celtics." (Becker, NYTimes). The Celtics were quickly down 2-0 and welcomed the chance to meet the Lakers at the Boston Garden.

At the beginning of the season, Larry Siegfried was the starting guard for the Celtics, but midway during the regular campaign he lost his job to Emmette Bryant. For the first two games of the playoffs, Siegried mostly came off the bench to give fouls and averaged 8.6 points per game. However, in game number three at the Boston Garden, Siegfried scored twenty-eight points and complimented Havlicek's thirty-four points as the Celtics pulled away in the fourth quarter to win by 111-105. A fourteen point fourth quarter outburst by Johnny Egan buoyed the Laker offense, but in the end the Celtics guards were just too much for Los Angeles.

The critical fourth game of the championship series was decided by a jump shot by Celtic veteran Sam Jones, who at age thirty-five had announced his retirement at the completion of the series. With two seconds left on the clock, Jones spun, stumbled and fired a shot that hung softly on the rim and then dropped through for an 89-88 victory by Boston. To the Lakers, the loss was hard to swallow. What might have been a 3-1 Laker edge heading home was instead a series tied at two games each.

After scoring but three baskets in the fourth game, Wilt returned to Los Angeles to finally dominate a game against the Celts. His numbers were thirty-one rebounds and thirteen points versus his counterpart Bill Russell (thirteen boards and two points). Jerry West continued his hot streak with thirty-nine points while Johnny Egan added twenty-three. Havlicek—who had averaged 33.7 points in the first three games—was held to eighteen, and the Lakers won by a 117-104 margin. Leading the series 3-2, the Lakers needed but one victory to take the NBA crown.

The sixth game in Boston lacked any last second heroics. The Celtics assumed a 32-22 first quarter lead and were never really challenged by the Lakers. Neither team looked especially sharp, but the well-balanced Celts won easily 99-90 to knot the playoffs at 3-3.

Since the Lakers had the better regular season record, they had the homecourt advantage for the final and deciding seventh game. After seven months of pro basketball, the season boiled down to just one game.

Confident of the Lakers home court advantage, Jack Kent Cooke hung purple victory balloons from the rafters of the Forum. The maneuver seemed to inspire the Celtics, as the visitors jumped out to an early 24-12 lead behind the shooting of Havlicek and Em Bryant. The Lakers clawed their way back into the game, however, and early in the third quarter the score was tied 60-60. The next five minutes of the game were a horror for the hometown Lakers. The Celts held the Western Division champs scoreless for a little more than five minutes. The Lakers had several open shots, but just couldn't convert. Chamberlain picked up his fourth personal limiting his effectiveness off the boards. Jones, Havlicek, and Don Nelson seemed to score at will. Near the end of the third quarter, the Celtics had a commanding seventeen point lead at 91-74.

But the Celtics aggressiveness had its price, and early in the fourth quarter Russell and Havlicek each had accumulated five personals. With the Celts playing a looser defense, the Lakers rallied to trail by seven points with a little more than five minutes left in the game. Then, the once physically indestructible Chamberlain complained of a knee injury and essentially removed himself from the game. "There was no doubt. Wilt was clear about wanting to come out," VBK remarked. Butch then inserted his other 7-footer, Mel Counts, as Wilt limped off the court.

VBK had his spirited five in the game, and the Lakers responded by closing the gap to 103-102 with 3:07 seconds to go. The partisan Forum crowd roared with approval as their team suddenly began to display its championship potential. With the game hanging in the balance, Wilt stood up off the bench and asked VBK to be reinserted into the game. Wilt's distinct height differential accentuated the discussion between the two men. But Butch was not intimidated by the Stilt, and instantly refused his request to reenter the game. Intuitively, Butch felt he owed it to the team on the floor, the team that had fought back to within one point of the Celts, to win or lose the game on its own. It was a matter of principle. He also felt that the momentum factor was on his side. In a quasi-military fashion, without hesitation, Butch glared at Wilt and stated in front of the team, "We're playing better without you." Chamberlain remained on the bench. The word "stumblebum" quickly crossed Wilt's mind as he sought to rationalize his festering disrespect for his coach.

In 1965, Don Nelson was traded by the Lakers to the Boston Celtics. He had an All-American career at Iowa and was regarded as a clutch substitute by player-coach Bill Russell. As Wilt Chamberlain sat sulking on the bench, Russell strategically inserted Nelson with little time left on the game clock. Nelson was the right man in the right spot at the right time, as he snared a carom off the hands of teammate John Havlicek and quickly shoveled the ball toward the basket. The ball hit the back of the rim, went straight up in the air, and miraculously dropped through the hoop for what was tantamount to the winning score.

The final score read:

Boston Celtics 108
Los Angeles Lakers 106

Butch had gambled on not reinserting Wilt "The Stilt" and came up short. Butch could live with his convictions. He had flipped the coin and lost. "Oh, what the hell!" It sure was better than being on the Navy cargo plane!

Some fifteen years later, a feature *Sports Illustrated* article about van Breda Kolff classified Butch's move as "probably the single most controversial courtside decision ever made by a professional basketball coach." The press at the time had a field day with the whole scenario. Wilt later wrote in his autobiography that Butch was "The worst coach I ever had." Upon hearing of Wilt's remark, he responded "That's a compliment!"

Butch defended his strategy. He wouldn't back down. He didn't blame the loss on his substitution strategy. Rather, he felt his team "missed the open man too often." He also complained about his team falling behind by seventeen points in the third quarter. When asked about reinserting Wilt, he simply stated, "I thought we were playing fairly well without him." At crunch time, Butch also wanted his better foul shooters on the floor. Wilt had gone 4-13 from the foul line before removing himself from the game.

The NBA Years: The Lakers 1967–1969

Jerry West was utterly disappointed by the loss. Unlike the 1968 team, he felt the 1969 Lakers were a vastly superior unit to the rapidly aging Celtics. He derived no satisfaction from the fact he set a new record for 556 points scored in eighteen playoff games, thus breaking the mark previously set by Rick Barry. Nor was he impressed by being named MVP for the playoff series. Especially since the Corvette that he was awarded was Celtic green! For Elgin Baylor, it was the seventh Laker title playoff loss to the Celtics. "This one really hurts," said Baylor, "especially when you come so close—two points in the seventh game."

Soon communication with the front office of the Lakers totally evaporated. On May 19, 1969, exactly two weeks after the title game, Butch van Breda Kolff resigned his position as head coach of the Los Angeles Lakers. Undoubtedly, he felt the pressure from Cooke & Co. Vintage von Breda Kolff, he made no excuses. He refused to comment when pressed by the media to discuss specific "personalities." He had no regrets. "No time for weeping or sour grapes . . . Time for a party . . . No sad songs please!" were his thoughts.

In 1972, Chamberlain led the Lakers to the league championship. Although Wilt truly dominated the scoring and rebounding statistics throughout his fourteen year NBA career, only twice did he earn a championship ring, once with the Lakers and once with the 1967 Philadelphia 76ers. Butch van Breda Kolff was a proactive coach who sought to mold a strong team effort wherever he went. Bill Bradley was a dominant yet unselfish player on a VBK coached team. Wilt Chamberlain resisted coaching and tried to carry the team totally on his own ability. Butch and Wilt. Two opposites. Two of the all time greats.

One of the sports writers—John Hall—wrote of VBK's departure:

> "A Silent Farewell. Los Angeles is losing a good man, a man deeply more sincere about life, family, and friendship than the public portrait."

BOX SCORE: 1969 CHAMPIONSHIP GAME

Boston (108)

	G	F	P
Howell	4	1-2	9
Havilicek	11	4-7	26
Russell	2	2-4	6
Bryant	9	2-3	24
Jones	10	4-4	24
Nelson	6	4-7	16
Siegfried	2	3-4	7
Totals	44	20-31	108

Los Angeles (106)

	G	F	P
Baylor	8	4-5	20
Erickson	2	2-3	6
Chamberlain	7	4-13	18
Egan	3	3-6	9
West	14	14-18	42
Hawkins	1	0-0	2
Counts	4	1-2	9
Totals	39	28-47	106

Boston	28	31	32	17	108
Los Angeles	25	31	20	30	106

Fouled out—Jones, Erickson
Attendance—17,368

Reversing history is impossibile, but it is interesting to speculate what might have happened if Nelson had missed his shovel shot and the Lakers had pulled out the win and the championship. Butch probably would not have resigned, but another season of the VBK-Chamberlain constant conflict probably would have led to a confrontational blowout between the two stubborn personalities. Barring the unlikely mellowing of either or both personalities, something had to give. As a guess, Butch probably would have resigned early in the following season. Also, Jack Kent Cooke, the one responsible for Wilt being in Los Angeles in the first place, was not really happy with Butch's leaving the Stilt on the bench during the championship game. Any slippage in the Lakers performance during the ensuing season, and Butch would be history. Regardless, there were other less stressful opportunities available in the professional and college coaching arena.

Butch's ability to "turn around" the Lakers from complacency to near NBA champions was a source of some self-satisfaction. As his career unfolded, Butch was frequently attracted by the prospect of reviving a deteriorating or dormant program. The opportunity to demonstrate his "touch" was out there waiting. The Detroit Pistons, a perennial doormat of the NBA, was looking to make a move on the coaching scene. Once Butch's resignation from the Lakers hit the press, the Piston management was quickly on the phone in search of his services.

Chapter 6

The NBA Years: The Detroit Pistons 1969–1971

"He salts the air around him and peppers it, and any honest description of his spoken prose must contain many blanks to protect those who have never been in the Marines or in the company of Leo Durocher."

Jack Olsen, *Sports Illustrated*, 1969

Butch van Breda Kolff was hired by the Detroit Pistons to bring winning basketball to the Motor City. For fourteen years, since moving from Ft. Wayne, Indiana, the Pistons had posted losing records and were perpetually mired in last place of the Western Division of the NBA. Generally speaking, the NBA practice of awarding the best college draft choices to the worst teams should have boosted the Detroit franchise toward the middle of the pack if not higher. Theoretically, Butch van Breda Kolff was the man to pull this team together.

The Pistons started to make some waves following their key draft choice of David Bing (Syracuse University '66) for the 1966–67 season. Bing averaged twenty points per game, led the team in assists, and was selected as "rookie of the year" in the NBA. Butch's Bradley-led Princeton team had played against Bing in the 1964 Holiday Festival.

Despite the contributions of David Bing, the Pistons again finished last in the NBA—which earned them yet another first pick in the draft of college players. This time, they selected Jimmy Walker, everyone's All-American from Providence College and the highest scorer in the nation (30.4 points per game). The positive chemistry between Walker and Butch van Breda Kolff was immediate as VBK admired Walker's team style and propensity to take "good shots." Butch liked Walker as much as Bing, playing both stars about equally. In addition to Bing and Walker, the Pistons listed veterans Eddie Miles (Seattle U. '63) and Terry Driscoll (Boston College) at the guard position. The Pistons had the raw material of a very strong backcourt.

Up front, Butch anticipated that he would have Terry Dischinger (6'7", 208) and Dave DeBusschere (6'6", 220) as his key operatives. Dischinger was a prolific scorer, when healthy, and DeBusschere was a dynamic power forward who had tried his hand as player-coach of the Pistons for three seasons. He constantly represented Detroit in the All-Star game, led the team in rebounds, and generally ranked as the team's third high scorer. For three seasons, he pitched for the Chicago White Sox.

Fred Zollner, the aging auto-parts magnate and owner of the Pistons, instructed his general manager—Ed Coil—to hire Butch van Breda Kolff in hopes of moving his team up in the standings. Coil offered VBK a two-year contract, implying a tidy raise from his Laker deal. Without missing a step from his experience in LA, VBK had a new project and/or coaching assignment in the Detroit Pistons.

Just prior to Butch reporting to the Detroit Pistons, the management consummated a major transaction in which they traded Dave DeBusschere to the New York Knicks for Walt Bellamy and Howie Komives. VBK had no voice in the trade, but would have to live with its consequences. Even more troubling, he would be accountable for improving the Pistons with Bellamy in the front court instead of DeBusschere.

On paper, the trade must have made sense. Bellamy was five inches taller than DeBusschere, had a slightly higher scoring average than his counterpart, and statistically out-rebounded the former Detroit Coach by a slim margin. In his fifth year out of Bowling Green, Komives was a streak shooter who led the nation in scoring in 1964 with a 36.7 average. Ironically, his nickname was "Butch" and he was left-handed.

But the value of Dave DeBusschere transcended the world of statistics. He was a great frontcourt passer, he was inspirational, he was a clutch player. He was a master at boxing out under the boards, which more often than not kept the opponent rebounder from grabbing the ball. He was at his best in the fourth quarter of a close game. Perhaps, he was the "ultimate slob." An overachiever, he eventually was instrumental in two New York Knickerbocker championships over the next four years. DeBusschere was like Thieben, Radcliff, and Thomforde all rolled into one player. He was a starter on VBK's theoretical All-Star team when asked who he deemed the best players of all time.

The Knicks seemed to steal DeBusschere. With Bellamy gone, they could move Willis Reed over to the center slot where he performed better than forward. Was there more than meets the eye to this trade? VBK eventually traded Bellamy away. When asked what he got for Bellamy, Butch replied, "Peace of mind."

Speculation on how well a VBK-DeBusschere combination would have done in Detroit remains just that. Butch van Breda Kolff never complained about the trade. He played the game with the cards that he was dealt.

Butch entered the season on a positive note. The headline in the *Detroit Press* read:

AN HONEST-TO-GOD BASKETBALL COACH MAYBE DETROIT'S FIRST EVER!

"I like the underdog role" and "Let's forget about Wilt" were just some of VBK's rallying cries.

At the reception welcoming Butch to Detroit, he wore a cardigan sweater while slurping beer from a can. It seemed that everyone else was gently sipping martini's and using cocktail napkins and the like. Early on, Fred Zollner expressed dislike for Butch's cardigan-mock turtle color combinations, but Butch insisted on doing his own thing. "I hate to wear a shirt and tie, but I realize it is necessary."

But 1969–70 saw the Pistons go 31-51, and thus marked the end of Butch van Breda Kolff's string of winning seasons (college and professional combined) at twelve. His last (and only previous) losing season had been at Hofstra when his make-shift 1956–57 team went 11-15. Butch continued to rant and rave at the officials, and his early departures seemed to mount. Butch soon came to the realization, "I'll have to think before I blow up!"

But the last place finish of the Pistons again gave them the top pick in the college draft. Conceivably, they could have opted for the services of "Pistol" Pete Maravich, the highest scorer ever in collegiate history. VBK liked the idea of going after Maravich, and perhaps trading Bing for an established big man. But the Piston's management was wedded to their backcourt of Walker and Bing, and selected the best big man available in the draft of 1970. Their pick was St. Bonaventure's graceful center, Bob Lanier. Lanier had led the Bonnies to the Final Four in 1970, and seemed on the verge of taking his team all the way to the title. Then, in a semifinal game against Villanova, Lanier went down with a disabling knee injury and he was done for the tourney. Still, optimism ran high that the 6'11" and 265 pound center had the tools to make the Pistons a winner. Lanier was immediately classified by the Detroit community as the "anti Edsel." He wore size twenty-two sneakers, representing the largest feet in the NBA.

Because of the limited services of Lanier, who could only go one quarter at a time, Butch van Breda Kolff experimented in the preseason with a platoon system. The new system was a success and so he carried it over to the regular season. As expected, he required a total team commitment and a special emphasis on aggressive defense.

Offensively, the team thrived on the scoring and passing of Mssrs. Bing & Walker. The platoon system produced great results as the Pistons started the season with a nine-game winning streak. But off the court, many of the Piston players complained about their reduced playing time. Their individual statistics were being sacrificed on behalf of the team. They were concerned about their bargaining chips come contract negotiating time. Lanier struggled with his nagging knee injury and originally voiced complaints in the press about VBK's platoon system. However, Butch worked closely with the "Giant from St. Bonaventure" and before long the two were on the same page. They grew to respect one another. Lanier even used Butch's Harvey Cedars house one summer.

As the season evolved, the 1970-71 Pistons were perhaps VBK's best NBA coaching accomplishment yet. The Pistons finished the season at 45-37. At long last, it was Detroit's best season ever!

Despite their great record, the Pistons finished fourth in their division behind Chicago, Milwaukee with Lew Alcindor, and the Phoenix Suns. The misfortune of being in such a strong division precluded the Pistons from playing in the playoffs. The 1970-71 Pistons epitomized Sisyphus pushing that rock up the hill.

The addition of rookie Curtis Rowe out of UCLA gave the Pistons the spark they needed to attain even higher goals for '71-72. But constant clashes with the Piston management, disagreement with his life style, his distasteful interchanges with the referees, and a myriad of intangibles led to VBK resigning his position from the Pistons early in the 1971 season. Although Butch rarely looked back to question any of his critical life decisions, he later admitted that leaving Detroit was possibly a mistake.

"It was stupid of me to walk out," he remarked some thirty years later. He confessed that a section of hometown fans near the Detroit bench were particularly annoying. They openly criticized his every decision. VBK speculated that they assuredly were fans of Wilt the Stilt.

Bob Lanier realized that the isolated but vocal fans were upsetting to Butch. Essentially, there were two identifiable fans who totally annoyed VBK. Taking a team leadership role, Lanier suggested that Butch and he face the fans directly over dinner. "We all want Detroit to be a winner," Lanier thought. But Butch turned down the idea. He just didn't want to capitulate to the renegade fans. Many years later, as he reviewed the cycles of his life, he felt he should have addressed the issue rather than leaving town.

Although he started the season with a 6-4 record, Butch resigned as coach of the Pistons and immediately sought the refuge of his Harvey Cedars retreat. Florence handled the sale of their home in the beautiful suburb of Grosse Pointe. It seems she had hardly unpacked the boxes from Los Angeles!

Butch spent the winter of 1971 with Florence at Harvey Cedars. He went to a lot of Princeton basketball games—he loved to watch Pete Carril coach a game! He cut a lot of wood and had a fire burning every evening. After 20 consecutive seasons of coaching, the time-off was therapeutic and relaxing.

Vanderbilt University in Nashville, Tennessee, is the only privately funded member of the Southeastern Conference. By most measures of scholastic rankings, it probably is the most selective of the twelve-member circuit.

Jan van Breda Kolff entered Vanderbilt in 1971 and subsequently played hoops for the Commodores for four years. In Jan's senior year, he was selected the Southeast Conference player of the year as Vandy finished 23-5 and won the SEC title. Jan averaged 10.9 points, 9.7 rebounds, and 5 assists that year. Jan set records for assists in a career, season, and a game while at Vanderbilt.

Following graduation from Vanderbilt, the younger VBK played for nine years in the NBA and the ABA. He played for Denver, Kentucky, and the New York and New Jersey Nets. In 1983, he retired from pro basketball. After a two year player-coaching position in Italy, he accepted a slot as assistant to Pete Carril at Princeton University.

The cycle was thus complete. Butch van Breda Kolff had coached Pete Carril at Lafayette College in the early 1950s. Pete Carril took over for Butch at Princeton in the late 1960s. Pete Carril would pass along the art of coaching to Jan van Breda Kolff in the 1987–1991 period.

Jan's first head coaching assignment was Cornell University where he stayed for two seasons. Subsequently, an opening at his alma mater Vanderbilt attracted him back to the Nashville campus.

The Southeast Conference ranks as one of the toughest leagues in the country. Kentucky and Arkansas won NCAA championship titles in the 1990s, while Florida, Georgia, and Mississippi State made trips to the Final Four. In his first season at Vandy, Jan van Breda Kolff went 20-12 and appeared in the NIT, the first of three such visits. Eventually he coached at Vanderbilt for six seasons and produced a 104-81 record, but third place in the SEC East Division was his best showing. His only appearance in the NCAA was 1997. Late in the 1999 season, Jan resigned his Vanderbilt post after a fourteen-fourteen season and a 4-11 record in the SEC.

On April 19, 1999, the news hit the sports wires that Jan van Breda Kolff, at age forty-seven, had been named head basketball coach at Pepperdine University in Malibu, California, just a few miles from Palos Verdes where he had played high school basketball when his father coached the Lakers. Pepperdine was to be a rebuilding project, but Jan produced an immediate winner at 25-9, winning the West Coast Conference regular season title, and taking the Waves to the NCAA. In the first round,

Pepperdine crushed Bobby Knight's Indiana University Hoosiers by 77-57.

Time will be the judge, but the combined records of the father-son team of Butch and Jan van Breda Kolff should eventually represent a high place in the annals of the NCAA for total victories and total games coached.

The Phoenix Sun Experience
1972

One of the big early season games for the 1972 Phoenix Suns was against the defending champion Los Angeles Lakers. Wilt Chamberlain was still the star for the Lakers. Butch van Breda Kolff had just taken over as coach of the Suns and relished the opportunity to potentially upset his former team. The game didn't go according to plan, however, and midway through the second half, the Suns fell well behind. Butch then conducted a wholesale substitution, effectively benching his starters including Charley Scott, Connie Hawkins, and Neal Walk.

Featuring the hustle of VBK's second platoon, the underdog Suns came roaring back—but ultimately lost 133-122. Butch kept his second unit in the game right up to the end. Jerry Colangelo, the Phoenix Suns owner, felt the starters should have been reinserted once the Suns started to catch up. Especially in defeat, he was not impressed with the hustling efforts of his lower-paid subs, and would have preferred to showcase his stars as the game ended.

Very shortly thereafter, just seven games into the 1972 season, with the Suns off to a 3-4 start, Jerry Colangelo fired Butch van Breda Kolff. Wilt Chamberlain felt vindicated by the action. Colangelo took over the coaching responsibilities of the Suns, as he had done when the previous Suns coach Cotton Fitzsimmons left to guide the Atlanta Hawks. In all reality, Colangelo seemed to crave coaching *and* owning the Suns. So be it! Without Butch, the Suns completed the season at 38-44, losing the finale to Fitzsimmons and the Hawks.

The NBA Years: The Detroit Pistons 1969–1971   147

Actually, Butch's discontent with the Suns was instantaneous. As soon as he had taken over as Coach, he was confronted by Suns star Connie Hawkins, who had three appearances in the NBA All-Star game to his credit. Butch liked Hawkins, but Hawkins didn't like Butch. Butch had little else to say about his short tenure with the Suns.

"I really could have done something with that club if they had left me alone and let me do what I wanted to," summed up Butch's thoughts.

In the "dubious distinction" category, Butch's 3-4 record with the Suns in 1972 represents the shortest coaching stint on record for any NBA coach. Actually, Dolph Schayes had coached the Buffalo Braves for an entire season, but was fired after the first game of the following season. Seven games and out represented Butch's entire record at Phoenix.

The van Breda Kolffs quietly left their Phoenix apartment and sped off to another winter at Harvey Cedars. Butch and Florence bought a boat rental business including fifteen rowboats and motors. They had their own little marina located right at the entrance to Long Beach Island. Butch continued to chop a lot of wood. He thoroughly relaxed in front of the TV at night as the fireplace burned away.

For fourteen years, Al Michaels has been doing the play-by-play announcing on ABC's "Monday Night Football." Back in the early 70s, Michaels was building his reputation as a quality announcer with his basketball production called "Saturday Game of the Week." Thanks to contacts made by Pete Carril and his friend Eddie Einhorn, Butch got a job providing the color for Michaels' broadcasts. Butch did a few games with Michaels, and was an apparent success at this new calling.

However, he was lured from the broadcast booth when Charles O. Finley offered him the job of coaching the Memphis Tams instead. Butch again second-guessed this decision later in his life. "I might have gone further as a broadcaster," he reflected.

The Memphis Tams Experience
1973–1974

"One comment about Butch van Breda Kolff. You either loved him or you hated him. There was absolutely nothing in between!"

John Sterling, Announcer for New York Nets

Charles O. Finley and Butch got along famously. "Charley was a great guy if he liked you. Not so if he didn't," Butch generalized of his only boss in the American Basketball Association. Unfortunately, Butch inherited a "slow" team, which included Johnny Neumann from Ole Miss, George Thompson of Marquette, and Randy Denton from Duke. Neumann twice in his collegiate career scored over sixty points in a game and was expected to provide a major portion of the Tams offense.

But Neumann's casual work ethic as a player was frustrating to Coach VBK. Despite having a pure shot, he failed to condition himself for the rigors of the pro game. His teammates were turned off when he was quoted in the media as saying, "I am the biggest thing to come out of Memphis since Elvis." Butch traded Neumann to the Utah Stars.

Butch tried to work with Randy Denton at center. But Butch preferred centers such as Billy Walton, who played aggressive defense and passed well. Denton's forte was his outside shooting ability. Will Jones was probably the Tams best player.

Before long, the Tams had traded away all their quality players. The season was a disaster, as indicated by a forty-point loss to the New York Nets (playing without the services of "Dr. J" no less), who were then coached by Kevin Laughery.

Butch encouraged Finley to go out into the market place and pay up for some faster players. But "Finley was tight as a duck's ass," and after the Tams lost eleven in a row, the Tams owner still felt the team was doing "fine." Butch commented to his owner, "If we lose thirteen in a row, do I get a raise?"

Prior to Butch's arrival in Memphis, the Tams of the American Basketball Association were not drawing well at the gate and their financial situation deteriorated as the season wore on. The Tams owed money to everyone, including the players, suppliers, and the city itself. On one occasion, in a game to be played against the New York Nets, just before they were to appear in the arena for their warm-up drills, the Tams had their uniforms confiscated under order by the local sheriff.

The Tams quickly improvised. The trainer taped their numbers to their T-shirts. They wore their practice shorts to portray some semblance of consistency. As the game progressed, the numbers gradually became "unstuck" and the contest transformed into a comedy. The Tams lost again.

That Butch was able to extract twenty-four wins from the Memphis team was probably more than anyone expected. The sixty games lost in the season represented the most ever incurred by a VBK team in a single season. Unfortunately, the 24-60 record with the Tams skewed his entire record in the professional coaching ranks.

Brief encounters with Wilt "The Stilt" Chamberlain continued to agitate VBK. During this period, The San

BUTCH VAN BREDA KOLFF'S OVERALL PROFESSIONAL RECORD

	Years	*Win-Loss Record*	*Pct.*
NBA	1967–77	266-253 (4 teams)	.514
ABA	1973–74	24-60 (1 team)	.285
Overall	1967–77	290-313	.480

Diego Conquistadors of the ABA were briefly coached by Wilt. He had been signed by the new franchise, but the Lakers were attempting to restrain the move with a "breach of contract" protest. During this "cooling off period," Wilt coached four games against his former adversary. In their four games versus one another, Butch never looked Wilt in the eye.

A *dashiki* is a loose shirt-like garment, often colorfully printed or embroidered, which is worn by many West Africans. A *dashiki* is put on by pulling it over the head. Although the ABA broke with tradition by employing a red-white-and-blue basketball, the league imposed a conservative dress code on its coaches, insisting they had to wear a collared shirt while on the sidelines. Wilt's wardrobe was resplendent with a broad assortment of *dashikis* and so he wore them regularly, along with sandals, while coaching the San Diego franchise. Only VBK was disturbed by Wilt's infraction. He also preferred to wear his casual clothes while coaching and so he too soon ignored the ABA formal dress code.

In 1969, Butch's former marine opponent "Bones" McKinney surfaced in the ABA as the coach of the Carolina Cougars. After eight years as head coach of Wake Forest University, he was lured out of retirement by a $100,000 multi-year contract.

Finley quickly became disenchanted with the Tams and the ABA. Within a year, he sold the team. Soon, the unemployed Butch van Breda Kolff vacated his Memphis apartment and was on his way back to Harvey Cedars.

As the Tams were fading into the sunset, the New Orleans Jazz was just getting started as an expansion team in the NBA. They started the season, not unexpectedly, by losing almost all of their early games. They needed a lift and soon they were in touch with Butch van Breda Kolff.

One of Butch's last official acts with the Memphis Tams entailed a scouting mission to Boulder, Colorado, home of

The NBA Years: The Detroit Pistons 1969–1971   151

the University of Colorado, for the purpose of checking out the abilities of the Buffalo's star forward, Scott Wedman. Butch liked what he saw, and made Scott a top draft pick of the Tams. However, Wedman was likewise pursued by the Kansas City-Omaha Kings of the NBA, which tapped him high in the league draft. Ultimately, he went on to play six years for the Kings, one year for the Cleveland Cavaliers, and five seasons for the Celtics.

To date, he is probably the most notable professional cager to list Colorado University as his undergraduate college. Cliff Mealy from the class of 1971 also had an impressive career with the Rockets and the Lakers.

Once Butch completed his scouting responsibilities, he returned to his hotel room and discovered a telephone message had been left at the front desk. When he checked with the agent on duty that night, he discovered that his father Jan—after a long bout with emphysema—had passed away that evening. Butch's father was seventy-eight years old. All those years of cigarette smoking had caught up with him.

Chapter 7

The NBA Years: The New Orleans Jazz 1974–1977

"You have to be hard headed and tough, but you can't be a drill sergeant or you lose the effervescence. At the same time, you can't let them do anything they want or you lose discipline. That's the struggle we go through all year."

Butch van Breda Kolff[1]

Part of Louisiana folklore implies that Pistol Pete Maravich wore the same pair of white socks in every game he played. Of course, he washed them out continuously, but be it for comfort reasons or a matter of superstition, he loved those socks. After a year or so of constant laundering, the well-traveled socks didn't have much elastic left, but Pete didn't mind. As a non-conformist, the floppy socks were Pistol Pete's trademark.

Pistol Pete was a gunner. Over a three-year span—freshmen were still not permitted to play varsity ball—he led the nation in scoring, averaging 44.2 points per game for his career at Louisiana State University. In his sophomore season, he broke the single season record held by Frank Selvy of Furman University. In his junior and senior years, he shattered the mark held by Oscar Robertson of Cincinnati University. His career and single season scoring marks easily represent

---

1 As quoted in van Breda Kolff article by Jenifer Quale, The Times Picayune, Nov. 8, 1975

the highest ever recorded in U.S. collegiate basketball history, with his nearest challenger averaging 34.6 (Austin Carr, Notre Dame). Pete's scoring records were even more astounding considering there was no three-point line. Nor was there a 45-second clock. In recognition for his accomplishments at LSU, Pete received a letter of achievement from President Richard M. Nixon following his final college game.

Pete was coached by his father Press Maravich, and the father-son combination revived interest in LSU basketball to a level not seen since the days of Bob Pettit (1954). The year prior to the Maravich family duo arriving at LSU, the Tigers were 6-20, finished last in the very tough Southeastern conference, and basically played in the shadow of a much stronger football program. Pre-Maravich, fewer than 100 fans signed up for season's tickets to the Tigers home basketball games.

Press Maravich established a team at LSU that totally accommodated Pistol Pete's offensive style. He surrounded Pete with players who could score from in close as recipients of Pete's spectacular passes. Otherwise, the supporting cast was distinctly "non-ego" driven, and enjoyed playing with the showman Pistol Pete. They just let Pete "do his thing," as he shot, dribbled and passed at will. Soon the word spread about the Pistol Pete scoring machine. Before long, the crowds mounted as they loved Pistol Pete and the high scoring LSU Tigers. It didn't matter that the team was absent from the Top 10 rankings. They were an exciting, high scoring team that won more than half of their games and that was what the local fans loved. In 1970, LSU played National Champ UCLA and lost by 133-89! Kentucky beat them 121-105. Still, they qualified for the NIT with a 20-8 regular season record, and they advanced to the semi-finals by beating Georegetown (83-82) and Oklahoma (97-94) before losing to Marquette. Pete could have been elected Governor of the State of Louisiana, hands down.

Upon graduation from LSU, Pete was drafted by the Atlanta Hawks of the NBA and the Carolina Cougars of the ABA. Pete opted to play for the Hawks and their coach Richie Guerin. The Hawks had just come off a strong playoff season, and featured a well-rounded lineup including Lew Hudson and Walt Hazzard. There was no superstar. The Guerin philosophy featured a strong inside game and an overall team effort. Although the Hawks were winning basketball games, they were not drawing at the gate. They needed a shot of charisma, and they undoubtedly drafted the entertaining Pistol Pete with that in mind.

For his first two years in the professional ranks, Pete struggled with personal health problems. In his rookie season, mononucleosis limited his performance. In his second year, a case of Bells Palsy distorted his appearance—he couldn't move the right side of his face. In his third and forth season, his new coach was Cotton Fitzsimmons. His health improved and he accumulated great statistics, but somehow his showy style never fit in with the Atlanta scheme of things. Behind the scenes, in private, as described in his biography *Forever Showtime* by Phil Berger, Pete gravitated from a "social drinker" to a "problem drinker" as a way of easing his frustrations. Soon the habit started to impact his playing ability.

Friction with Fitzsimmons intensified. On the return flight from a game with Houston, after Pete had consumed several beers on the plane, Pistol Pete and Fitzsimmons got into a heated argument. The coach demanded that Pete meet with him privately, but Pete failed to show. Fitz then suspended Pete for disciplinary reasons, and after two games Pete agreed to the meeting. The meeting, held at Morehouse State in Atlanta, failed to rectify the differences between the two professionals. The end result was that the Hawk coach demanded his management trade the former LSU scoring machine.

Meanwhile, the New Orleans Jazz was in its first year as an NBA franchise, and the top management of the Jazz had a burning desire to obtain the services of Pistol Pete. They craved his flamboyant playing style. The Jazz management was obsessed with his fancy dribbling, his spectacular passes, his long-range shooting ability, and even his floppy socks. For sure, Pistol Pete would pack the house! Thus, the Jazz gave up three first round draft choices for the first three years of its existence, three qualified players from the expansion draft (including "Dean the Dream" Meminger) and a lot of cash. The transaction was satirically tabbed "The Louisiana Purchase."

The Jazz got off to a horrible start in the 1974–75 season, winning only two games in their first 20 outings. The team was on track to recording the worst record in NBA history, which was held by the 1972–73 Philadelphia 76ers at 9-73. From the college ranks, the Jazz had selected Scotty Robinson as its first coach. Scotty had turned in a consistent record over a ten year period at nearby Louisiana Tech where he was 165-86. However, his leadership in the pros proved totally ineffective, he lost control, and chaos ensued. Perhaps he was too nice of a guy. Regardless, he was quickly fired. He apparently cried when he faced the team and said the problems of the team were "his fault." The ever compassionate Neal Walk, a supposedly rugged All-Star center and new addition to the Jazz via the Phoenix Suns, also wept when he heard of Robinson's ouster.

The Jazz decided to hire Butch van Breda Kolff to hopefully point them in the direction of winning basketball. The Jazz needed a disciplinarian. Friends warned Butch that he had to be a masochist to take the job. While en route back from his Harvey Cedars retreat, Butch simply replied,

"It's good for me to work . . . I'm not a fixer of motors . . . It makes for a very long day when I'm not working."

When Butch arrived on the scene, he discovered that Pete Maravich was grossly unhappy. His mother had committed suicide during the summer months, he was still drinking heavily, he wore a huge ugly bandage on his knee, and frequently asked to be traded. Unlike the Atlanta Hawks, he was virtually the entire offense for the Jazz, but the defeatist attitude of the Jazz was wearing on Pete. He loved to win *and* score.

But Butch had a tremendous impact on Pistol Pete. After Pete tried one of his patented behind-the-back passes during a practice session, Butch pulled him aside and instructed him to make sure that the pass hit its target. Soon Butch toned down—but did not eliminate—the gunner impulses of Pete Maravich. Pete blended more of his outstanding passes with sensible shots. He ran continuously with the team. Everyone on the team touched the ball. He played *real* defense. Butch called it a "barbed wire" defense. The results were remarkable, as the Jazz went 18-17 over its next 35 games to finish with a 23-59 record. Butch's ally in the press, John Hall of the *LA Times,* labeled him "Coach of the Century." Butch's reaction to Hall's statement was, "They like to exaggerate on the West Coast!"

Preseason hype for the 1975–76 schedule escalated to a feverish pitch. The Jazz optimistically hoped to attain a .500 record by season-end. Adding to the fan enthusiasm was the fact the Jazz was slated to open its colossal new arena, The Superdome, in December against Butch's former employer, the Los Angeles Lakers. Publicity about the game generated a buying frenzy, and the once perceived unlimited supply of tickets evaporated overnight. By game time, every seat in the Superdome was taken. Despite a monsoon type storm, a record crowd of 26,511 came to watch Pistol Pete. The Lakers were led by Kareem Abdul Jabbar (nee Lew Alcindor) and were coached by former Celtic great Bill Sharman.

The atmosphere of the contest resembled a playoff game. The partisan crowd's cheers echoed within the new stadium. Pistol Pete brought his "A" game (thirty points), VBK brought his best coaching strategies, and the Jazz upset the Lakers by a narrow margin, 113-110. As the Jazz seemed to lose its grip on the game, VBK self-induced a technical foul call which seemed to act as a "wake up" call to his team and helped preserve the win. Sharman called the technical the turning point and recommended VBK be selected "Coach of the Year."

New Orleans is a party town where the pubs are open twenty-four hours a day, and certainly they hummed the night of the Jazz victory over the Lakers. Butch van Breda

Kolff was suddenly the second most famous person in the State of Louisiana. The aura of an expansion team whipping the NBA West leading Lakers, the possibility of a winning season, a fabulous new stadium—all these vibrations were stirring at Pat O'Brien's pub and other establishments in New Orleans that night. And early into the morning!

When you mention New Orleans to Butch, a big smile crosses his face and his eyes light up. "Now, that was a town." He loved the social life there as there were plenty of "blue-collar" pubs for him to find new friends. He enjoyed Pat O'Brien's on St. Peter Street in the Old French Quarter or "Vieux Carre" where he was frequently joined by Hot Rod Hundley, the Jazz' broadcaster. Although Butch drank mostly beer, the local favorite was "Hurricane Punch," a mixture of light and dark rum, grenadine and papaya juice. Everywhere he went in town, the locals recognized him. Not only was the team doing well, but he was having fun, the best of possible worlds!

Hundley, a star in his own right at West Virginia University and in the NBA, used to play "pick up" basketball with Butch at the local YMCA and other gyms around town. Most of these anonymous pick-up teams consisted of businessmen who were exercising for fun or possibly just to lose weight. Rarely did you ever get to know anyone's last name. Forever the coach and drill sergeant, Butch instinctively took charge of these teams as if they were miniature NBA franchises. He would yell at his fellow players, exhorting them to cut and go for the rebounds. "Pick and roll," he shouted. Regardless of the level of play, Butch van Breda Kolff wanted to see the game *played right*.

Shortly after the conclusion of the 1975 season, Butch's daughter Kaatje (Dutch for "Little Cat") graduated from Vanderbilt University and she gravitated to New Orleans where she got a job with the municipal government. She married a club golf pro by the name of Gene Zimmermann and lived in the Lake Ponchartrain area. Kaatje was perhaps the most loyal of VBK's offspring and she continued to go to almost all his games. She was indeed his best supporter, "People look at my dad and say the guy is crazy. Away from the limelight, he never goes bozo. He's not loud!"

Or when the local fans criticized one of VBK's moves, she would yell out: "Listen, smartie, why aren't you out there?!"

In one contest, she actually chased NBA official Richie Powers all the way into the Detroit locker room.

Between seasons, Pistol Pete went on a personal training vendetta. Everyday, he worked out with the New Orleans Saints football team, lifting weights regularly. He shaved off his beard. He gained fifteen pounds. His major sacrifice was that he gave up his floppy socks. He had become a serious basketball player and less of a showman.

Butch continued the 1975-76 season with the Jazz where he had left off. As an expansion team in their second season, the Jazz compiled a very respectable 38-44 record for the season. What made the season even more remarkable is that Pete Maravich missed twenty games with a separated shoulder injury. While Pete was sidelined, the Jazz posed a 6-14 record. Pete was selected to the NBA All-Star team for the first time in his career. Conceivably with a healthy Pete Maravich, the Jazz might have made the playoffs in its second season, the first expansion team to do so in NBA history.

While playing for Florida University and the Phoenix Suns, Neal Walk at 6'11" and 240 pounds was a powerful force under the boards. In the 1969 NBA draft of college players, he was the number one selection of the Suns. He averaged 20.2 points per game and 12.4 rebounds while playing in the NBA All-Star game in his fourth season. He holds the Suns record for 1,006 rebounds in one season. However, during the expansion draft, the

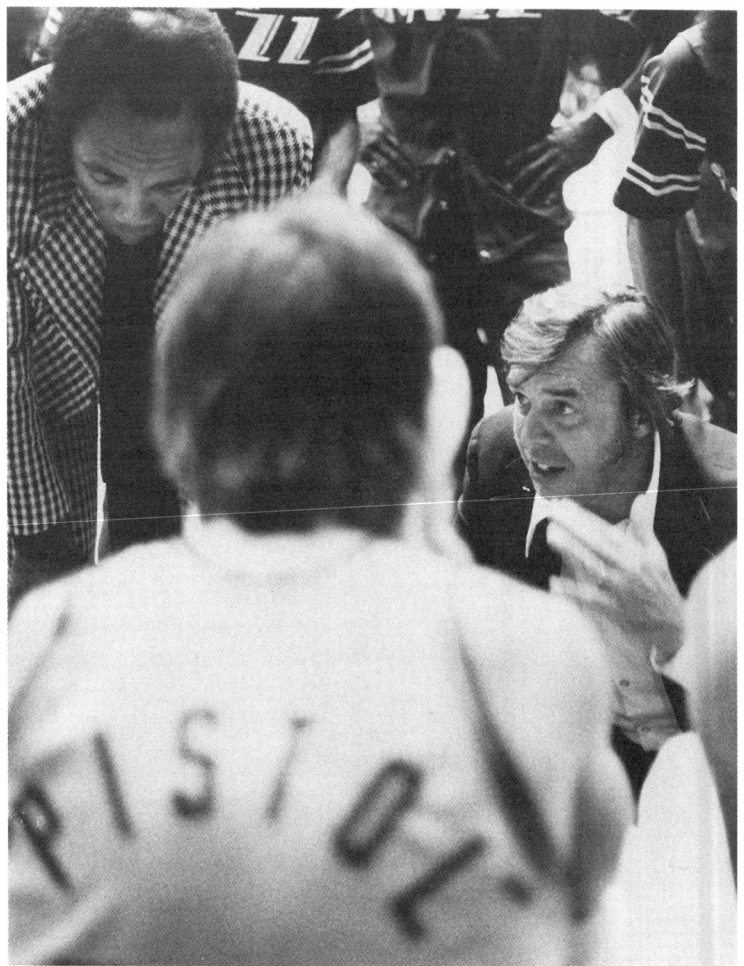

Assistant Jazz coach Elgin Baylor and Butch give Jazz star Pistol Pete Maravich some strategy pointers during a NBA contest. Credit: VBK private collection

Suns made his services available and the Jazz with Scotty Robinson as coach anxiously picked him up.

    Conspicuously obvious to the Suns but unknown to the Jazz, Walk had mysteriously altered his diet and had become a total, macrobiotic vegetarian during the off season. He had lost fifty pounds and weighed 190 pounds. He had adopted a form of Eastern Religion. He talked to him-

Bill van Breda Kolff Head Coach. Credit VBK private collection

self all the time. Although Walk was a selection of Scotty Robinson, VBK was bagged with the slender center. Actually, Butch and Neal got along very well in his brief stint in Phoenix. Walk was a good passer, strong rebounder, and played with intensity. However, when Butch spotted Walk in the showers following his trade to the Jazz, he felt the hairy Walk looked like a latter-day Jesus. When Butch inserted the slenderized Walk into the game, he complained of being "brutalized" by the beefier competition. Soon, VBK found Walk to be totally useless and placed him far on the end of the bench—where he continued to talk to himself.

The Knicks were in the market for a backup center, and they felt they could rehabilitate Neal Walk under the

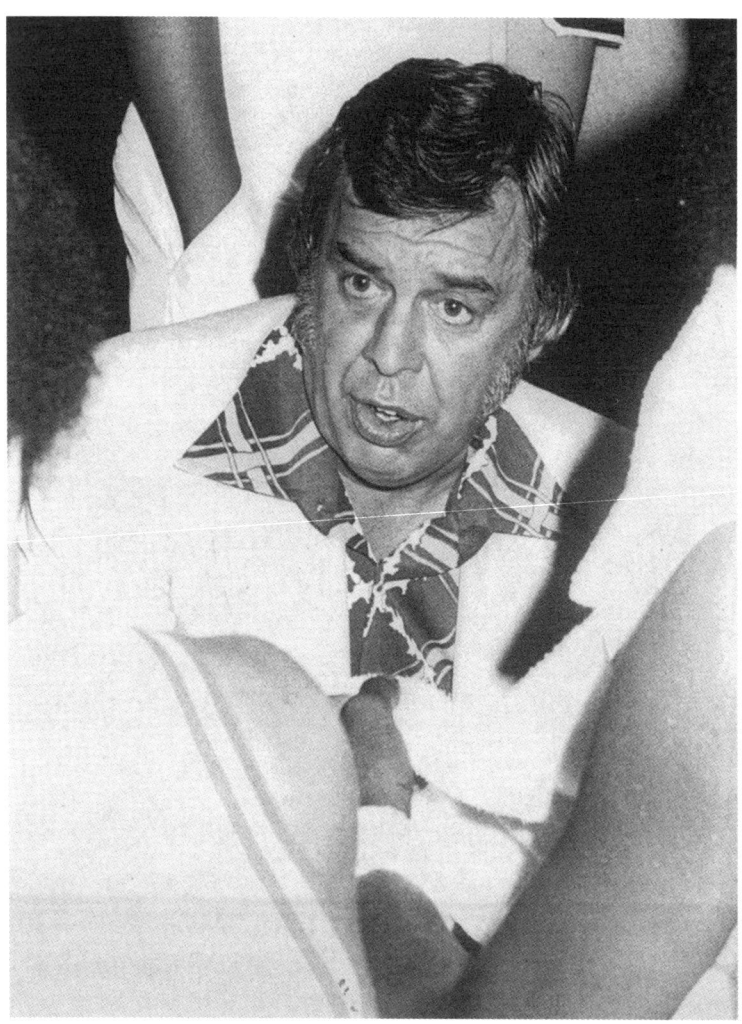

tutelage of Phil Jackson, likewise a vegetarian. The Jazz management was afraid to trade Walk lest he would start to eat meat again and restore his All-Star status. VBK was convinced that Neal was too far gone! He craved the Knicks guard Henry Bibby, who incidentally wore the same number 17 that he had worn as a Knick. Eventually, the Jazz management relented and the Bibby-for-Walk trade (the Jazz added Jim Barnett) was consummated.

The NBA Years: The New Orleans Jazz 1974–1977   163

Butch and his daughter Kaatje enjoying a post-game celebration at Pat O'Brien's Pub in New Orleans. Credit: O'Brien's photo

With Butch and Elgin Baylor at the negotiating table, the Jazz additionally received a third round draft choice and $100,000. The third round draft choice turned out to be Jim McElroy, who helped the Jazz a lot. Butch regarded it as a "great trade," one of his best. VBK felt he orchestrated some better trades than his management gave him credit for.

Bibby and Pistol Pete complemented one another extremely well. After Walk landed on the Knicks, he regained thirty of the fifty pounds he had lost while on his vegetarian binge. Knick coach Red Holzman toted around peanut butter sandwiches, and awarded Walk $10 each time he ate one. The incentive program worked, and the Knicks drew some mileage from the Bibby trade. Walk eventually developed cancer and currently works in the Phoenix Suns office, paralyzed from the waist down, and employs a wheelchair.

Former Detroit Piston Otto Moore was unemployed when he attended a New Orleans Jazz basketball game in 1975. During the warm-up drills preceding the second half, Otto chatted briefly with VBK and apprised him of his personal situation. In a few days, Butch signed Otto as a free agent and got a lot of mileage out of the energetic center.

With Maravich and Bibby leading the way, Butch's popularity soared accordingly. After four frustrating stops in the professional ranks, Butch had finally landed where he was appreciated.

The friendship between Butch and Pistol Pete strengthened during these two seasons in New Orleans. The two enjoyed playing racquetball against each other, and one particular day Pete challenged Butch to a match at a newly opened club in downtown New Orleans. The two-some talked the new owner into letting them use a court for free. Butch defeated his younger counterpart. Following a delayed reaction to the loss, Pete called Butch at home that night and challenged him to a rematch at the same spot the next day. When the two returned to the club and requested court time, they were informed by the matronly attendant that the free trial was only available for one day. If they wanted to use the court, they would have to pay the annual fee of $500. Without hesitation, Pete pulled out his checkbook and wrote out a check to the club. Butch could be his guest for the day. The second day, Pete bested his senior counterpart. It was well worth the $500.

When Butch got back to his apartment and unpacked his gym bag, he noticed that he had inadvertently taken Maravich's sweat-suit. He would launder and return the garment and its prominent "Pistol Pete" logo the next time they played raquet-ball.

A new face appeared on the New Orleans Jazz management team. Barry Mendelson, whose previous position was that of a radio announcer in Ithaca, New York, was hired as general manager in hopes of building attendance at the already popular Jazz home games.

Mendelson's emphasis was on marketing—promotions and pregame entertainment—and soon he broadened his thrust into decisions affecting the makeup of the team and its playing style. The very ambitious Mendelson learned quickly that Butch was no sycophant. Butch confronted Mendelson, whereas others were more diplomatic in their dealings with the young executive. Almost immediately, the two were at odds over trades, which players to waive, and the like. Constant bickering took place early into the 1976–77 season as the Jazz stood slightly over .500 with a 14-12 mark.

In January 1977, Mendelson decided he had had enough of the hard-headed Dutchman. He fired VBK on the spot.

The city of New Orleans was totally shocked. At the first home game after the announcement, fans brought crying towels with "We Want Butch" marked thereon. Mendelson, fearing repercussions for his actions, arrived at the game with a police escort. Kaatje van Breda Kolff cried when she learned of her father's fate. "I cried every time he got fired!"

Behind the scenes, Pistol Pete apparently harbored a desire to lead the NBA in scoring, but Butch's "team-style" offense capped Pete's potential average at about 22 points per game. Quite possibly, Pete turned on Butch and expressed his feelings to Mr. Mendelson. Pete was quite outspoken, and used to argue openly with his father. Butch was not averse to pulling Pete from the game if the move was warranted. He averaged roughly thirty-eight minutes per game with Butch making the substitutions. When Assistant Coach Elgin Baylor's took over as head coach of the Jazz, Pistol Pete played forty-eight minutes and went on to lead the NBA in scoring by averaging 31.1 for the 1977 season. The night that Butch was fired, Pete racked in fifty-one points.

In the press release following his departure, Butch was consistent as ever about airing the reasons behind the decision. "I never believe in sour grapes or washing dirty laundry in public." Privately, however, he seethed at the mere mention of Mendelson's name. "A liar" was as descriptive as he would get with words. His facial expression told how he felt.

A few months later, the Jazz ownership fired Alan Mendelson. The ownership was inclined to move the franchise to Salt Lake City. The move eventually came about in 1979.

Further turbulence erupted between Butch and his wife Florence. After twenty-seven years of marriage, they separated in 1977. Forced to resign in LA, throwing in the sponge in Detroit, fired by the Jazz and the Suns, and now in effect Butch was fired by his wife.

The University of New Orleans
1977–1979

The job offer from the University of New Orleans came very quickly. The decision was a no-brainer, as Butch wanted to stay in coaching and he loved his surroundings in the Crescent City. Butch seemed ready to be rid of the constant management infighting and turmoil implicit to the professional game, although when asked if he missed the pros, he responded "The first and the fifteenth of every month." He frequently talked of "the fun" of basketball, and it appeared the "fun" had been taken out of the game as long as he stayed in the pros.

So Butch took over the position as head basketball coach for $25,000 per year. He eventually took over the responsibilities of athletic director in addition to his duties as basketball coach. Butch was a BMOC (Big Man on Campus) at UNO.

UNO was a state-supported institution with an enrollment of approximately 14,000 students. The school had only one dormitory and most of the students were commuters. Unlike Lafayette and Princeton, little "campus life" existed. But the Privateers were on a mission to upgrade their basketball program, and they had just completed their second year in Division I with a respectable 18-10 record.

The school competed in the highly competitive yet newly formed Sunbelt Conference, which launched its debut for the 1975–76 season. As a new league, the conference champion was not entitled to an automatic bid to the NCAA annual tournament. In its inaugural season, the league champion—the University of North Carolina at Charlotte—was denied an at-large bid to the 1976 "Big Dance," but was selected by the NIT. Nicknamed the 49ers, UNC-Charlotte was led by star forward Cedric "Cornbread" Maxwell, and they advanced through the entire field only to lose in the finals to Kentucky University at Madison Square Garden.

"Cornbread" returned for the 1976–77 season, leading the 49ers to the Sunbelt Title, and thus UNC-Charlotte earned the recognition of the NCAA selection committee by receiving an at-large berth in the Tournament. Among UNC-Charlotte's victories was a narrow one-point win over the University of New Orleans Privateers. Again, UNC-Charlotte roared through the field, advancing all the way to the Final Four, eliminating Central Michigan, Syracuse, and Michigan in the process. In their semifinal game against Marquette, a game-ending dispute over the clock was decided in favor of the Warriors and the Sun Belt champs were defeated by a mere two points. Upon graduation, Maxwell went on to star for the Boston Celtics.

The Sunbelt Conference had arrived, however, and the 1977–78 season belonged to the University of New Orleans. In Butch's first season as their coach, the Privateers went 21-6 and won the year-end Sun Belt Conference Tourney over the University of South Alabama by a 22-20 margin. The stalling techniques of the South Alabama coach Cliff Ellis (the current coach at Auburn University) were widely criticized in the press and greeted by extensive booing by the fans, but Butch simply noted that it was the coach's prerogative to play the game any way he could in order to win.

Despite Butch's gracious remarks, the slow-down game had its impact. The operators of the Charlotte Arena threatened to withdraw its sponsorship of the Sun Belt Conference Tourney. In the off-season, the Sun Belt Coaches voted to experiment with a 40 second clock for all but the last two minutes of the game. After the season, the coaches were unanimous in approving a clock.

But the nature of the game probably tarnished the profile of the Sunbelt Conference. Despite UNC-Charlotte's prior year's run, both the NCAA and the NIT snubbed the University of New Orleans as a possible entrant.

Butch was indeed disappointed by the actions of both tournament committees. UNO had compiled several "quality" wins including a victory over state rival LSU at the latter's home court while accumulating its twenty-one wins. They also had beaten the University of Alabama at Birmingham three times. Butch felt some of the reaction of the NIT committee may have been spiteful based on his remarks from back in the early '60s when he was coaching at Hofstra. At the time, while filling a temporary seat on the Coaches Committee for the NIT, he referred to the tournament as the CIT, thus criticizing the tourney's reliance on Catholic institutions. Right or wrong, Butch felt that the snub of his UNO team—in his mind, one of the best he ever coached—reverted back to his CIT comment years ago.

En route to their successful season, the Privateers won the Stetson University "classic," an early season tournament. Coincidentally, the only other time the Hatters didn't win their own tourney was in 1990 when Hofstra Universitiy, under the leadership of Coach VBK, upended host Stetson by 64-62 and Mississippi 78-73. The two local voids in the banners stretched across the Stetson Gym were the responsibility of Butch van Breda Kolff.

The following season, UNO finished a sub-par 11-16 record. Butch found the job of athletic director more than he could handle. It was just that—a job! Too much paperwork! He found he was stuck in an office, "signing checks and answering phones." The job of athletic director was much bigger than he thought, and so he resigned from the dual position at UNO after the completion of the 1978–79 season.

In March of 1979, Butch was appointed an "honorary ambassador of goodwill for the State of Louisiana." His next position would be that of coaching the New Orleans Pride, the local representative in the WBA.

The New Orleans Pride
1979–1981

After shedding his duties as athletic director of UNO, Butch was approached by the ownership of the newly formed New Orleans Pride, a charter member of the Women's Professional Basketball League (WPBL). They were in the market for a coach who could win and, perhaps more importantly, sell tickets! As one of the most popular men in New Orleans, Butch was definitely what the club was looking for.

Butch greatly enjoyed coaching the women. He treated the female players just like the male! They coined the label "The Al Jolson Move" whereby VBK in his classic sideline plea to the referees gets down on his knees and places his forehead on the floor.

He relished the opportunity to congratulate one of his Pride players upon her making a game winning shot. "I sure enjoyed hugging a beautiful blond more than some sweaty guy!"

In the team photographs with the Pride, Butch has his hair neatly combed as if he just came from the beauty parlor. In most other photos of VBK, he has a more casual sweep to his hair.

Butch summed up his experiences with the Pride: "The first year, I knew more than they did. The second year, they *thought* they knew more than me. The third year, the league folded."

After coaching four college teams, five professional teams, and one women's pro team, Butch was unemployed. He had made a total of ten stops in a thirty-year span. He had coached a total of 1,141 games while compiling a record of 666-475 over the period.

**Picayune Memorial High School
(Mississippi)
1982–84**

"Of all insults to The Game, his pure and beloved game, this perfect Mona Lisa hanging in the Louvre of his life, the most contemptible is hot-dogging."

William Nack, *Sports Illustrated* magazine,
February, 1984

Only three coaches in the history of the game have coached teams in both the Final Four of the NCAA Tournament and the finals of the NBA playoffs. Jack Ramsey, who coached St. Joseph's University in 1961 and the NBA champion Portland Trail Blazers in 1977, is the last to reach this spotlight.* Fred Schaus qualified for the list as coach of West Virginia University in the 1959 finals and the LA Lakers in both 1965 and 1966. Butch van Breda Kolff coached Princeton University in 1965 and the Los Angeles Lakers in 1968 and 1969. After completing his coaching career, Ramsey undertook various business ventures and was a frequent TV commentator on collegiate and professional basketball. Like many coaches and players, he capitalized on the reputation he attained while at the peak of his success.

After being succeeded by Butch van Breda Kolff, Schaus continued on as general manager of the Lakers for several years.

*Subsequent to Ramsey's St. Joseph's apparent third place finish in the 1961 tourney, the Hawks were disqualified upon discovery of "point shaving" by three of its star players. Thus, some trivia buffs say that only VBK and Schaus coached teams that made it to both the college level Final Four and the NBA championship finals.

Butch, however, wanted to coach forever. He tried his hand at being an athletic director, obviously a related interest to coaching, and spurned the job because of all the paperwork. He tried selling tuck tape in Pennsylvania and shrimp products in Louisiana. He tried running a marina in New Jersey. He derived little satisfaction, let alone income, from any of these projects.

Butch surely would have been a colorful commentator on the sports networks. His short test-run with Al Michaels on the Saturday "Game of the Week" was an apparent success. Tact and diplomacy were not on his resume, however, and undoubtedly the network executives feared his succinct mode of expression. In particular, his "big bullies" theory was not a favorite of the broadcasting world. On the coaching sidelines, he could belittle Elgin Baylor and motivate the superstar to greater heights. In the broadcast booth, the media is expected to subtly embellish the public's perception of the legends of sports. There was nothing subtle about Butch van Breda Kolff.

Unlike Bud Palmer in the '50s and Digger Phelps in the '90s, Butch was unable to leverage his athletic achievements into financial gains. Butch was a coach, no matter how you sliced it. He craved having a team to coach regardless of the level of play. For two lonely years, 1980–82, Butch was "teamless" as he yearned for another coaching opportunity. After accepting the Laker position, he had quickly assumed the coaching slots in Detroit, Phoenix, Memphis, and New Orleans as soon as he was "available." But upon leaving the New Orleans Pride, he found his phone ceased to ring. Time moved ever so slowly, his days and nights were long. Aside from a few visits from his daughter Kaatje, he saw virtually no one.

Virtually overnight, his life, once a hyperactive arena of games and crowds, had been reduced to a lonely void. Subsistence, puzzles, and long walks filled out the day.

He even approached Princeton University, volunteering to run their intramural program. His former employer never returned his phone call.

Once a hot commodity on the coaching circuit, Butch van Breda Kolff's stock seemed to turn ice cold. It seemed as someone turned a switch and he just disappeared. Suddenly, there were no photos of Butch on the sidelines. There were none of his pointed quotes in the press.

Approaching sixty years old, Butch was at the low point in his life.

☆ ☆ ☆

Picayune, Mississippi is a town of about 10,000 located roughly four miles over the Louisiana-Mississippi state line on Route 59 connecting New Orleans with Hattiesburg. Butch heard that the local high school was in the market for a basketball coach, and he put a call into the athletic director.

It was probably indicative of the remote life style of Picayune that the athletic director was not immediately familiar with Butch's reputation. But the athletic director—Charley Triplett—recognized and was indeed impressed

Special Photo: VBK Spinning Basketball While Pete Maravich Looks On in Awe

with Butch's vast experience. After further discussions, he extended Butch a $20,000 a year coaching offer contingent on his teaching a history course as well, and Butch quickly accepted. It wasn't the Princeton Tigers or the LA Lakers, but Butch had a team. His two-year nightmare was over. At any rate, "Oh, what the hell," he gave Picayune a shot!

Butch's team at Picayune was the opposite of his teams at Lafayette, Hofstra, and Princeton. While there were virtually no black players on his early college teams, there were no white players on his Picayune team. Jim Radcliff's father was a Pennsylvania car dealer, Bill Thieben was an honors history student, and Bill Bradley was a Rhodes Scholar as well as the son of a prominent Missouri bank president. On the other hand, Butch's Picayune players were barely passing their high school courses and were essentially fatherless.

Regardless, Butch attacked his new post with gusto, almost as if Picayune were the latest expansion entry in the NBA. After two years of being out of the game, he relished being called "Coach" as he poured his entire personality into his new job.

Soon, he had the Picayune team practicing the same "and fours" drill he taught Jim Radcliff back in his early Lafayette years some thirty years ago. Back-and-forth, run-run-run, miss the layup at the end of the drill and you do it all over again. Butch worked his young players hard, almost but not quite to the point of exhaustion. The boys from Picayune were known as the Maroon Tide. They were learning *to play the game right*.

Come game time, Butch's involvement from the sidelines was as animated as ever. He is ecstatic over a successfully executed pass which results in an uncontested scoring lay-up. He waves his arms frantically, screaming at his team to hustle back on defense. He engages in some incidental chatter with the referees. Then one of his star players tries a slam dunk and misses the open lay-up. Butch is beside himself! "Oh no!" he bellows. Butch is back—again!

The manic-depressive nature of coaching continued on at Picayune. In Butch's eyes, there was no real difference in coaching the players, just a matter of degree. He was oblivious to the differences in lifestyle when he rode first class with the Lakers versus riding in a drafty bus at Picayune. What mattered most to Butch van Breda Kolff was the quality of the game. High school, college, or pro— he sought to see the game *played right.* That principle overrode any other possible impulse in life.

Butch guided Picayune to a 14-8 record. "I wouldn't trade those days for anything." Deep down, Butch had derived a ton of psychic income from coaching the young men from Picayune. Butch never regretted any of his decisions in life, he never looked back. A sequence of coin flips had landed him in Picayune, and he made the most of it.

Teaching world history to some eighty-five students at Picayune Memorial High School was a new experience to Butch. Without much preparation, he had passed the national teacher examination and thereby secured his teaching license. He certainly enjoyed teaching more than the other jobs he had tried in the "real economy," but was somewhat disheartened by the fact that close to thirty of his students were failing. Butch felt challenged to motivate these students as well as those who were satisfied to just get by with Ds. To Butch's credit, he sought to teach the youngsters "why things happened" in history rather than stressing the memorization of a lot of names and dates.

Butch's star student was Sarah Bridges, who posted a straight-A record at Picayune High School. Butch quizzed Sarah as to where she was thinking of going to college.

"Mississippi State, Mississippi University, and Southern Mississippi University," she replied.

"Sarah, you must appreciate that there are many great colleges that exist outside the borders of Mississippi," Butch advised.

Sarah Bridges went to Mississippi University.

Taken a step further, Butch was proactive in trying to improve the quality of education for young Mississippians. He openly advocated that school officials, teachers, and parents should attend cook-outs where the teachers outlined their programs before the parents, which hopefully would be translated into the parents being more supportive of the homework efforts of their offspring.

Soon, he purchased a navy-blue blazer sports jacket, a button-down blue shirt, and a red-striped tie. Officially attired, he even made a special pilgrimage to Governor William F. Winter's office in Jackson to make a statement about the inferiority of the state's school system. The governor indignantly replied, "What do you mean, I just signed an appropriation giving every school in Mississippi a computer or computers!" Bill replied, "What good are computers if the kids can't read or write?"

Butch lived alone in a small two-bedroom home in Bay St. Louis, Mississippi and found few social undertakings while coaching and teaching at Picayune. Yes, there were a few late nights of shuffle board at the local "knock-knock" bar, but he missed the collection of friends that he seemed to accumulate at every stop in his life's journey. He cooked his own meals, mostly hot dogs in the microwave, sipped a few beers, did the crossword puzzles, read a few pages of history to stay two days ahead of his students, and took long walks with his dog. Occasionally, his faithful daughter Kaatje stopped by to visit him. She also attended many of his games and as always cheered as vocally as anyone in the stands.

☆ ☆ ☆

The February 20, 1984 edition of *Sports Illustrated* featured a 10-page article by William Nack entitled "I Made My Own Bed and I've Got to Lie in It." The article detailed the ups and downs of Butch van Breda Kolff's coaching career, and dwelled at length on his "dead end" stop in Picayune. The author spent some four days living in Butch's small house in Bay Saint Louis. The article was like a mini-biography of Butch himself.

Dr. "Doc" Stein, the general physician for Lafayette College, brought the article to the attention of Ollie Kollevoll, the athletic director of Lafayette College, who was in the market for a new head basketball coach at the time. Lafayette had experienced three straight losing seasons, and was looking for a proven winner. Ollie liked what he saw and the rest was history.

Butch soon said good-bye to Picayune. Among his parting recommendations was the suggestion that they serve beer at the PTA meetings. He was on his way back to Easton, Pennsylvania, to coach Lafayette College. Twenty-nine years had passed since he coached the Leopards to their first postseason tournament ever and their best record ever 23-3. Butch salivated at the opportunity to recreate that scenario.

PROFESSIONAL COACHING RECORD "PHASE II" BUTCH VAN BREDA KOLFF (MIDDLE COACHING YEARS)

Los Angeles Lakers (NBA)

1967–68	52-30
1968–69	55-27
2 years	107-57

Detroit Pistons (NBA)

1969–70	31-51
1970–71	45-37
1971	6-4
2 years	82-92

Phoenix Suns (NBA)

1972	3-4

Memphis Tams (ABA)

1973–74	24-60

New Orleans Jazz (NBA)

1974–75	22-44
1975–76	38-44
1976–77	14-12
3 years	74-100

Totals for 10 Years of Professional Coaching:

1967–77	Won 290	Lost 313	.480 pct

Chapter 8

The Later Lafayette College Years 1984–1988

"It was a joy playing for him."

Matt Roberts '90

"Digger" Phelps, the impeccably dressed Notre Dame basketball coach, had his team on a roll early in the 1987–1988 season. Led by All-American guard candidate David Rivers and a corps of power rebounders, Phelps' Fighting Irish jumped out to a 7-2 record and seemed on the verge of making some serious noise on the national scene, thus justifying their preseason number twelve ranking in the polls.

As Phelps and the Irish worked their way through a tight four-game road schedule, they successfully downed St. Bonaventure in Upstate New York and LaSalle at the Palestra in Philadelphia and were en route to meeting Marquette University in Wisconsin. The "throw in" or "breather" game sandwiched between these three matchups was against Lafayette College. Conceivably, Notre Dame would easily walk over Lafayette, fatten up its record, and cruise confidently into the Milwaukee Arena and confront the Marquette Warriors. Lafayette was coached by Willem "Butch" van Breda Kolff and was struggling along at 3-4 when the Irish invaded Allen P. Kirby Field House in Easton, Pennsylvania. New York's *Daily News* listed Notre Dame as fifteen point favorites.

Butch on Cover of Lafayette Alumni Quarterly.

The Later Lafayette College Years: 1984-1988   181

As the two teams went through their warm-up drills, "Digger" Phelps was on the sidelines flawlessly attired in his expensive business suit, white shirt and power gold tie. His hair was neatly combed, and he looked as if he just walked out of a corporate board meeting. Feeling confident of his chances versus the lesser-rated Leopards, "Digger" elected not to wear his patented green boutonniere in his suit jacket lapel.

On the opposite side of the scorers' table, "Butch" van Breda Kolff wore a V-neck gray sweater with an open collared navy-blue golf shirt underneath. Charcoal slacks filled out his outfit. Unlike the infamous Bobby Knight who has always worn sweater and shirt combinations to match the official colors of Indiana University, Butch made no apparent attempt to tie in with Lafayette's maroon and white. "If they had given me an outfit, I would have worn it," exclaimed VBK when asked about wearing the school colors. If it weren't for Butch's expressive facial features, somewhat exaggerated by an aggressive gum chewing habit, you might have guessed he was one of the 4000 fans who packed the local gym for the game. In essence, Butch was one of the boys.

Actually, van Breda Kolff resembled Pete Carril in his attire on the basketball court. Sounding distinctly like VBK, Carril wrote of his own wardrobe,

> "My clothing, often ridiculed, is not Armani style, but it's good, it never prevented me from doing what I know I have to do. I have always tried to be on the outside what I am on the inside. What you see is what you get."

Digger Phelps was at or near the pinnacle of his career. His previous year's team had gone 24-8 and achieved the Sweet 16 of the NCAA tournament. In 1986, his forces finished at 23-6 and were ranked tenth in the final AP poll. At age forty-eight, he was in his seventeenth season at Notre Dame and stood as the winningest coach in the school's history. Digger's teams continuously exhibited strong rebounding skills, consistently ranking in the top

10 nationally in "rebound margin." He was at the helm of one of the nation's most visible sports programs, and ultimately on the fast track to the TV broadcast booth as a nightly regular for ESPN during the college hoop season. Butch van Breda Kolff was sixty-five years old, coaching at one of the smallest colleges in Division I, and struggling to stay close to the .500 mark. Speculation ran that this could be the last coaching assignment of the itinerant VBK. Butch admitted openly, "Lafayette was where I began, and where I'd like to finish. It's worked out extremely well, and this is where I'd like to be."

The contrast in the two schools was also enormous. Notre Dame's undergraduate enrollment was close to 8,000 whereas Lafayette stood at just over 2,000. In football, the Irish had a multimillion dollar national TV contract with NBC, often competed in postseason bowl games, and generally played one of the strongest schedules in the country. Coast-to-coast, Notre Dame was claimed by many an American as his or her adopted alma mater. Over the years, seven Notre Dame football stars had won the Heisman Trophy award, with wide receiver Tim Brown winning the award in 1987. Meanwhile, Lafayette played football in the NCAA's Division 1-AA as part of the Colonial League (soon to be renamed the Patriot League) and was rarely seen on TV outside the Lehigh Valley area. The fact that the Lafayette Leopards were national football champions in 1926 when they posted a 9-0 record was buried in the collegiate gridiron archives.

Nonetheless, Lafayette prided itself on the character of its athletic profile. In 1948, the football team posted a 7-2 record and was invited to play a postseason game in the Sun Bowl in El Paso, Texas. There was one stipulation in the Bowl committee's invitation: Lafayette would have to leave home its one black player. The team voted unanimously to decline the invitation.

But this was a basketball game, and essentially a game of five-on-five. "Many good teams have only a few strong players," observed VBK. In basketball, Lafayette competed in Division I and, in that respect, was on a par

The Later Lafayette College Years: 1984–1988   183

with Notre Dame. However, Lafayette College did not offer any athletic scholarships *per se* to its students. Following the model of the Ivy League, only need-based financial aid was available, whereas Notre Dame basically had an open checkbook for potential athletes. Regardless, both teams had a shot at going to the NCAA tourney, and for Notre Dame it was an opportunity to bolster its record while underdog Lafayette had a chance to vault itself into the national picture. Digger's objective was simply to garner a "W" and move on. Butch's mission was to resuscitate a career.

There was a trace of irony in the comparison of the two schools. One of the most prominent basketball players to ever wear a Notre Dame uniform was Kelly Tripucka, who later went on to star for the Detroit Pistons in the professional ranks. Meanwhile, Kelly's older brothers Tracy and Todd ranked as Lafayette's first and fourth all-time leading scorers and both were inducted quickly into the College's elite Hall of Fame. Frank Tripucka—who was the father for all three boys as well as three other athletic offspring—played quarterback for Notre Dame in the late 1940s. It seemed that the only name missing from the Tripucka drumroll was that of the second leading scorer in Lafayette's basketball history. His name was included on Lafayette's roster for the evening. The Irish would soon be introduced to Otis Ellis.

Otis Ellis was a classic small forward, and listed program stats of 6'5" and 200 pounds. An African-American, he had been recruited by then assistant coach John Leone, who ventured into the back streets of Philadelphia to secure Otis' enrollment at Lafayette. On the afternoon of the Notre Dame game, in keeping with his standard pregame ritual, Otis went down to the APK Field House to practice his jump shot for hours on end. He was modestly upset when he was informed that "Mr. Phelps" wanted to use the gym and would he please vacate. "This was my gym," he thought to himself, but he soon relented and allowed the Irish to practice.

The presence of national TV channel WGN9 of Chicago had many of the local fans doing "Hi Moms," a rare treat for Lafayette loyalists. At precisely eight P.M. on January 4, 1988, the TV cameras were rolling and the local public address announcer Jim Finnen bellowed "Let's Play Basketball." The referee held the center jump and the Lafayette-Notre Dame game was underway. In the early minutes, Lafayette adopted a strategy of setting up Otis Ellis. Using picks, screens, ball motion, the van Breda Kolff blueprint to isolate Ellis quickly paid off as the Leopards ran out to an early 37-33 halftime lead. Phelps' scouting report seemed more focused on shutting down VBK's patented high-post scissor maneuvers and backdoor moves. For sure, Digger didn't anticipate a game of clear-out by four players and a weak side one-on-one show by Ellis. The van Breda Kolff plan worked to perfection as Ellis accumulated twenty-one first-half points, hitting eight out of nine shots from the field and five for five from the foul line.

During the halftime intermission, Digger tried to inspire his players but the tight road schedule seemed to be taking its toll on the Irish. He ultimately put the ball in David Rivers' hands, his diminutive point guard, and Dave responded with a thirty-one-point effort for the night. VBKs players, on the other hand, hadn't played a game for over three weeks.

A five day study period followed by final exams took priority over athletics at Lafayette. Following the testing period, Butch instructed his players to work out at home and be back on campus by December 31. As such, the Lafayette players were well rested and hungry, and they effectively neutralized the expected Irish rebound edge. Quite a feat considering that Notre Dame—just a few days earlier—had outrebounded LaSalle by a twenty-three margin!

Butch opted to keep his game plan in place as he continued to exploit the hot hand of Otis Ellis. Jump shots, spinning layups, and converted free throw opportunities were all part of Otis' repertoire as he would eventually score a career high thirty-five points. His achievement was made even more astounding when coupled with his ten-rebound effort against the taller and presumably more physical Irish front court. Lafayette built a second-half lead of twelve points, and was never really challenged by the Irish late in the game. VBK had coached his young team well in the art of handling the full-court pressure applied by an increasingly desperate Phelps.

Butch's emphasis on conditioning played a role as he relied primarily on seven players to combat the Irish. Unlike Dr. Tom Davis and Fran O'Hanlon, who employ virtually unlimited substitutions during the course of a game, Butch usually made personnel changes on a very selective basis. Against Notre Dame, he had to take out the energetic Kevin Davis because of foul trouble. Occasionally, he gave one of his starters a breather. He used Stu Murray as a sixth man in the '50s to come in and generate some offensive firepower. Even in the professional ranks, as illustrated by the final game of the 1969 Championship series, he frequently only used seven players during the course of a game.

In college basketball, many late-game rallies take place because of the exponential power of the three-point shot. But the Fighting Irish were only marginally effective from three-point range, and essentially traded baskets with the upstart Leopards. On one occasion, the Notre Dame "zone buster" Sean Connor had an open look at the three, only to have the ball slide out of his hands and fall backwards over the end-line. Digger watched helplessly as his team's full-court pressure aimed at trapping the Lafayette guards was ineffective against Butch's well-trained crew, which passed over the press and scored several uncontested layups. When fouled, the Leopards converted most of their key free throws. Late in the game, as Notre Dame compressed the lead to nine points, Butch inserted Paul Staubi. The Irish immediately fouled the senior Leopard guard, assuming he would be ice cold coming off the bench. To the contrary, Staubi sank four straight foul shots to squelch Digger's strategy.

The partisan crowd of over 4,000, the largest ever to witness a game at the Kirby Field House, collectively held their breath until announcer Jim Finnen said, "One minute remains in the ball game." A huge roar erupted as victory was assured. When time finally expired, Lafayette had achieved an 83-68 upset win, which exactly reversed the spread published in the *Daily News*. The local fans went berserk as Otis Ellis completed several victory laps of the gym floor.

In effect, Bill "Butch" van Breda Kolff had coached a perfect game.

At first, Butch gave a muted response to the victory. "Their style suited us. We can't stay with teams that make us run." But then the reality sank in and he said, "When they want to, when they play their game and run their offense, these kids can play with anyone in the country. Tonight, they did it all."

The normally glib Digger Phelps was indeed succinct in the media. In the *Daily News,* he said "They just totally outplayed us."

Following the loss, Notre Dame vented its frustrations with a 62-44 victory over Marquette. Eventually, Notre Dame posted a 20-9 record and received an "at large" invitation to the NCAA tourney. David Rivers had a strong season, averaging twenty-two points per game and accumulating 158 assists and forty-seven steals. According to *Street & Smith's 1988 Annual,* David was basketball for Notre Dame for four years. They also wrote, "He did everything but straighten out Digger's boutonniere." After losing to Lafayette, Digger wore the boutonniere to all of his team's remaining games.

Otis Ellis had indeed shown Digger Phelps that the Allen P. Kirby Field House was *his* gym. Nine years later, following the Tripucka brothers, Otis would be inducted into the Lafayette College Hall of Fame. Three of Otis' teammates—Matt Roberts, Andy Wescoe, and Bruce Stankavage—would eventually join the Leopards exclusive 1000 point scorers ranks. Over the school's long sports history, only thirty-three players have achieved this plateau. The fifth member of the squad was team captain Billy Hughes. He fell short of the 1,000 point mark, but probably led the country in floor burns. His unlimited hustle was particularly frustrating to the exhausted Irish. Although he fouled out of the game, Kevin Davis' aggressive defense kept the Irish from penetrating inside as he constantly double-teamed the ball. Scott Lewis appeared physically outsized inside, but his timely baskets, foul shots, and rebounds helped sustain the Pard momentum.

Although Otis was the superstar of the evening, the entire team played a role in the triumph.

Andy Wescoe alluded to the confidence instilled in the team by VBK's lecture the evening of the team's last practice session before the Notre Dame game. VBK sat the team in the new stands erected for the expected overflow crowd, and pronounced "If you guys rebound the ball with Notre Dame we will win." Following Butch's forecast, "Nobody said a word and you could tell at that moment we were focused and knew we could pull it off."

The day after the Notre Dame game, Butch strayed from his office at the Field House to revisit the scene of the victory. As he set foot on the Tartan surface, alone, he savored perhaps the greatest single win of his collegiate coaching career. As he rewound the tape in his mind, the satisfaction of his team's flawless execution against Notre Dame just about brought him to tears. But out of the corner of his eye, he caught the clean-up crew making strides in his direction. Assuming additional congratulatory praise, Butch braced himself for a series of handshakes and back-slapping. Not so! The custodians went out of their way to complain about the extra work and clean-up effort that 4000 fans implied. So many paper cups!

Butch decided to return to his office and prepare for his team's next game, against Navy. His phone was ringing as he neared his desk. He surmised that the president of Lafayette or some top administrative official might be calling him to acknowledge the great win over the Irish. Butch had guessed wrong. The caller was an old friend from New Orleans, and the news was bad. Pistol Pete Maravich, one of the most exciting players in basketball history, had died of a heart attack at age forty. The reaction of the custodians, the immediacy of the Navy game, the silence of the school's officials, and Pete's death all made the Notre Dame game seem like ancient history to VBK.

Butch had one last guilty thought. He never had returned Pistol Pete's sweatsuit from the time they played squash in New Orleans. It was somewhere packed among his life's belongings.

Perhaps Butch was a bit sullen at the practice session that evening. According to Wescoe, "We were all hung over and Coach had us doing a conditioning drill and we were dragging." Then VBK said, "Well you want to hoot with the owls you gotta soar with the eagles." The Coach proceeded to add a few extra sprints to the drill, and took the time yelling at his young team, stressing that the Notre Dame win was only one game and that the team had better get refocused.

The upset of Notre Dame acted as a springboard for the Leopards, who went 15-6 for the balance of the season and finished at a respectable 19-10 for the season. The Leopards went undefeated at their home court. They won the regular season East Coast Conference championship with an 11-3 record. For his achievements, Butch van Breda Kolff was named conference Coach of the Year. More importantly, Butch had revived the spirit of winning basketball at Lafayette.

In its current format, the NCAA invites sixty-four teams to its season-ending tournament. For many years, the NCAA has invited not only the conference champions from a vast array of leagues, but also the runners-up from "power" conferences such as The Big East, The Big Ten and the Atlantic Coast Conference. The East Coast Conference that Butch van Breda Kolff knew while at Lafayette partially evolved into the Patriot League. In all reality, the ECC then and the Patriot League now ranks as a second or third tier league in the eyes of the NCAA selection committee. A multitude of "at-large" bids—some years as many as six bids—are extended to teams who play in the above-mentioned "power" group. The ECC, however, would only send one team to the "big dance," and that "automatic" bid would be awarded to the winner of the league's yearend tournament. In recent years, approximately seventeen conferences receive their one automatic bid to the tourney and that is all. For the teams who fail to win those year-end conference tourneys, the season is effectively over. No runners-up need apply!

The rivalry between Lafayette and Lehigh University is well documented. The two Pennsylvania schools are separated by approximately fifteen miles along Interstate Route 78. Playoffs aside, the schools conclude their football seasons with the annual Lafayette-Lehigh game. The contest is almost always the Saturday before Thanksgiving, the same day that Michigan plays Ohio State, Harvard plays Yale, and UCLA plays USC. The Lafayette-Lehigh game has been played 135 times, the most of any collegiate rivalry in the nation. The Princeton-Yale series ranks second in number of games played with 122. Lafayette holds a modest 71-59-5 lead over Lehigh in the football series which dates back to 1888. Lehigh has been the more successful team over the last 20 years, posting 12 wins while dropping 8.

Lafayette's historical edge over Lehigh is more substantial on the basketball front, with the Leopards leading the series by a 125-63 margin. But for the 1987–88 season, Lehigh basketball was experiencing an unprecedented level of success. The Engineers (subsequently re-nicknamed the Mountain Hawks) were led by Mike Polaha and Daren Queenan. Queenan, in fact, finished second in the nation in scoring with a 28.5 point per game average and was named the East Coast Conference player of the year for the 1987–88 season. As you enter Lehigh's Stabler Arena, you see Queenan's number 12 and Polaha's number 24 hanging from the rafters as the only two players so recognized in the school's history.

More than rivalry was at stake when Lafayette squared off against Lehigh in the semifinal round of the

ECC "sudden death" conference tournament. The automatic bid to the NCAA "big dance" was still alive for the victor. Lehigh prevailed by 67-65 in a real thriller, and the defeat ended the season for Lafayette. The defeat was especially hard since Lehigh was a team Lafayette had defeated twice during the regular season. For Coach van Breda Kolff, the win over Notre Dame was a distinct highlight, but missing the NCAA by such a close margin ended the season on a pronounced downer. The NIT—increasingly a clone of the NCAA Tourney—also snubbed the Leopards even though they had a quality win over Notre Dame and won their conference during the regular season by a two-game margin over Delaware and Drexel. The NIT, whose number of entrants had grown to thirty-two, was void of any teams from the Top 20 in the AP final poll. In lieu of a smaller college with a strong record, the NIT of the '80s preferred a college with a "big-name" program, a home arena with a large seating capacity, and a minimum regular season record of .500 or better.

However, Butch had achieved quite a record in his second tour of duty at Lafayette. In 1984, he had assumed the head coaching position from Will Rackley, whose teams posted losing records in three of four seasons. The Lafayette alumni and fans were spoiled by an extended series of winning records during the 1970s. At first, there was Dr. Tom Davis who led Lafayette to six straight winning seasons (1970–1976) before moving onto Boston College and other major collegiate programs such as Stanford and Iowa. The Davis-led Leopards most memorable victory was in the National Invitational Tournament at Madison Square Garden when they upset highly rated Virginia University from the Atlantic Coast Conference in 1972. While at Lafayette, Davis' principal assistant was Gary Williams, who has coached a winning Maryland University program for many years.

Dr. Davis was followed by Dr. Roy Chipman, who treated the Leopard fans to three more winning seasons. Chipman guided the Leopards to a NIT berth in 1980, and Lafayette lost in the first round to Ralph Sampson's University of Virginia. Soon, however, Lafayette again acted as a stepping stone for coaches when Chipman moved onto Pitt of the Big East. Leopard fans craved the return of the likes of Tracy and Todd Tripucka.

Just four years prior to Lafayette's upset victory over Notre Dame, a February 20, 1984, edition of *Sports Illustrated* contained a special article about Butch van Breda Kolff. The lengthly article pointed how Butch had fallen on hard times and was teaching history and coaching a high school basketball team of fatherless youths in remote Picayune Mississippi. His annual salary was $20,000. The consummate coach, he derived great satisfaction from teaching and guiding these young men. "The *Sports Illustrated* article gave me more publicity than all my years in the NBA," Butch observed.

Lafayette Athletic Director Olav "Ollie" Kollevoll was under the gun to bring back some of the glow from the Davis & Chipman years. His search committee sifted through 126 applications before narrowing the field down to seven finalists. After interviewing the seven, Ollie staked his reputation on the rehire of Coach van Breda Kolff. In his second go-around, there would be no soccer or lacrosse coaching responsibilities.

An air of excitement immediately filled the Lafayette campus. "Butch is Back" T-shirts were circulated and widely displayed by the student body. Attired exactly as he was when he visited the Governor of Mississippi, Butch wore his new blazer, tie, and blue button-down shirt to the reception acknowledging his return. VBK commented:

> "I enjoyed it here before and if our record is as good as it was then, I'll definitely enjoy it here now."

And so, at age sixty-one, Butch van Breda Kolff began his second career at Lafayette. After reviewing films of prior games, Butch recognized the raw talent at his disposal but thought the players were "a little hesitant." "I'd like to see the games a little more fluid," he commented early on.

One of Kollevoll's reservations about VBK was his zeal for recruiting. But within days of his rehire, Butch was on the road on his first recruiting trip. If a potential recruit showed any resistance, Butch jokingly threatened the prospect that he would be marched down to the gym and Larry Holmes would "knock his block off." VBK assured Kollevoll, "Chronological age doesn't matter. It's how you feel."

One of the leading players returning for the 1984-85 season was senior Tony Duckett. Duckett still holds the Lafayette record for assists in a career (622). But Duckett feared that Butch might opt to create a whole new lineup to snap the Leopards from its slump of the last few seasons. Duckett said, "If he could bench Wilt, he could definitely bench me! Once I sat down and talked with him, I realized I could play for him. He became my friend right there. I love this guy!"

In his first game in 1984, the VBK Leopards opened up the season against Ohio State from the Big Ten. As expected, Lafayette was crushed by an 85-67 margin. Double digit road losses at the hands of Tennessee, St. John's, and Pitt didn't help the overall record, but helped prepare the club for its slate of East Coast Conference games. As the season progressed, Butch shaped the team into a stronger unit as the team posted a 15-13 record and finished in the middle of the pack of the ECC. Butch stressed a man-to-man defense as "Number One." "The idea of the game is good defense, and making them take the bad shots," he commented.

A battle of wits occurred early in Butch's first season of Phase II of his coaching experience at Lafayette. On January 26, 1985, Lafayette entertained Princeton University at the APK gym. The duel between Pete Carril and Butch van Breda Kolff was set. In a classic defensive thriller, VBK bested his prize pupil by a 45-43 margin. The following year, Princeton won the grudge match with a 62-49 win over Lafayette.

Oddly enough, the Lafayette-Princeton game was discontinued for four years and has been played every year since 1990. Perhaps Butch and Pete felt an "on court" confrontation might jeopardize their friendship!

During the 1980s, many college and professional coaches departed from the traditional suit and tie attire and wore more casual outfits during regular season games. Lou Carnesecca (St. John's) and John Thompson (Georgetown) received wide publicity for their colorful sweaters. Butch wore some bright-colored striped shirts while coaching in New Orleans and Memphis. At Lafayette, he experimented with wearing a maroon and white warm-up outfit, and the team reeled off three straight wins.

However, the higher ups at Lafayette felt the warm-up suit was too casual and suggested he wear something more businesslike. Butch accommodated, but he sincerely felt that warm-up suits—given the amount of animation and perspiration he generated during a game—were more practical.

A high point of his first season came on February 6, 1985 when Lafayette routed Hofstra by an 85-62 margin. But less than thirty days later, as fate would have it, a one-point loss to Hofstra in the conference championship tournament dashed any hopes of advancing to the NCAA tourney.

For the 1984–85 season, Lehigh finished sixth out of eight teams in the ECC, posted a 12-19 overall record, but most importantly won the year-end conference tournament. As a result, they received the automatic bid to the NCAA. The "winner-take-all" syndrome of the conference tourney had again abruptly ended Butch's season. For the Engineers, the euphoria was short-lived, however, as they were immediately annihilated 68-43 by number one seeded Georgetown and their All-American center Patrick Ewing. Meanwhile, the coaching experience, the life of Butch van Breda Kolff, continued on its emotional roller coaster.

☆ ☆ ☆

During this second tour at Lafayette College, Butch van Breda Kolff was indeed a living legend. He certainly was not cast in the "gentlemanly" mold of his predecessor coaches such as Drs. Davis and Chipman. On one occasion, Butch was invited to play as a "celebrity" guest in a twenty-fifth year reunion golf tournament for the class of 1960.

The site of the outing was the serene Oak Hill Country Club in Milford, New Jersey. Like most private golf clubs, Oak Hill had a strict dress code as well as other regulations governing player behavior. The outing chairman had sent letters to participating classmates as well as to VBK about how the course required players to wear collared golf shirts, Bermuda-length shorts, and the like. Coolers to be loaded on the back of the golf cart were specifically banned.

Punctuality is probably not one of Butch's strong suits, as he arrived just before his slated T-off time. The chairman realized immediately that Butch had either not read or chosen to ignore his letter concerning Oak Hill's local rules. He wore a gray basketball shirt with the logo "Lafayette Basketball." He opted not to tuck in his shirt, which hung out over his gray-colored basketball shorts. He toted a maroon golf bag over one shoulder and a beer-filled cooler on the other, in effect his own build-in speakeasy. A beautiful young blond in a short white skirt accompanied Butch to the first tee, and Butch introduced her as his daughter Kaatje. Suddenly, prominent on the first tee, there sat a five-some, four sets of clubs, two carts, and one cooler. The reunion golfers were amused by the display, but the chairman was concerned about getting by the starter without being reprimanded. Undoubtedly, the starter was mesmerized by Butch's daughter and the group teed off without invoking any criticism.

Once on the golf course, the outing chairman tried to strike up a conversation with VBK. He volunteered to help him recruit in the northern New Jersey area.

"Where do you live," he asked.
"Chatham," he responded.
An instant profile of the Jersey suburb passed in front of his eyes. Tony Mack, a member of the 1954–55 Lafayette NIT team, was the coach of Chatham (Borough) High School and was noted for his deliberate tactics and a style of setting up the "sure shot." Mack's win-loss percentage was admirable, but featured many low-scoring, almost annoying victories. One of Mack's stars—Eric Kambour '85—selected Lafayette but opted to play soccer instead, subsequently rising to be the captain of the ECC champions in his senior year. Butch had recruited Mack when he starred for Bloomfield High School in 1953, but rarely used his talents during the 1954–55 season when VBK guided the Leopards to the NIT. Mack's key role, it seemed, was that of a member of the Red Caps. Under George Davidson, however, Mack blossomed and captained the NCAA representative in 1957.

"I don't need any more 6'1" shooting guards!" he exclaimed, as he seemed anxious to change the subject.

Butch's portfolio was well stocked with a redundancy of long-range shooters. Ideally, the VBK offense depended on well-conditioned athletes who could penetrate and create back door plays. In the win over Notre Dame, Butch's guards were scoreless from three-point range.

While at Lafayette, Butch never coached a team which would "live or die" by the three-point play. He explained his main ax, and said, "I need some 6'8" power forwards who can clean the boards." Butch's plea was certainly justified. His leading rebounder for three of the four years was none other than the slender Mr. Otis Ellis. The tallest Leopard on the squad was 6'7" Matt Roberts, who weighed in at a lean 210 pounds. Matt's main contribution to the team was his passing capability, foul shooting, and clutch scoring. Even during the successful run of 1987–1988, Butch's teams were consistently outrebounded by their opponents.

One of Butch's strong points as a recruiter was that he sought players to fill specific positions. He was averse to "wholesale" recruiting and rather sought to fill out the components of a strong team. He didn't need an army of players. Three strong players in the front court, a power rebounder, and three hustling guards (including a good shooter or two) were all he needed. He would teach the group to be a winner.

But Butch seemed more interested in the little intramural golf wager that the group had arranged. He admonished the chairman to forgo any further shop talk—he wanted to focus on winning some money from his hosts. A potential pot of $15 challenged VBK. He would deal with recruiting at another time.

Part of Butch's winning strategy on the golf course was encased in his cooler. Soon everyone in the foursome was sucking down *Miller Lites* and before long the finer points about golf had gone by the wayside. Upon completing the ninth hole, the Lafayette alums beelined their way to the clubhouse to use the men's room. Meanwhile, Butch disappeared to his car and restocked the cooler with more beer. The chairman of the Twenty-fifth Reunion Golf Tournament and his playing partners were all set for the back nine at Oak Hill.

Lafayette reunionists John Hickman (left) and Bill Clearwater (right) join Kaatje and Butch von Breda Kolff at the Class of 1960 Golf Tourney. Credit: Paul Luscombe

The Later Lafayette College Years: 1984–1988

Butch exhibits his golf swing on the first hole of Oak Hill Golf Club in Milford, NJ.

Midway through the back nine, the beers caught up with VBK and he had to relieve himself. Just off the fairway, on one of Oak Hill's famed oak trees, Butch elected to take care of the "inconvenience." "Ahhhh," he said. "Oh, Dad," remarked his daughter.

Somehow, the details of who scored what on that day are long forgotten but suffice it to say that Butch collected the $15 prize from his playing partners at the completion of the round. The celebrity from the Roaring Twenties was some competitor!

In another golf-related incident, Butch was invited to play the prestigious Saucon Valley County Club in Allentown, Pennsylvania. SVCC is the epitome of serenity, as the majestic clubhouse sits elegantly among the multitude of willow trees which outline the course. In 1992, the course was the site of the U.S. Seniors Open won by Larry Leoretti. The seniors returned in June of 2000 and Hale Irwin emerged the winner.

As you might expect, the dress code at Saucon was even stricter than that prevailing at Oak Hill. For example, no shorts of any kind are permitted at SVCC. Golfers are required to wear long pants. However, no rule concerning footwear prevailed and so when Butch arrived in his high-top sneakers, he was actually in compliance with the local code. His hosts would have been a bit more comfortable had he worn Gucci loafers instead. When the hosts handed over their standard business shoes to the locker room attendant for cleaning, Butch submitted his sneakers for polishing as well. Obviously, the country club set was not his bag. Butch was one of the boys.

Local Lafayette fans and alumni frequently gather before home basketball games at the College Hill Tavern. The friendly pub is located on Cattel Street, just three blocks from the APK Field House. Three TV sets are invariably tuned into some sporting event, and the bar is more or less dimly lit. Adjacent to the bar is a restaurant section with a nominal seating capacity. The traditional pinball machines, jukebox, and neon signs decorate both areas. Although prices are modest by New York standards, there is an ATM machine available for those who run out of cash.

For over twenty-five years, Bob Trimble has been the proprietor of the College Hill Tavern. Bob and his wife Dawn are avid basketball fans and frequently travel far afield to see the Leopards in action. For example, they flew out to Columbus a few years ago to see the previously mentioned Ohio State game. More likely than not, Bob is your bartender or waiter and he loves to reminisce about basketball history at Lafayette and otherwise. Recently, before a Lafayette-Holy Cross basketball game, Bob was asked if Coach van Breda Kolff frequented the CHT. "Oh yeah, he drank *Miller Lite,*" Bob replied. Sure sounded familiar!

Butch made constructive use of his barroom time, however, as he soon encouraged the locals to reorganize the struggling fan-club supporting the Lafayette Leopards. Known as the "Friends of Lafayette," the group consisted primarily of non-alumni men and women whose interest had waned during the losing seasons under Coach Rackley. Energized by VBK's presence, the group soon became more evident at both home and away games.

The Later Lafayette College Years: 1984–1988   199

Bus packages to distant locales on the Lafayette schedule were a distinct highlight. Inspired by the imposing figure of Butch van Breda Kolff, the group congregated at the CHT and would set out for destinations near and far.

Butch took his responsibilities with the "Friends" very seriously. Between coaching commitments, he would order, negotiate and pick up the postgame catering package from "Sal's" just a few blocks off campus. Following the games, he would set up the entire spread for the benefit of the fans. According to one original member of the "Friends," "Beer was never a problem."

Ultimately, "The Friends of Lafayette" would take on a sanctioned status as a booster organization for the College. "The Friends" in its present form sells sweatshirts and other clothing at home games, and members and their guests participate in postgame receptions held at the recently renovated Allen P. Kirby Sports Center. In effect, VBK revitalized the "sixth man" rooting section for his teams, the institutional structure of which remains in place to this day.

Back to basketball: One of the most famous college players to ever play against Lafayette was Navy's David Robinson. During the 1986–87 season, the Robinson-led Middies were nationally ranked and were still savoring their 30-5 season, in which they had made it to the the "Elite Eight" of the NCAA tourney. On January 14, 1987, Navy invaded the Easton environs to play the 5-7 Leopards. Lafayette gave Robinson all kinds of headaches as the future NBA star had to turn his game up to full throttle in order to narrowly defeat the Pards by a 75-71 margin.

VBK was severely disappointed in the loss. He was never one to take solace in "moral victories." Following the game, he was quoted in the press as saying that David Robinson would never make it at the professional level. Perhaps Butch was offended by Robinson's prior comments that he never "got himself up" for teams like

Lafayette. Obviously Butch, if taken literally, had miscalculated the potential of the man who would lead the San Antonio Spurs to the NBA title in the 1998–1999 season. Butch claimed that the press had twisted his words and that he felt he was implying that Robinson would have to play with more intensity in order to succeed in the NBA. Butch alluded to the eighty-plus game schedule of the pros, and mentioned that Robinson needed to build his strength to be a star. As events unfolded, Robinson went on a vigorous weight program and built himself up. Perhaps David read between the lines of VBK's comments.

In addition to the tough loss to Navy, the 86-87 season was marred by some other "near misses" against strong opponents. The Pards lost to Rutgers by one point, Boston College by six, and St. Peters by two. Against their peers of the ECC, the Leopards finished 11-5 and 16-13 overall. Then a sophomore, Otis Ellis lead the team in scoring (21.0 average) and rebounding (9.4 average).

While coaching Lafayette in the '50s and the '80s, Butch's only losing season occurred during the 1985–86

David Robinson, playing for nationally ranked Navy against Lafayette in 1987. Navy won 74-71 in an unexpectedly close contest. Otis Ellis of Lafayette, who starred in the Notre Dame game a year later, is shown guarding Robinson. Credit: Paul Luscombe campaign. Even then, his team barely slipped below .500 as a loss to Drexel in the final game of the ECC Tourney brought the record to 14-15.

Midway through the 1987–88 regular season, following a win over Drexel, Butch checked into the Easton Hospital saying he was suffering from chest pains. He was diagnosed as having an arrhythmic murmur, or, in laymen's terminology, an irregular heartbeat. Butch was forced to miss the February 17 Rider game because of what he labeled "the heart thing." Ironically, Bill Bradley was affected by the same condition, which may have impacted his run for the presidency in 2000.

The doctors immediately directed Butch to change his lifestyle. They prescribed a diet of apples instead of beer. "I'd definitely say that I've matured. Long walks and crossword puzzles have replaced all the parties. Now instead of coming home at six in the morning, that's when I wake up." Despite the scare, the Rider game was the only game he missed because of health or any other reasons throughout his 1300 plus game career. By the way, Digger Phelps is a Rider alumnus.

Keith Van Auken was one of Butch's targeted high school recruits for his 1988–89 teams and beyond. Keith was a 6'6" forward who had averaged 16.6 points per game and eleven rebounds for Tunkhannock High School in Northeastern Pennsylvania. Butch visited with Keith and his parents at his Dalton, Pennsylvania, home and entertained the Van Aukens with many stories of the Knicks, the Lakers, and Lafayette in the past. Details of the Bradley-led Princeton team's march to the Final Four, details of the NBA Finals of 1968 and 1969, stories of the run-ins with Chamberlain—all these walks down basketball's memory lane kept young Keith and his parents absorbed for hours. When Butch departed for the evening, Keith's father said to him, "You have got to go to Lafayette and play for Butch."

In mid-April, 1988 the phone rang in VBK's office at the field house. The caller was Jim Garvey, the athletic director of Hofstra University. Hofstra had just completed a dismal 6-21 hoop season, finishing dead last in the East

Coast Conference. It probably was the worst season ever for the Hofstra Flying Dutchmen. Garvey was in the market for a new head basketball coach, and he asked Butch if he had any recommendations. Butch responded, "Why not me?" Undoubtedly, Butch craved another "turnaround" project.

Thus, VBK abruptly closed the record on his bookended Lafayette coaching career, which included two stints, 1951–55 and 1984–88. In both instances, VBK took his respective athletic directors—Anderson and Kollevall—by surprise.

He was succeeded by assistant coach John Leone, who assumed his first collegiate head coaching job. VBK's overall record for the two periods was 132-85 and a winning percentage of .608. Butch's combined number of wins put him in third place among Lafayette coaches. His 16.6 wins per season ranked second only to Dr. Tom Davis' 19.3 wins per season among those coaches who had 100 or more wins at the college.

Soon, Coach van Breda Kolff was on his way to Hofstra University. Keith Van Auken, who heeded his father's advice and matriculated at Lafayette, would never have the pleasure of being coached by VBK. The heritage of VBK continued at Lafayette, however, as Butch's ace recruiter—the thirty-six year old John Leone—kept his mentor's program in place. According to Ed Louboch of the *Easton Express,* the first order of business for John was to "rearrange the furniture in van Breda Kolff's office." John did even better than his goal of maintaining the "status quo" as he quickly led the Leopards to their first twenty win season in ten years. The Pards went to the finals of the East Coast Conference only to lose to Bucknell 71-65. Otis Ellis finished his college career just 113 points behind Tracy Tripucka as the college's all-time leading scorer.

Butch would again recycle his life as this would be his second tour at Hofstra. In 1955, he left a relatively successful Lafayette program to coach the Hofstra Flying Dutchmen. Obviously, a catalyst for change had disrupted Butch's initial vow that Lafayette was where he would finish his career. Butch seemed always to feel uncomfortable whenever he felt comfortable. Or perhaps it was those griping custodians the day after the Notre Dame game! Butch harbored a desire that Lafayette make more of a commitment to athletics, particularly basketball. The silence of the administration after the Notre Dame victory led him to believe that commitment was somewhat tentative.

Butch felt that schools like Lafayette and Princeton really didn't want *overly successful* athletic programs. For sure, they wouldn't tolerate continuous losing seasons. But unlike the Big Time sports colleges and universities, a high profile athletic program implied a compromise on the side of academic excellence. A continuous winner was cause for suspicion. Butch intuitively felt that the Lafayette's and the Princeton's of the world preferred to major in "M" (mediocrity) instead of "W" (winning). Currently, Lafayette's President Art Rothkopf uses the word "competitive" to succinctly capture the school's overall objective of athletic policy.

Regardless, Butch needed another challenge. He was leaving a very strong team at Lafayette and he looked forward to building another one at Hofstra. In view of the Hofstra's 6-21 season, the challenge would be formidable.

BOX SCORE OF LAFAYETTE-NOTRE DAME GAME: JANUARY 4, 1988

Lafayette 83

	FG	FT	PF	PTS
Ellis	12	11-14	3	35
Hughes	1	8-10	3	10
Roberts	5	4-4	4	14
Davis	2	3-3	5	7
Wescoe	0	0-0	4	0
Stankavage	2	2-2	5	6
Staubi	0	4-4	0	4
Lewis	2	3-5	2	7
Totals:	24	35-42	26	83

Notre Dame 68

	FG	FT	PF	PTS
Rivers	11	7-8	4	31
Connor	1	1-2	1	4
Jackson	2	1-4	5	6
Stevenson	5	3-4	3	13
Voce	1	2-2	4	4
Ellery	0	0-0	0	0
Paddock	0	0-0	3	0
Robinson	2	0-2	5	4
Singleton	1	4-6	2	6
Totals:	23	18-28	27	68

3 point goals: Lafayette 0. Notre Dame 4 (Rivers 2, Jackson 1, Connor 1)

FINAL STANDINGS OF EAST COAST CONFERENCE 1988

	Conference			All Games		
	Won	Lost	Pct	Won	Lost	Pct
Lafayette College#	11	3	.786	19	10	.655
Delaware University	9	5	.643	19	9	.679
Drexel University	9	5	.643	18	10	.643
Lehigh University*	8	6	.571	21	9	.700
Bucknell University	7	7	.500	16	12	.571
Rider College	6	8	.429	9	19	.321
Towson State University	4	10	.286	14	16	.467
Hofstra University	2	12	.143	6	21	.214

#Regular season champions

*Winner conference tournament, automatic bid to NCAA tourney

Chapter 9

The Later Hofstra University Years 1988–1994

"Coach van Breda Kolff never played the best players. He played the players that played the best together."

Steve Balber

Perhaps the greatest of Butch van Breda Kolff's considerable talents as a coach is his knack for making basketball fun for his players."

Christopher D. Jones, Jr., *Princeton Alumni Weekly*

Hofstra University represented perhaps the most appreciative collection of fans, alumni, and administrative personnel associated with Butch van Breda Kolff's career—college or pro. Typical of this recognition was their offer to provide VBK with air transportation and lodging which would have enabled him to witness Hofstra's first round appearance in the 2000 NCAA Eastern Region bracket in Buffalo, New York. The Flying Dutchmen were making their first appearance at the "big dance" since 1977.

The setting in Buffalo had a lot of appeal to VBK. Lafayette College was making its second straight NCAA appearance under the leadership of Coach Fran O'Hanlon. Butch's son Jan was coaching Pepperdine University in a matchup with Indiana University and its famous coach, Bobby Knight. And Hofstra had earned a slot by virtue of its winning the America East Conference tournament. Hofstra was led by its star guard—Craig "Speedy" Claxton—who some say was the best player in the country under six feet tall. Butch relished the thought of reuniting with friends from the Lafayette and Hofstra communities. Better yet, he could have seen his son's Pepperdine squad totally dominate Indiana. And then, there was the nostalgia of his first team at Lafayette, and their fun-filled pilgramages to play the University of Buffalo in the 1950s. At age seventy-eight, given the choice of sunny Florida or snowy Buffalo, Butch opted not to make the trip. But the generous offer reconfirmed his inner feelings about Hofstra. They liked him as a person and they recognized his achievements as a coach, even some six years after he had retired from coaching at the Hempstead institution.

The Hofstra loyalists had reason to appreciate Butch. Hofstra had the distinction of being his longest uninterrupted coaching experience. From 1955 through 1962, for seven solid seasons, Butch compiled a 136-43 record, including five seasons of twenty wins or more. Upon his return, from 1988–1994, his teams recorded a 79-91 log. Overall, his 215 wins over thirteen seasons easily made him the winningest coach in Hofstra history.

The Hofstra University of the 1980s was vastly different from the Hofstra College which Butch coached in the 1950s. The enrollment of the school mushroomed to 12,000 and shifted from an exclusive dependence on Long Island commuters to a broader base of some forty-five states and seventy-two countries. Some 120 buildings including dormitories stretch out over the now 238 acre campus. During Butch's first coaching phase at Hofstra, the Flying Dutchmen played in the small college division of the NCAA, but in 1973 they made the move to Division I and actually competed with Lafayette College in the East Coast Conference during the 1987–88 season.

The atmosphere surrounding the Hofstra campus was "garish" in comparison with the subdued rustic setting of

The Later Hofstra University Years 1988–1994

Lafayette. Bright colors and modern architecture were a prevailing theme at the Hempstead campus. Butch lived in the Twin Oaks Apartments located just two blocks from the school.

Over the last fifteen years or so, Hofstra has adopted a very ambitious program to elevate its sports performance profile. In football, the Flying Dutchmen moved from Division II to the more competitive level of I-AA, playing its first official season in 1993. The 1994 team went 8-1-1 and ranked twenty-second in the country. The school completed Phase I of its plan to increase the capacity of its football stadium from 7,000 to 15,000. During the 1999 season, the football team went undefeated in the regular season and lost in the quarterfinal round of the Division I-AA playoffs to Illinois State by 37-20. The New York Jets all-pro receiver Wayne Chrebet adds notoriety to the program. One of the most popular Jets, many fans wear his number 80 green jersey to the games.

In January of 2000, the New Hofstra Arena opened featuring a basketball capacity of 5,124. The 1998–99 Hofstra cagers won the ECAC Holiday Festival and advanced through three rounds of the NIT.

Just prior to this string of successes and the upscaling of Hofstra's overall athletic program, the Flying Dutchmen basketball team finished last in the East Coast Conference and posted a dismal 6-21 regular season mark for the 1987–88 hoop season. Meanwhile at Lafayette, Butch was conquering Notre Dame and piling up nineteen wins. Hofstra then ditched Coach Dick Berg and encouraged Butch van Breda Kolff to leave his rapidly improving Lafayette situation in order to restore the program to its former prominence. Without doubt, the "appreciation factor" played a role in Butch's decision to move. Ed Laubach, sports editor of the *Easton Express,* mentioned "Lafayette will miss the crusty, gravelly-voiced guy who was able to bridge more than two generation gaps with his basketball savvy. But can he go home again? We'll see."

Although every coach sets out to win all the games, Butch realistically hoped he could get the Flying Dutchmen back on track with a .500 season. Senior floor leader Frank Walker, who averaged fifteen points per game, was the heart and soul of the team at point guard. Carlos Dicenta was the ace from three-point range, hitting 49.7% from beyond the circle for the single season record at the school. Gerald King, the younger brother of NBA stars Bernard and Albert King, and Matt Tucker (6'6", 230 lbs) were the key inside players for Hofstra.

Assessing his prospects for his first season in his second stop at Hofstra, VBK remarked, "I'm realistic, not optimistic or pessimistic . . . don't think we're going to be that bad." Delaware University coach Steve Steinwedel mentioned, "I am sure Butch will do a good job once he clears the debris. They could take off around mid-season."

And take off they did. Hofstra quickly responded to VBK's coaching ways and by season's end, they had consummated a 14-15 season. One of the defensive gems for VBK was his 48-34 win over conference foe Rider. It marked the last time that a Hofstra team held an opponent to less than forty points. An overtime loss to Bucknell in the second round of the postseason tourney ended Butch's hope for the ultimate turnaround. The "Screaming Dutchman" was back on Long Island and the Hofstra locals had reason to be appreciative again.

The 1989–90 season was a "bad news-good news" affair. The Dutchmen lost seven of their first 10 games, but fought their way back to finish at 13-15 overall. Virtually written off as a rebuilding year, Hofstra wound up tied for first place in the East Coast Conference. Butch employed as many as ten underclassmen, all of whom would be at his disposal for the 1990–91 season.

While coaching the New Orleans Pride women's team, one of Butch's favorite sideline maneuvers was when he fell to his knees, elevated both hands over his head, and then placed his forehead and hands on the floor. The Pride labeled the action the "Al Jolson Move," and encouraged him to use the motion as a protest to some of the referees questionable calls. At Hofstra, he resurrected the Jolson

"Jazz Singer" impersonation, and one game he accidentally hit his head a tad too hard on the playing surface. He was quite dazed, and actually was treated by a doctor a few days after the game.

The ECC garnered some recognition in the 1989 NCAA Tourney as the league's representative—Towson State University—fought high scoring Oklahoma down to the wire, just losing at the buzzer.

Butch had a well-balanced squad on hand for the 1990–91 season. *Street & Smith's* preseason college annual predicted that Hofstra would finish second in the ECC behind Delaware. As for manpower, in the frontcourt, he shuttled the below-listed players:

6'5" Derrick Flowers (11.8 ppg 5.8 rbd)
6'6" Anthony Knight (7.7 ppg 4.3 rbd)

Butch demonstrates his infamous "Al Jolson" maneuver while coaching the Memphis Tams in the ABA in 1974. The move usually served to insult the referees and led to a technical foul. Later on in his career, while coaching Hofstra, Butch hit his head so hard that he required modest hospitalization. Credit: VBK private collection

6'5" Ernie Atkinson (6.5 ppg 3.1 rpg)
6'7" Pat Cosgrove center

At point guard, Erroll Flanigan (7.8 ppg, 2.7 assts) replaced Walker as floor leader. Other lettermen included: Joe Lalrsen, Stephen Kiernan, and Keith McMillan.

Butch's charges had another hot and cold, hard luck season as they finished up 14-14. In the first round of the ECC Tourney, they lost to University of Maryland of Baltimore County by 68-67.

The best season for Butch in round 2 at Hofstra was 1991–92 when he constructed a 20-9 record. They won the ECC regular season title with a 10-2 record. Post season accolades included Butch being named ECC Coach of the Year. The Flying Dutchmen featured ECC conference Player of the Year Demetrius Dudley, a transfer student from St. Peter's College in Jersey City. A deadly three-point shooter, Dudley averaged 21.7 points per game while leading the team in rebounds and assists. "Fast Freddy" Nason anchored a strong defense as he led the team in blocked shots. Offensively, the squad was the last Hofstra team to break the 100 threshold when they romped over UMBC by 103-87. Butch was again denied an NCAA Tourney berth when his team lost to Towson State in the second round of the ECC tournament, 69-61.

The Demise of the East Coast Conference

Constant conference reshuffling and newly created leagues were a way of life in the NCAA basketball world of the mid-1980s. For example, The Big East added Rutgers, Notre Dame, West Virginia, and Miami to bring its membership up to thirteen participants. The Big 10 added Penn State while the ACC added Florida State. The Southwest Conference pooled its stronger schools with the Big Eight, as the second tier colleges mostly wound up in the Western Athletic Conference. Arkansas switched from the Southwest to the Southeast Conference. Once one of the top conferences in the country, the Southwest Conference disappeared overnight.

Similar activity led to the establishment of the Patriot League. The Patriot League took on independents Army and Navy plus three schools from the East Coast Conference (Lafayette, Lehigh, and Bucknell). The league also adopted Holy Cross and Fordham from the Metro Atlantic North, and Colgate from the ECAC North Atlantic. Excluding the special cases of Army and Navy, none of the original members of the Patriot League offered athletic scholarships.

As a scholarship-dependent school, Hofstra elected to stay in the ECC, only to see its membership drift away. Soon, Drexel, Delaware, and Rider realigned with the North Atlantic Conference. Towson State joined the Big South. By the end of the 1991–92 season, the ECC ceased to exist as a viable conference. Although the ECC held onto a thread of conference stature along with sister ECC members Central Connecticut State and Buffalo University, Hofstra essentially played its entire 1992–93 season as an independent. Dipping below the NCAA's requirement of six membership schools, the ECC lost its automatic bid to the NCAA tournament. Unlike the earlier years of college basketball, independents in the 1990s had little or no standing. The NCAA had sent out the message: You had to be part of a recognized conference in order to qualify for its lucrative year-end tourney. No independents need apply!

The 1992–93 season was a four-month struggle. Effectively playing as an independent, the Flying Dutchmen had to play twenty of their twenty-seven games on the road. Thirty point or more losses were registered against USF, UNLV, and Villanova. Two wins were against ECC foe Central Connecticut. Demetrius Dudley again led the team in all categories, even adding the team foul shooting title to his achievements. Hofstra finished at 9-18. On March 3, 1993, Butch's forces lost resoundingly to Richmond University by 79-48 as Butch's old friend and playing partner from the Verona Inn—Dick Tarrant—closed out his twelve-year coaching career for the Spiders.

On January 13, 1993, Butch van Breda Kolff took his Hofstra Flying Dutchmen to Cornell University to play The Big Red and their coach Jan van Breda Kolff. Cornell represented Jan's first full-time college coaching assignment after a brief training assignment with Pete Carril at Princeton. The game was the only meeting between Jan (then age 41) and his father (then 70 and the oldest Division I college coach in the nation). Both coaches claimed to enter the game without any serious emotional involvement, and opted to focus on winning the game at hand.

During Jan's high school and college playing years, Butch sincerely enjoyed watching his son play, but viewed any coaching on his part as implying a "conflict of interest," in effect a form of interference. Butch speculated if he had intervened with Jan's coaching, he would have to "offer him a $6 million no-cut contract, and tell all the other players on the team to set picks for him. Then I would retire!" Jan gives Pete Carril the credit for teaching him how to rotate the ball on his jump shot. Oddly enough, Butch offered Jan some incentives to improve his soccer game. (For example, he offered one cent for shots made with his right foot, five cents for those made with his left.)

Early on, Jan saw the classic movie *Fears Strikes Out—The Jim Pearsall Story*, which portrays the role of a dominant father (Karl Malden) and his psychological impact on his son (Tony Perkins), and this seemed to influence Jan's relationship with his dad. "Looking back, I am just as glad my dad stayed away."

Sports columnists of the times noted that Jan was probably closer to his mother Florence, whereas better chemistry existed between Butch and his daughters.

On the evening of January 13, 1993, Cornell beat Hofstra by 70-56.

Attempts to create a viable East Coast Conference led to a massive scheduling overhaul and for Hofstra in the 1993–94 season. From the Midwest corridor, three other

VBK (seated in stands in upper left hand corner) observes his son Jan (10) playing high school basketball. Credit: VBK privsate collection.

"orphaned" independents (Troy State, North East Illinois State, and Chicago State) joined Central Connecticut and Buffalo to form the new ECC. Still, the far-flung six-team conference was lacking NCAA recognition. Again, Hofstra experienced a tough winter, suffering through a 7-20 regular season. At the age of seventy-one, the oldest coach in the country of a major college program, Butch van Breda Kolff announced his retirement effective after the completion of the ECC year-end tournament. The last two seasons, saddled with the stature of quasi-independence, just didn't allow him and his players to focus on *"playing the game right."* Recruiting for a lame duck conference had become next to impossible.

Providing the venue for the final ECC tourney was the University of Buffalo's spacious Alumni Arena. The new gym had a seating capacity of 9000, but only a little more than 100 fans were on hand for Butch's last hurrah. The tourney encompassed six teams with losing records. Generally speaking, ESPN televised all the conference tournament finals leading into the NCAA "big dance," but there was no TV coverage in Buffalo that weekend. The tournament was played for pride. More important to Butch, the tournament was played for fun.

The Flying Dutchmen played their hearts out for their charismatic coach, posting back-to-back overtime wins over Troy and NE Illinois. "We played the tourney just for fun. It turned out to be pretty exciting!" Ironically, it marked the second time in Butch's career, at University of New Orleans and at Hofstra, that his teams won year-end conference tourneys only to be denied an NCAA berth.

At the ECC tournament finals, Butch van Breda Kolff was under constant medical surveillance. He had been hospitalized for an irregular heart beat, and had not been at courtside for several weeks. According to the *New York Times,* Butch was most upset that he couldn't take advantage of the social amenities associated with the tourney. "It's a terrible thing—they got a hospitality room here and I can't drink beer," VBK recalled. Fearing a potential relapse, some of his doctors advised him not to make the trip to Buffalo, but Butch assured them he would remain calm.

Butch van Breda Kolff calm? On the sidelines of an overtime game? Slowly, he worked the refs and suddenly he had a technical called. He claimed to the *Times* that it was his first technical of the year.

Some 1,357 games after coaching his first game at Lafayette College in 1951, William Hendrik van Breda Kolff—at age 71—had coached his last game.

Butch's Retirement Dinner: June 9, 1994

Butch's retirement dinner was held at the Crest Hollow Country Club in Woodbury (Long Island), New York on June 9, 1994. Senator Bill Bradley was there, as was Pete Carril. Lou Carnesecca from St. John's was there also. Jim Garvey, the last athletic director to lure Butch from his "previous stop" was there as well. Stu Murray and Cary Ahl made it from the Lafayette teams.

To a man, Bradley and Carril included, everyone referred to Butch as "Coach." Peter Reinke, who acted as an assistant under VBK in 1985-86, felt he was slighting his legendary boss by referring to him as Butch. Soon, Pete adopted the "Coach" moniker as well.

Most important to Butch was the presence of his twin daughters and his daughter Kaatje. When asked if they were in attendance, he replied, "Look for the loudest part of the party and that's where they will be!" Carry Ahl observed, "They are very handsome women and look a lot like their father."

When Pete Carril stepped out of one of the two busses from Princeton, he was attired in a sports jacket and tie. Butch had to tease his lifelong buddy. "Pete, you've been an Ivy Leaguer so long that you're starting to look like one of them!"

(Note: See end of chapter for others in attendance or others recognized.)

Butch eventually settled in Sun City Center, Florida, a retirement suburb located twenty-five miles south of Tampa off Interstate 75. He continues to visit Harvey Cedars during the summer months. Although retired, he seemed to crave contact with his vast array of friends. He often returned to Lafayette and Hofstra for sporting events. He frequently thought he should have found another coaching job after Hofstra, perhaps at the high school level. Picayune was a truly gratifying experience for him. Was there another Charley Triplet looking for an "experienced" coach?

His successor was announced shortly thereafter. Jay Wright, an assistant under Rollie Massamino at both Villanova and University of Nevada-Las Vegas, would take over the reigns from Butch. By 1996, Hofstra was aligned with the America East Conference and in 2000 they represented the Conference in the NCAA. Wright also took the Dutchmen to the NIT in 1999 where his team made it to the third round.

In recent years, institutions of higher learning have sought to broaden their profiles by changing the school's nickname. Lehigh sought to strip itself of a mundane occupational identity when it dropped the nickname of "Engineers" and adopted the allegedly ferocious "Mountain Hawk" as its mascot. Using the principles of separation of church and state, Elon College (North Carolina) scuttled its long standing nickname "The Fighting Christians" and now is known simply as "Phoenix." A pattern of dropping nicknames associated with the Indians was evident as St. John's University ceased to be known as the Redmen, adopting "The Red Storm" instead. Likewise, Marquette became the Golden Eagles (nee "Golden Warriors"). Midway through 2000, the Hofstra University administration changed the school's nickname. Despite outward and visible signs of Dutch loyalty, Hofstra dropped the name "Flying Dutchmen," preferring to be known as the "The Hofstra Pride."

(replica of invitation)

WILLEM H. "BUTCH" VAN BREDA KOLFF TESTIMONIAL DINNER COMMITTEE

Honorary Chair
James M. Stuart

Co-Chairs
Stephen M. Balber   Joel F. Solomon

Vice Chairs
Brian S. Appel
Michael B. DeLuise
M. James Fellman
Barry H. Kurtz

Master of Ceremonies
Mike Francesca

Honorary Vice Chairs

Elgin Baylor	Hon. Thomas S. Gulotta	Hon. Joseph Margiotta
Hon. Bill Bradley	Robert Gutkowski	Dick McGuire
Carl Braun	"Hot Rod" Hundley	Hon. Joseph Mondello
Lou Carnesecca	Larry Lacchino	John C. Schmidt
Pete Carril	John Leone	Dean Smith
George G. Dempster	"Fuzzy" Levane	Bill "Babe" Thieben
Irving Freiman	Tom LaSorda	Jan van Breda Kolff
Hon. James Garner	Leonard Lewin	George Vecsey
James V. Garvey		Jerry West

"The best college coach I ever saw."

Bobby Knight,
coach of Indiana University

Dinner Committee
(in formation)

Martin J. Batey
James Boatwright
Curtis W. Block
Patrick Cameron
Raymond Cuneen
Joseph Cynar
Kenneth Cynar
Stephen E. Dunn
Stanley Einbender
Joeseph Famighetti
Lewis Freifeld
John H. Frew

Roger Gaeckler
Joseph T. Gardi
Sam Goldstein
Stanley Grossman
Lionel Harvey
Joseph Jakubauskas

Thomas E. Kennedy
Donald G. Laux
Frank V. Martin
John J. McGowan
Robert McLaughlin

Jonathan Otto
Michael Pollack
William J. Rathje
Kenneth J. Rood
Peter Salit
Henry R. Schwab
George Sempke
Jim Shannon
Edward A Soukup
Bernard Tomlin
Sam Toperoff
Peter S. Treiber

HIGHLIGHTS

Butch van Breda Kolff's Career Awards

"Coach of the Year," 1955. Lafayette College. Metropolitan Writers Association of New York.

"Coach of the Year for a Visiting Team," 1955. Lafayette College. Philadelphia Sportswriters Association.

"Coach of the Year," 1965. Princeton University. U.S. Basketball Writers Association.

"Coach of the Year," 1988. Lafayette College. East Coast Conference.

"Coach of the Year," 1992. Hofstra College. East Coast Conference.

Postseason Tourney Appearances

National Invitational Tournament, Lafayette College, 1955

NCAA Tourney (Division II), Hofstra College, 1959

NCAA Tourney (Division II), Hofstra College, 1962

NCAA Tourney (Division I), Princeton University, 1963

NCAA Tourney (Division I), Princeton University, 1964

NCAA Tourney (Division I), Princeton University, 1965
Final Four Representative

NCAA Tourney (Division I), Princeton University, 1967

Sun Belt Conference Tournament Champion, University of New Orleans, 1978 (Sunbelt ineligible for "automatic" NCAA tourney bid. Despite 21-6 record, NCAA and NIT spurned UNO.)

National Basketball Association

NBA Championship Series, Los Angeles Lakers, 1968
Lost to Boston Celtics 4-2

NBA Championship Series, Los Angeles Lakers, 1969
Lost to Boston Celtics 4-3

NBA Regular Season, Detroit Pistons 1970–71
Takes Pistons to first winning season in fourteen years

NBA Regular Season, New Orleans Jazz 1974–75
Takes over 2-20 expansion team and guides them to eighteen wins in their next thirty-five contests

COLLEGE COACHING RECORD
Phase III   Butch van Breda Kolff

At University of New Orleans

1977–78	21-6
1978–79	11-16
2 Years	32-22

At Lafayette (part 2)

1984–85	15-13
1985–86	13-15
1986–87	14-14
1987–88	19-10
4 years	64-51

Overall Lafayette Record: 8 years   132-83 (.608 pct)

At Hofstra (part 2)

1988–89	14-15
1989–90	13-15
1990–91	14-14
1991–92	20-9
1992–93	9-18
1993–94	9-20
6 years	79-91

Overall Hofstra Record: 13 years   215-134 (.616 pct)

OVERALL COACHING RECORD
"Butch Van Brenda Kolff"
(Phases I-II-III)

College:	28 years	482-272
Professional:	10 years	290-313
Total:	38 years	772-585

Number of Games: 1,357
Win-Loss Pct: .569

Chapter 10

Retirement? 1994–present

"Old soldiers never die. They just fade away."
General Douglas McArthur 1952

"Someday, I'll retire . . . What the hell. I'll move to Florida, play some tennis and golf. I'll sit around and look at the water . . . Nah . . . Never happen."
Butch van Breda Kolff in article from *Long Island Weekly* by Charley Rosen in December 1988

Sun City Center is a neat and tidy retirement community located roughly twenty-five miles south of Tampa, Florida. As you drive down the local streets, you are impressed with the lack of clutter and the overall serenity of the area. You almost wonder if any of the houses are lived in! Given the heat of the mid-day April sun, most of the retirees are probably sitting comfortably in their air-conditioned living rooms while watching the "soaps" or major league baseball on TV.

There is one exception to this picture. A narrow strip forming a front porch reveals a timeworn sweatshirt and an old pair of sneakers, which are strewn somewhat haphazardly over a lounging chair. Underneath the chair is a set of fifteen-pound bar-bells. It's a dead giveaway that you are at Butch van Breda Kolff's house. His garage door is open, revealing two refrigerators. Plastic bags serve as recycling conduits for beer and soda cans.

Soon Butch pulls into the driveway in his 1991 Ford Taurus and he quickly apologizes to his visitor for being late. His tennis match ran a little bit into overtime, but at least he emerged the winner!

"I just found out I have Parkinson's," Butch reveals to his visitor. Butch had been wondering what was wrong with his body and had seen several doctors in the process. For months, he had been bothered by a numbness in his hands and feet, rendering his limbs virtually useless to any form of athletic activity. He "wiffed" on his tennis serves. He had no power on the golf course. Putting was impossible. Finally, after observing how he walked on his toes and heels, a local neurologist quickly diagnosed him with the Parkinson's affliction.

Up to now, there is no known cure for Parkinson's, but a steady flow of medication in the form of pills can dramatically reduce the affects of the disease. The prevalent medication to date goes under the name of "Sinemet," but others include "Mirapex," "Comtan," and "Eldepryl." Off this menu, most patients take a daily combination depending on the severity of the case.

Butch felt the pills helped his walking and overall physical prowess. Side effects vary from patient to patient, but Butch felt the medications just made him sleepy during the course of the day. Forever one to fight the system, Butch always took one less pill than the doctor prescribed. Frequently, he would fall asleep while doing his time-honored stretching exercises on the floor of his living room.

Some form of exercise was part of Butch's daily routine. He frequently took 2–3 mile walks on the beach or to the local marketplace. Stretching everyday, walking everday, these were the key activities that kept him going. He would not allow his seventy-eight-year-old body to atrophy.

And then there is always the "heart thing," his arrhythmic murmur, which must be monitored.

Dehydrated from his tennis match, Butch snaps open a non-alcoholic beer. Simultaneously, he asks of his out-of-town visitor, "Want a beer?" Before long, two of his neighbors are over. "Grab yourself a beer," Butch orders. As the day progresses, there is a constant flux of visitors who just stop by. Everyone has something to say to the mailman.

One of the visitors is Tom Bertrand, who hails from New York City and occasionally makes the trip to visit VBK. For years, Tom followed VBK's volatile career, and kept all sorts of statistics and clippings on Butch's coaching experiences. When Butch fainted after a Hofstra game in 1994, his last year of coaching, Tom tried to visit VBK at the hospital, only to find he had already checked out. Not to be denied, Tom went to Butch's apartment, rang the door-bell, introduced himself, and Butch invited him into chat for a while. It was the first meeting between the two and they have been solid friends ever since.

☆ ☆ ☆

There is a coffee mug that sits prominently in Butch's living room, and it overflows with small change. If the spirit moves you, you can place a small donation in the cup to help finance the "beer fund." Also if you borrowed Butch's newspaper and didn't return it, you can likewise make a contribution. You need only return the section with the crossword puzzle. Also, along side the coffee mug, sits a copy of Bill Bradley's book entitled *Life on the Run*.

Butch's house is a "functional" five-room facility, which is attached to another unit of comparable size. No particular decorating scheme prevails. The furniture just blends together. There is no conspicuous color scheme or attempt at "balderdash." The living room is resplendent with pictures of Butch's children at various stages of their lives, plus a wealth of photos and trophies from his illustrious past. On a coffee table, near the kitchen, sit two major scrapbooks and other memorabilia collected by his wife Florence. Over the scrapbooks hangs a plaque constructed by John Leone, his assistant coach at Lafayette College, which outlines his entire career and is simply entitled "Sweet Ole Butch."

The living room subtly merges into the kitchen. A somewhat cluttered, large table with unopened bills and unread newspapers stands ready to be organized. The refrigerator is stocked with a vast array of TV dinners and a huge microwave stands ready to function upon command. Bagels sitting in a shopping bag await consumption.

The units in Butch's development lack swimming pools, but he and his pals aren't shy about using the nearby hotel pool.

"How's Pete doing?" inquires Ben Richards, one of Butch's buddies. Ben is the retired chairman of Numerica Corp, a New Hampshire banking company which merged out of existence in the mid-1990s. He was inquiring about Pete Carril who had just suffered a heart attack and was hospitalized in Sacramento. Butch replied, "I think he is doing OK . . . at least that's the report I get."

"The Kings are really playing great thanks to him," Ben mentions.

"They just tied the Laker series up 2-2 the other night." "Would love to see them win the deciding game for ole Pete!"

The men that stop by are mostly Butch's golf and tennis buddies. Some are younger than Butch, just a few are older. They each seem to have one or maybe two beers, just enough to loosen up the vocal chords. They don't get drunk or sloppy.

They all seem to have varying schedules, and so it often becomes confusing as to what day they play tennis, where they play golf, whose car is broken, who has tennis elbow, and on and on. Nobody seems to write anything down. For a Parkinson's victim, this is a matter of practicality. You can't read your own writing anyway!

They all seem excited about the new local executive golf course which charges a mere $10.50 for greens fees. And they only charge $1.00 per beer! You can't afford not to drink!

Ken Pason, one of the younger participants and a race car driver, asks Butch if he can change the TV channel. Butch had been watching ESPN's sports highlights, but Ken had interest in mentally updating his stock portfolio. As an active trader in the market, he was contemplating making some moves in his portfolio. The tape scrolled mysterious ticker symbols across the bottom of the screen thereby reflecting the changes in the market value of an infinite number of equities. Some were in red, indicating they were trading lower in value, and some were in green, indicating they were "in the money." Ken got quite excited when some of the stocks he followed—and probably owned—portrayed some volatility. "Look at Sun Microsystem this morning. It's up 3 points!" Butch was not nearly as excited and in fact soon became very uncomfortable with the constant flow of price changes. He instructed Ken to put the channel back to the sports network. Ken obliged.

Financial matters, particularly minute details, just weren't overly interesting to Butch. He had enough money to support his modest lifestyle, and didn't wish to divert his attention from the world of sports. He invested his savings through a broker from Salomon Smith Barney in Morristown, New Jersey named Mario Milelli, a former soccer player from Penn State University.

In the fall of 1986, while Butch was coaching at Lafayette College, Mario "cold called" Butch from his post at Smith Barney while sifting through names in the Princeton University directory. Butch liked Mario's approach, and the two have been working on his modest portfolio ever since. Their mutual love for the game of soccer was their bond. As their association grew, Mario began to handle accounts for Florence, the children and the grandchildren. Butch attended Mario's wedding.

"Often I call Butch with the intention of making some suggestions about his financial holdings, but almost invariably the conversation shifts to the world of sports, soccer in particular," Milelli remarked. Butch's only complaint about Mario is that he continuously makes it necessary to pay quarterly taxes to the federal and state governments.

Another contact in the financial arena is Ted Winpenny, Butch's chum from his high school days in Montclair, New Jersey. Ted has been with Merrill Lynch for over forty years and maintains an office in New Canaan, Connecticut. Perhaps no one has been a friend for a longer time than Ted Winpenny.

Butch's tennis pal Bob Geleverti then makes reference to how Butch likes to use drop shots to take advantage of his artificial knee. Butch laughs off the criticism as if to say he would never do anything so unsportsmanlike. Of course, assigning the duty of scorekeeper to Kenny Sherman, their friend with Alzheimer's disease, was just a part of their sick humor. Ken's tennis partners frequently yell at him, "Just hit the ball! Don't worry about the score!" Mid-way through their most recent game, Ken just walked off the court as if the game were over.

Butch prided himself on his long-term memory and his amazing recall of details of games played over thirty years ago. If only he could remember where he parked the car!

Butch prefers to sit outside in the Florida sun. While coaching the Lakers years ago, he spent many hours sitting on the beach and obtained a deep tan. Upon returning for the opening of the season, Elgin Baylor observed his dark tone, and remarked, "Now you are one of us!" Butch is not a big fan of air-conditioning. Besides, sitting on the small porch encourages more social activity, although none of the locals seems too inhibited when the action is inside. Butch's friends just walk right in and make themselves at home.

Occasionally a golf cart drives by. For many residents, this is their primary mode of transportation around town.

"Want to play tennis on Friday?" asks one of the regulars.

"Can't. I am going to Jersey," Butch replies.

"Will you see your wife?" one of the other guests asks.

"Briefly. We say 'hello' and 'good-bye' and that's about it. When I arrive, she leaves. It's better that way."

"What will you do in Jersey? Hear it's cold up there."

"One of my former assistant coaches is getting married. Also, one of my friends says he may have a coaching situation lined up for me in Bound Brook." Butch answered.

There was suddenly an air of silence. The fire, the passion for coaching, was still burning inside his body. It didn't matter that Butch was seventy-eight years old—he still harbored thoughts of returning to coaching. "Maybe I should have looked for another coaching job right after

Hofstra in 1994," he remarked recently. Like his original players at Lafayette, his new Florida buddies didn't want him to leave. Butch was the epicenter of their social life. They loved Butch. They didn't want him to destroy himself.

The Sun City Center Inn

"When Butch walks into the room, the party starts."

Florence van Breda Kolff

One of the more important facts to note is that it is Tuesday. Most retirees are not too concerned with what day of the week it is. However, Tuesday is the day that they have beans and franks for $2—"all you can eat"—at the nearby Sun City Center Inn. The dinner special is only available between 4:30pm and 6:30pm, and a lot of local citizens are at their tables just as the special falls into place. Discounted early-hour dinner specials are common in the state of Florida, as restaurants seek to capture the senior citizen market. Some pejoratively call the practice "Blue Hair Specials."

Regardless, Sergeant Butch soon gives marching orders and before you know it a patrol was on the way to the Inn. Butch whispers to his out-of-town visitor that the other two guys like martinis, as if they were from another planet. Butch is a beer man from the word go. His friend ordered a chardonnay. Once the chardonnay glass was empty, Butch refilled it with beer from his pitcher. The party was just warming up.

The lounge at the Inn is very crowded. Everyone laughs at the sign indicating that the price of the beans and franks dinner was just raised to $3—a 50 percent increase! Doubtless, few if any of the locals will change their Tuesday eating habits because of the extra dollar fee! A view of the courtyard from the lounge shows a golf-school group taking putting lessons on the Inn's lush green. Their golf instructions would last them beyond the time of the beans-and-frank special. They would have to pay the full price for dinner.

Soon, after just one martini, Bob—Butch's friend who has an artificial knee cap—challenges this massive guy to arm wrestling. After extensive conversation, Butch dissuaded the parties from any physical exchange. Soon the martini guys are on beer instead. Everyone calms down.

As the visitor reaches into his wallet to potentially pay his share or the entire tab, Butch gets quite upset as he *always* pays the bill. "Big Hearted Bill" comes to mind as the visitor put his wallet away.

Then, Butch temporarily breaks away from the group to talk to the hostess in the Inn's dining room adjacent to the lounge. She is a very attractive, poised middle-age woman. They briefly hold hands and exchange a few words.

The participants can hardly wait to get back to Butch's house to relieve the pressure of all those beans! Coins flow into the coffee cup in payment for whose relief is the longest and loudest.

The phone rings and it is Fran O'Hanlon's secretary Judy Cambell on the phone. When Butch was the coach, she was his assistant as well. She wanted to remind Butch that the Lafayette College basketball banquet was scheduled for later in the week. Because of O'Hanlon's success, a larger-than-normal crowd of some 200 participants was expected. Butch acknowledged that he would try to attend and he thanked Judy for remembering him. There was a "name tag" for Butch at the dinner, but he was unable to attend.

On February 29, 2000, Wilt "The Stilt" Chamberlain died at sixty-three of an apparent heart attack. Wilt was not indestructible after all.

☆ ☆ ☆

Butch's two-story home in Harvey Cedars, New Jersey, is located right next to the local fire house. He rents out the first floor to a single middle-aged woman and he lives on the second floor of the unit. To reach his living quarters, you must proceed to the rear of the building and then walk up a vertical incline of nineteen steps. A sprawling deck featuring Butch's outdoor grill and rod-iron furniture provide a comfortable entry setting. From inside the screened in living room, you hear the voice "Come on in!" as Butch beckons his latest guest.

The second floor of the house is set up like an apartment. You first notice the multitude of photographs about Butch's past experiences with the Knicks, the Lakers, and others. A collage of the *Sports Illustrated* article from 1984 is a prominent feature as you walk down the hall between the living room and bedroom. A portable bar houses the cordless phone and a myriad of clutter relating to Butch's immediate social engagements. Traditional bar stools sit in front of the facility.

A small kitchen houses the barest necessities including a well-stocked refrigerator. Beer and non-alcoholic beer are the main offerings.

Butch and his friend sit glued to the TV as the NBA playoffs start their second round. The Lakers had eliminated the Kings, so the hopes of a Cinderella season for Pete Carrill had drawn to a close.

Butch is master of the TV remote as he constantly switches from baseball to soccer to basketball. Soon, the Knicks-Heat game is on, and the score is 81-81 with about 1:34 to go, when Miami coach Pat Reilly calls a time-out. Following the TO, the Heat back court works the ball into Alonzo Mourning inside, he spins and has an easy bucket. Butch yells at the TV, "They play a 90 game schedule and they have to call a time out to remember to move the ball!" Following a Knick turnover by Patrick Ewing, the Heat again works the ball to Mourning for an open jumper. Bingo! The Knicks are dead meat and the game is over.

"Do you like Van Gundy?" his friend inquires on behalf of the Knicks coach.
"Yes."
"He's Dutch, isn't he?"
"He better be!" Butch replies.
Another flick of the remote and Lakers-Suns game is on. "Bill Walton has to be the world's worst announcer," Butch quickly judges. "He was a great player, but a lousy announcer."
"His son played for Princeton this year," his friend volunteered.
"Yes, I hear he was a good passer."
Butch then offered some criticism of Shaquille O'Neal's foul shooting style. He observed that Shaq's one handed right-handed shot had little chance of going in because it was unguided by the shooter's left hand. A dart-like shot, Shaq's foul shots were line drives with little or no touch. Butch even tried to call one of Coach Phil Jackson's assistants (Bill Griffin) to offer advice on Shaq's foul shooting style. Butch's phone call somehow got lost in the sea of recorded messages and voice-mail surrounding most institutional enterprises.
Butch replaced the remote with a rolled up version of the *New York Times* crossword puzzle. He had his eye on an annoying New Jersey fly. When the fly landed on his sun-tanned leg, Butch took a quick slap at the fly. "Damn, missed the sucker," he commented.
Butch's friend has Parkinson's as well, and soon the two are discussing any recent changes recommended in their pill selection. Butch reveals that he is low on his supply and must return to Florida to get his exact prescription refilled. Being a Sunday, his doctor is off the airwaves. The local CVS doesn't play ball with the pharmacist in Sun City Center. His friend's pills don't compare, so it seems, and Butch, sensing some urgency, wants to get back to Florida.
He is further upset by the fact he will have to miss his former assistant coach's wedding. Butch relished maintaining a continuing relationship with his former players

Retirement? 1994–present   **235**

and assistant coaches. Coaching was much more than a job. It was a lifetime commitment. He dreaded making the call to cancel.

In another mood shift, Butch is off to his outside deck exhorting his friend to look at his new gas grill. "It's a beauty, isn't it?"

"Sure is." The friend knew Butch just relished the possibility of using the new grill to support any kind of social gathering. However, Butch did harbor a fear that the grill might set fire to the nearby pine trees and set the house ablaze.

Butch's guest, seeing that it is almost five P.M. and factoring in Sunday night traffic on the Garden State Parkway, says a quick good-bye to Butch. Tired from the heat

Various Photos from VBK Private Collection; "Expressions"

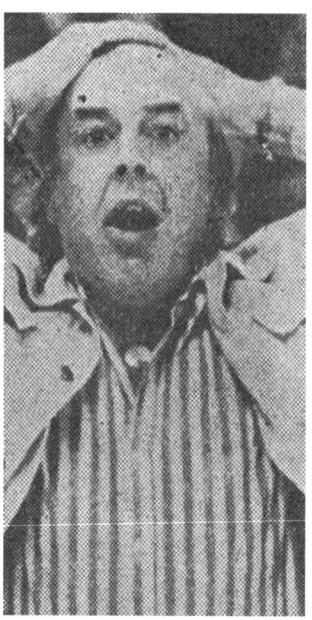

Butch van Breda Kolff never lacked for expression or enthusiasm while coaching college, professional, or even high school basketball.

Retirement? 1994–present

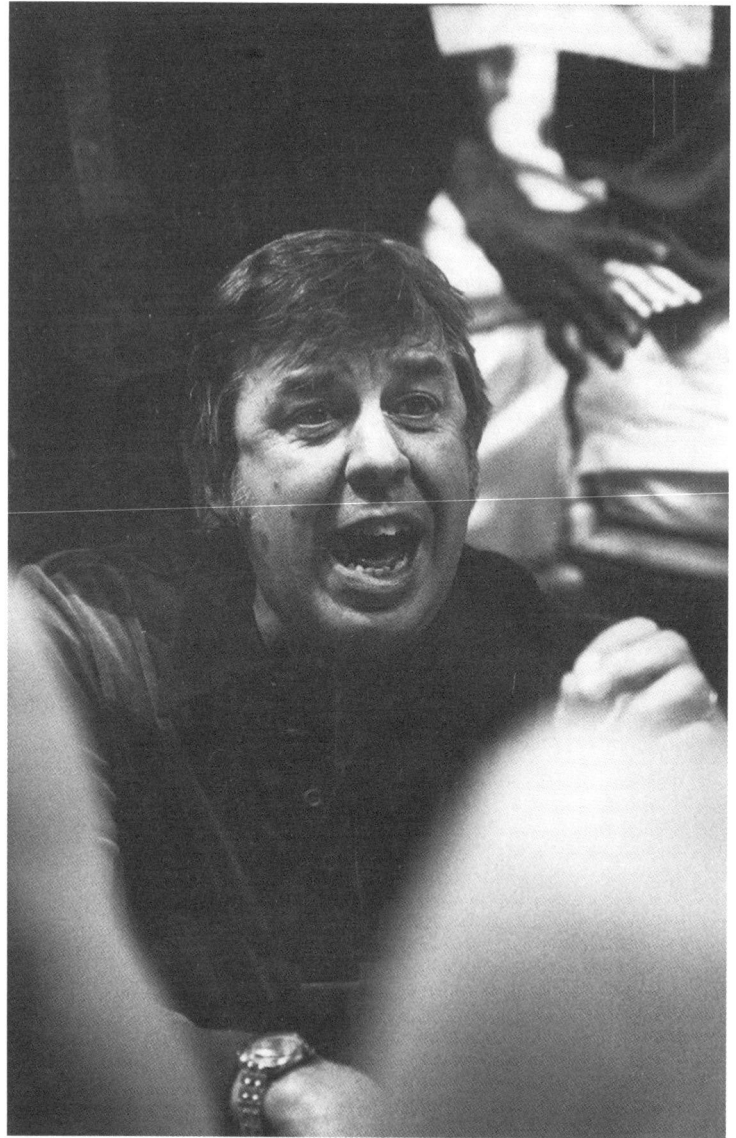

Retirement? 1994–present

and all the weekend guests, Butch is somewhat relieved to see the friend leave. He needed to do some laundry for his trip to Florida. He always did his own laundry and prepared his own meals. There was no maid service or room service in Harvey Cedars.

Also, he definitely needed a little nap.

☆ ☆ ☆

The Pomona Golf Course is a nine-hole course located between Absecon and Atlantic City in southern New Jersey. The course has a lot of attraction to Butch von Breda Kolff and his golfing buddies. The moderate price of $17.00, which covers greens fees for eighteen holes of golf (you go around twice) and half of a power cart, fits well with the budgets of retirees in their mid to late seventies. A local membership can reduce these numbers even further.

The layout accommodates the game of the senior citizen golfer. The course consists of two par threes and seven par fours. The total yardage is 4,852. Holes number eight and number nine are over 340 yards, all the rest are less than 295 yards. The greens are in good shape, just a bit slower than those seen at finer country clubs. The hardpan nature of the fairways enables the ball to travel a longer distance than at courses less dried out. Almost anywhere on the course, you get a flat lie. The course offers sufficient challenges without being "unfair." Perhaps, you would use the euphemism "executive course" when referring to the Pomona layout.

Butch introduced his friend Paul Albert to his playing buddies Phil and Bill. Bill Claren is a former race-car driver and Butch refers to him as "Crash Helmet." A graduate of Montclair State University, Bill has a local real estate business and his friend Phil is one of his coworkers. Bill is one of Butch's old teammates from the Verona Inn team of the late '40s and early '50s.

Butch and Paul ride in one cart, Phil and Bill in the other. A friendly match is created whereby the players from one cart are pitted against those from the other. When Butch's playing partner indicates that he rarely breaks 100 and shows a handicap card indicating that he is an "official" twenty-nine at his home course, Phil and Bill immediately become skeptical.

The stakes are set. Initially, the winners of the eighteen holes would be treated to beers at the clubhouse. Double-up bets were also permitted. The two carts proceeded to the first tee for a competitive round of golf.

On the first tee, Butch teed off and hit the ball a weak thirty yards. Phil and Bill offered Butch a "mulligan" or a free shot, but he refused. Butch, disappointed in his first shot, growled, "I can't take a mulligan when we have a match at stake!" Paul then hit a decent drive followed by a second shot just off the edge of the green. As Bill hit his third shot onto the green, the ball seemed to move slower than Paul had mentally calculated. As a result, he gave his chip shot a rap and soon he was over the green with the same shot coming back. One more chip, three putts and Paul had a seven. Butch's team was down one after one hole.

The second hole was a par three and both Paul and Bill parred the hole. Butch continued to have trouble, and he carded a six. Now his team was down two with just two holes completed. Butch remarked, "The bad news is that we are two down. The good news is that we are two down." Two holes later, VBKs team was all even and by the end of the first nine held a seven-point lead over Bill and Phil. Hoping to avoid paying for the beers, Bill and Phil made a separate "double or nothing" bet covering the back nine.

Paul soon deflected the challenge and birdied the tenth hole. Later, he parred three of the last four holes to finish with an even eighty for the day. The Bill-Phil team (scores ninety-seven and 107 respectively) was caught in a buzz-saw and they lost the second round of beers to Butch and Paul (100 and eighty respectively).

The ride home from the golf course was gratifying to Butch and Paul as they savored their victory. The beers tasted especially good considering the hot humid playing conditions. With their windows wide open, the two partners enjoyed riding the twenty-five miles back to Long Beach Island. Neither liked riding in an enclosed air-conditioned vehicle.

As they proceeded north on the Garden State Parkway, they passed the exit for Absecon and the Seaview Country Club. Paul asked Butch if he had ever played there, and Butch admitted that he never had. He was, however, familiar with the bar where the caddies stopped upon completion of their rounds. "The 19th Hole" pub on Route 9 had to be one of the earthiest bars in South Jersey. Butch had been there several times, particularly after some winning times at Atlantic City's casinos. As if to apologize for his taste in bars, he remarked "I think they have spruced it up a bit."

As Paul's car crossed over the bridge marking the entrance to Long Beach Island, the temperature drop was quite noticeable and indeed welcome. Appropriately, the first restaurant you see is Dutchman's. Butch instructed Paul on a special route to avoid unnecessary traffic lights and stop signs. One turn was particularly designed to ogle at the young mothers sunning themselves on the beach.

As the two golfers approach Harvey Cedars, Butch tells Paul about his desire to someday own property on the water. In a rare reference to his age, he smiled and said "It had better be soon!". Then he remarked, "I guess we never should have sold the marina." He had his eye on a house where no one lived in hopes that it someday would come onto the market.

Once back to his residence at Harvey Cedars, Butch returned his oversized golf bag to the storage shed on his property. Butch preferred a lighter weight bag and often carried his own bag when he played in Florida. The bag displays the logo of the Baylor University Bear, and Butch mentions that the bags were gifts for the coaches of the 1991 Baylor Invitational tournament sponsored by Dr. Pepper when he was at Hofstra University. Ironically, Hofstra played Princeton and Pete Carril in the first round of the tourney. Butch lost to his prize pupil by 54-42.

Butch and Paul were a bit drained from the heat and humidity of the late June sun, and so they slowly ascended the nineteen steps up to Butch's living quarters. Florence van Breda Kolff was spruced up and ready to go to dinner. Paul cracked open a bottle of chardonnay for Florence and himself, while Butch opted for a cold can of non-alcoholic beer. Gradually, Butch started to strip out of his sweaty golf attire. Soon, he was on his way to the outdoor shower with merely a towel wrapped around his body. Paul filled Florence in on the details of their golf victory at Pomona. She rolled her eyes in amusement.

Butch was definitely a new man after his shower. He had played golf in a tattered gray T-shirt and sweat shorts. He looked like he hadn't shaved in several days. In fact, generally speaking, Butch regarded shaving as a "waste of time." But now he was clean-shaven, and sported a pair of navy Bermuda shorts over his scotch plaid boxers. A collared Hofstra blue and white basketball shirt completed his outfit.

Dinner entailed a short walk to the Harvey Cedars Shellfish Company. "Crash-Helmet" Bill and his wife, Bonnie, were scheduled to join the VBKs and golfing whiz Paul. Bill arrived separately since his wife was wrapped up in closing a real estate transaction. Bill seemed still upset at having lost so badly on the golf course. Like Butch, he was a helluva competitor. He continued to accuse Butch of bringing a "ringer" into town. Following dinner, the group adjourned to Butch's place for Dutch chocolate ice cream.

The next day is travel day for Florence van Breda Kolff. Butch and Florence can only take each other in short doses! Florence must catch a five o'clock plane from Philadelphia to New Orleans. Although Butch has no car of his own in New Jersey, he has access to one as a result of his rental agreement with his first floor tenant. He has ready access to her car in trade for a weekly supply of vodka. The barter system works!

Florence admonishes Butch to take his Parkinson's pills on a regular basis, rather than when he feels the disease's impact on his physical activity. Parkinson medicine is designed to preempt the symptoms from occurring in the first place. Most other medications aim to eliminate pain or conditions that have already surfaced. When possible, she attends Parkinson support group activities on Butch's behalf.

As the summer wore on, Butch continued with his active schedule. First he visited Lafayette College where he had a meeting with his attorney Norm Seidel in Easton, and then went to lunch with John Leone and Judy Campbell. As the month of July 2000 progressed, Butch made a trip to see his pal Bill Thieben on Long Island. Late in the month, Pete Carril visited him for a few days. The two chronies continued to exchange stories of their experiences. They were most annoyed with each other when neither one could remember the name of Clyde Drexler. For a man who used to know the name of every ballplayer in the majors, this was a most upsetting development! Pete and Butch took some long walks on the beach, had dinner together, and rehashed some more of the past.

Dating back to his youth in Montclair, Butch always woke up early in the morning, usually rising in the area of 5–5:30 a.m. Butch always liked to have the competitive edge on his comrades! On one occasion, Butch got up early, did the crossword puzzle, then quickly placed a call into Bill Thieben. In their meeting in July, the two old friends were discussing an athlete who ruined his career by walking into a plate glass window, but somehow neither gentlemen could remember the player's name. When Butch got through to Thieben's answering device, he left the athlete's name: Stacey Arcineaux. To Butch, reminiscent of his Montclair youth, it was like winning a game of twenty questions!

The phone rang and Butch thought it would be Thieben calling to congratulate him on recalling Arcineaux's name. Instead, it was George Vecsey of the *New York Times* who was gathering information for a report on Princeton basketball.

Butch complained to Pete that he just couldn't find the type of bar that he liked. It was too long of a drive to The 19th Hole in Absecon!

Overall, Butch felt an element of satisfaction in his modest golfing victory. Butch wanted his golfing buddy Paul to visit him again so that they could take on the Bill and Phil team. About a month or so later, he was anxious to show Paul his altered golf swing, which encompassed more of a rocking action while staying behind the ball. Butch claimed he was hitting his drives thirty yards further. Also, he had converted back to putting left-handed, and felt the results were positive. He had many of his friends on the lookout for a left-handed putter at local garage sales.

After spending most of June and July in New Jersey, Butch set off for Florida around the middle of August. His friend "Crash Helmet" Bill picked him up at five-thirty A.M. in order to catch the seven A.M. direct flight on "Spirit Airlines" to Tampa out of Atlantic City. His friend Bill the tennis player with the artificial knee was waiting on the other end to pick him up to take him to Sun City. He was attracted by the fact the plane originated in Atlantic City. Given the convenience, he vowed to return sometime in September.

The Lafayette College Hall of Fame Dinner in November 2000 featured the school's "Fifteen Greatest Athletes of the Twentieth Century." Two of Butch's pupils—Pete Carril and Otis Ellis—were among the elite, as was his original boss athletic director Bill Anderson, who was posthumously cited. Marty Zippel, the closing speaker for the evening, introduced Butch as a member of the audience and the Coach received a standing ovation from the 180 attendees. Following the event, Butch and many of his friends adjourned to the College Hill Tavern.

The next day, as Butch drove home to Harvey Cedars, the weather channel on his car radio indicated that a string of twenty-degree weather was in the offing. Soon the December weather pattern generic to Southern New Jersey would entice Butch to return to his Sun City Center abode. Within a few days, he was on a plane to Tampa. He relished the thought of playing golf and tennis with his pals in Florida.

After spending the months of December and January in Florida, Butch again returned North for some special occasions. Hofstra University was enjoying its third straight twenty-win season under coach Jay Wright, a feat last accomplished by VBK's 1961–64 teams. The appreciative Hofstra authorities paid special tribute to Butch and allowed him to sit on the bench in its game against Delaware.

On February 24, Princeton University honored Pete Carril and Butch in its celebration of "100 Years of Basketball." Bill Bradley presented Butch with a trophy while Pete Carril received his award from Geoff Petrie. As Butch strode onto the court, he shuffled his feet in short choppy steps, a sign of his intensifying Parkenson condition. In the ceremony that followed after the game, young fans sought his autograph as he struggled with his signature. "I should just sign VBK," he lamented after struggling with his three-part surname. Nonetheless, Butch was the last to leave the party.

Prior to attending the ceremony, when Butch arrived at his home in Harvey Cedars, he discovered that his property had suffered substantial tree damage from the Valentine's Day storm that struck New Jersey. Although the cleanup entailed extensive work in the near-zero wind chill, Butch attacked the project immediately and was "glad to have something to do." He wanted to continue being active. He didn't mind getting older. In his words, he just hated to get old.

Selection to the Lafayette College Hall of Fame

The Lafayette College Hall of Fame is a very selective group. Over the entire history of the college, dating back to 1826, only ninety-one athletes have been chosen for this elite society. Of the ninety-one so honored, only seventeen have been basketball related (players, coaches, and one announcer).

On March 31, 2001, the name of Willem "Butch" van Breda Kolff was approved by the Board of Trustees of Lafayette College to be inducted into the Lafayette College Athletic Hall of Fame. His induction would take place at the school's Annual Hall of Fame Dinner in November 2001. Another inductee named was Tony Duckett '85, the school's alltime career assist leader, and a star of Butch's 1984–85 team. Rounding out the selections were Erik Marsh (who holds the College's career rushing yardage record), Heidi Caruso (who holds the Lafayette record for steals), and Frank Kirkleski (an All-American from the great LC football teams of the mid-twenties). The Annual Hall of Fame dinner to be held November 16, 2001, promised to be a banner evening for Lafayette athletics.

When Butch was asked about the subject matter of his acceptance speech, he responded: "One thing I am *not* going to do is thank everyone in my family and everyone I know. So many acceptance talks are diluted with an endless array of *thank you's.*" He was unsure of exactly what his theme would be. He simply stated he would think of what to say while en route to the ceremony. A natural extemporaneous speaker, he seemed inwardly confident that he would inspire and entertain the audience (expected to exceed some 200 Lafayette loyalists) when called to the podium on the eve of November 16, 2001.

Over twenty-five coaching jobs opened up at the end of the 2000–01 college basketball season. When UMass let their coach go, they replaced him with Steve Lappas of Villanova. The Villanova opening was then filled by Jay Wright, leaving an opening at Hofstra. Tommy Amaker left Seton Hall for the University of Michigan. Speedy Morris was axed at LaSalle, and Kevin Bannon was fired at Rutgers. After thirty years at the helm, Louisville University's Denny Crum retired and was replaced by the charismatic Rick Pitino. Jettisoning the marvelous climate of Malibu, California and his coaching assignment at Pepperdine University, Jan van Breda Kolph took the job at St. Bonaventure in Olean, New York.

Texas Tech forgot that their coach James Dickey finished 30-2 in 1996 and replaced him with the infamous Bobby Knight. With all the shifting of college basketball coaches following the 2000–2001 season, you almost expected the name of VBK to show up as a candidate for one of the openings. He still harbored the dream that he could return, if only as an assistant or an advisor. Maybe we will see those "Butch is Back" T-shirts again!

Resources

Mokray, Bill, ed./pub. *Basketball's Best,* Major League Players, NBA Pictoral Preview 1967–68 Season, Revere, Mass., 1967.

Rappaport, Ken, *The Classic: A History of the NCAA Basketball Championship,* pp. 30–31. National Collegiate Athletic Association, 1979.

Chamberlain, Wilt, *A View from Above.* New York: Penguin Co., 1991.

Frankl, Ron, *Wilt Chamberlain.* New York: Chelsea House Publishers, 1995.

McPhee, John, *A Sense of Where You Are—Bill Bradley at Princeton.* New York: Farrar, Straus, and Giroux, 1965.

Princeton Basketball 1999–2000, Basketball Media Guide Sports Information Department, pub. Princeton University, 1999.

Pepe, Phil, "The Night that Bill and Cazzie Met." *Knickerbockers Basketball Magazine* 1, no. 2 1967–68. New York: Harry M. Stevens, 1967.

Berger, Phil, *Forever Showtime—The Checkered Life of Pistol Pete Maravich.* Dallas: Taylor Pub. Co., 1999.

Klein, Moss, "Holiday Festival's Magical Mystique." *Holiday Festival Magazine,* 1974.

13th Annual ECAC Holiday Festival, Game Program, December 30, 1964

Vecsey, George, "Sports of The Times," *New York Times,* 6 February 2000, sec. SP3.

Lipsythe, Robert, "Sports of The Times," *New York Times,* 27 April 1969.

Lipsythe, Robert, "The Titans," *New York Times,* 27 April 1969.

Rogers, Thomas, "Celts Brinkmanship," *New York Times,* 26 April 1969.

Anderson, David, "Celts Control Rebounds," *New York Times,* 21 April 1968.

McCrovan, Deane, "Lakers Conquer Celts," *New York Times,* 24 April 1968.

Becker, Bill, "Baylor, West Combine for 68 Points," *New York Times,* 28 April 1968.

Anderson, Dave, "Celtics Beat Lakers," *New York Times,* 30 April 1968.

Becker, Bill, "Howell Hits 30 Points," *New York Times,* 2 May 1968.

United Press International, "Lakers Set Back Celtics," *New York Times,* 23 April 1969.

Becker, Bill, "Second Setback Shakes Celt Confidence," *New York Times,* 26 April 1969.

Rogers, Thomas, "Jones Goal Sinks Lakers," *New York Times,* 30 April 1969.

United Press International, "Lakers Set Back Celtics," *New York Times,* 1 May 1969.

Rogers, Thomas, "Celts Win 111-105," *New York Times,* 3 May 1969.

Koppett, Leonard, "Celts Conquer Lakers, 108-106," *New York Times,* 5 May 1969.

National Invitational Tournament, Game Program, 19 March 1970.

Horowitz, Paul, *Newark Evening News,* March 1955. (see George Young scrapbook)

Smith, Craig, "VBK Rides Again." *Lafayette College Alumni Quarterly,* Spring 1984. pp. 11–15. Easton, Pennsylvania: Lafayette College Alumni Association.

Lafayette College, Basketball Media Guide 1988–89. Published by the Easton, Pennsylvania: Sports Information Dept. Lafayette College, 1988.

Lafayette College, Basketball Media Guide 2000–2001. Published by the Easton, Pennsylvania: Sports Information Dept., Lafayette College, 2000.

The Lafayette, various issues of school newspaper; 1951–55 and 1984–1988.

Hofstra University Football Program, 16 September 1995

Hofstra University, Internet e-mail from Hofstra University public relations department relating to "Dutch Connection" of Hofstra.

Hofstra University, Basketball Media Guide, 1999–2000. Hempstead, New York: Hofstra University Sports Information Department, 1999.

Rosen, Charley, "Give and Go." *Long Island Monthly,* December 1988, pp. 56–59.

Carril, Pete, *The Smart Take from the Strong,* New York: Simon & Schuster, 1997.

Nack, William, "I Made My Bed and I've Got to Lie in it." *Sports Illustrated,* 24 February 1984, pp. 61–76.

Olsen, Jack, "Hedonist Prophet of the Spartan Game." *Sports Illustrated,* 23 September 1968, pp. 28–38.

Sports Illustrated, Bobby Knight of Indiana. January 26, 1981.

Additional Sources: The meticulous scrap-books constructed by Fran van Breda Kolff were invaluable in capturing her husband's story. However, the names of the periodicals from which many of the articles were drawn were not posted in her books. The following are just some of the articles used in writing *Play the Game Right.*

"Completing the Cycle," The Center Piece by Dave Rosner, p. 163: quote about Tony Duckett "loving" VBK.

"Dad wasn't the Pushy Type" by Bernice Beglionee.

"Jan Felt Further Away" by Felipe Bundy, Daily News.

"VBK and Coaching Rivals" by Associated Press, 1-15-93.

"ABA West" by Woodrow Page.

"Pistons are Set" by Bill Hall.

"Along the Sports Trail" by Robert Makus, p. 109, cause of $250 fine from Walter Kennedy.

Cage, Tom, "Unthinkable but Jazz Wins Again," 5 November 1975.

Hicks, David, "VBK Ranked Top Masochist," p. 135 quote: "It's good for me to work" upon his return to NBA as coach of the expansion New Orleans Jazz.

Quale, Jennifer, "Coach Butch did it His Way." *Times Picayune New Orleans,* 11 November 1975; general: preference for "scroungy" bars; specific: "You have to be hard hearted and tough."

Hall, John, "VBK—Coach of the Year" from column "Around Town," *Los Angeles Times,* 12 March 1975.

Hafner, Dan, "VBK Resigns, May Coach Detroit Pistons." *LA Times.*

Fain, Don, "The NBA . . . Same Cellar."

Larue, Mark, "Lafayette's Stroke of Genius."